the New
Explorers

Bill Kurtis

WTTW/Chicago

COMPANION TO THE INTERNATIONALLY ACCLAIMED TELEVISION SERIES FROM WTTW/CHICAGO

The publishers would like to thank WMX Technologies, Inc. for their sponsorship of this publication.

Companion to the Internationally Acclaimed Television Series from WTTW/Chicago

WTTW/Chicago

Published by WTTW/Chicago
5400 North St Louis Avenue, Chicago, Illinois, 60625, USA

Based on The New Explorers television series produced by WTTW/
Chicago and Kurtis Productions, Ltd.
Executive Producer and Correspondent: Bill Kurtis
Project Manager and Executive Producer, WTTW: Edward Menaker

Conceived and produced by Weldon Owen Pty Limited
43 Victoria Street, McMahons Point, NSW 2060, Australia
A member of the Weldon Owen Group of Companies
Sydney•San Francisco•London
Copyright © 1995 Weldon Owen Pty Ltd

Chairman: Kevin Weldon
President: John Owen
Publisher: Sheena Coupe
Project Editor: Julia Burke
Text Editors: Regina Elkan & Christopher Carroll, Elkan & Carroll
Copy Editors: Margaret Olds, Kate Etherington
Design: Janet Marando/Burk Associates
Picture Research: Jenny Mills
Illustration Research: Julia Burke
Vice President International Sales: Stuart Laurence
Coeditions Director: Derek Barton
Production Consultant: Mick Bagnato
Production Manager: Simone Perryman

ISBN 0-9647457-0-4

Manufactured by Mandarin Offset

Printed in Hong Kong

A WELDON OWEN PRODUCTION

PAGE 2: *The majestic bald eagle fishing for prey.*

PAGE 3: *Astronauts have to be able to build structures in space as part of
NASA's planned space station progam. Here an astronaut is attached to
the space shuttle's remote manipulator arm by feet restraints.*

PAGES 4–5: *Plants from rainforests have many uses. Here, a Yanomami
Indian dries a coating of virola resin on arrowheads.*

PAGE 7: *An observer watches lava and a steam cloud at the Volcanoes
National Park, Kilauea, Hawaii.*

PAGE 8, LEFT: *Plants from the rainforest provide the basis for many
modern medicines.*

PAGE 8, RIGHT: *Light micrograph of a thin section of silicon.*

PAGE 9, LEFT: *A Siberian crane in its wetland habitat.*

PAGE 9, RIGHT: *Responsible disposal of all types of waste is necessary
if we are to protect the environment.*

PAGES 10–11: *As landfills such as this one in New York gradually fill
up, recycling and incineration become important alternative ways of
managing our garbage problem.*

Victor Englebert/Comstock

Contributors

Dr. George Archibald
Director, International Crane Foundation,
Wisconsin, USA

Dr. Randall L. Brill
Scientist, Naval Command, Control and Ocean
Surveillance Center—Research and Development Division,
Hawaii, USA

Dr. Leonard J. Cerullo
Medical Director, Chicago NeuroSurgical Center,
Chicago, Illinois, USA

Mr. Christopher John Chiaverina
Physics teacher, New Trier High School, Winnetka,
Illinois, USA

Dr. Betsy L. Dresser
Director, Center for Reproduction of Endangered Wildlife,
Cincinnati Zoo and Botanical Garden;
Research Associate Professor, Department of Obstetrics/
Gynecology, University of Cincinnati College of Medicine,
Cincinnati, Ohio, USA

Dr. John W. Fitzpatrick
Executive Director and Senior Research Biologist,
Archbold Biological Station, Florida, USA

Dr. Steven P. French
Co-founder Yellowstone Grizzly Foundation;
Adjunct Assistant Professor, Montana State University,
Montana, USA

Ms. Marilynn Gibbs-French
Co-founder Yellowstone Grizzly Foundation;
researcher, lecturer, writer,
Evanston, Wyoming, USA

Dr. James W. Grier
Team Leader, Northern States Bald Eagle Recovery Team;
Professor, Zoology Department,
North Dakota State University, North Dakota, USA

Dr. James L. Hicks
Advanced Placement and Honors Physics teacher,
Barrington High School, Barrington, Illinois, USA

Dr. Mae C. Jemison
Astronaut, Mission Specialist, National Aeronautics and
Space Administration, Johnson Space Center,
Houston, Texas, USA

Mr. Daniel Kraus
Co-director Cheetah Preservation Fund, Windhoek, Namibia

Dr. Walter C. McCrone
Director, McCrone Research Institute, Chicago, Illinois, USA

Ms. Laurie Marker-Kraus
International Cheetah Studbook Keeper;
Co-director Cheetah Preservation Fund, Windhoek, Namibia

Dr. Martin V. Melosi
Professor of History and Director, Institute for Public
History, University of Houston, Texas, USA

Ms. Sy Montgomery
Author, columnist, freelance writer, and naturalist,
Hancock, New Hampshire, USA

Ms. Phyllis Burton Pitluga
Senior Astronomer, The Adler Planetarium,
Chicago, Illinois, USA

Dr. Marleta Reynolds
Associate Professor of Clinical Surgery,
Children's Memorial Hospital, Chicago, Illinois, USA

Dr. Linda Schele
John D. Murchison Regents Professor in Art,
University of Texas, Austin, Texas, USA

Dr. Paul C. Sereno
Assistant Professor, University of Chicago,
Chicago, Illinois, USA

Dr. Larry L. Smarr
Director, National Center for Supercomputing Applications;
Professor of Physics and Astronomy,
University of Illinois, Urbana, Illinois, USA

Dr. William B. Stapp
Director, Global Rivers Environmental Education Network;
Arthur Thurnau Professor and Professor of Natural Resources,
School of Natural Resources, University of Michigan,
Michigan, USA

Ms. Karen B. Wachs
Conservation Officer, Center for Reproduction of Endangered
Wildlife, Cincinnati Zoo and Botanical Garden,
Cincinnati, Ohio, USA

Dr. David E. Willard
Collection Manager, Field Museum of Natural History,
Chicago, Illinois, USA

Dr. Robert N. Yonover
Director of Research and Development, Vision Safe,
Kaneohe, Hawaii, USA

Contents

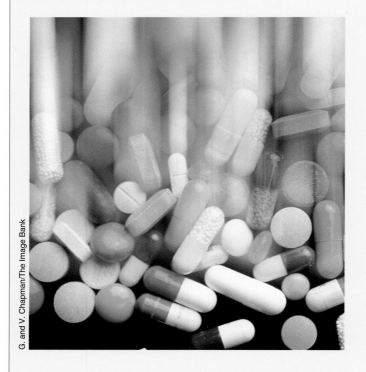

G. and V. Chapman/The Image Bank

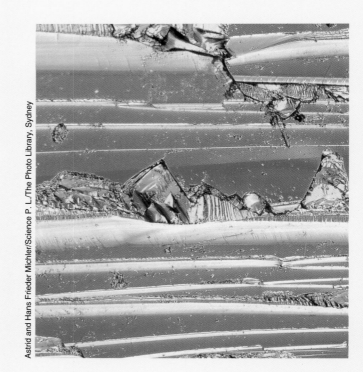

Astrid and Hans Frieder Michler/Science P. L./The Photo Library, Sydney

Medical Advances

Great Mysteries

Tom Ulrich/Oxford Scientific Films

John W. Banagan/The Image Bank

Introduction

Every generation, in its own time, relives the age of exploration. The human quality that asks why and where is the same in the fifteenth or the twenty-first century. We are linked by the intoxication of the promise of discovery.

It is the thrill that Galileo must have felt when he first saw mountains on the moon using his improved telescope. And it's no different from Watson and Crick's realization, one day in 1953, that the helical shape of DNA appearing before their eyes would explain how life replicates itself.

Each moment of discovery, one in a grand exploration of the heavens, the other in a microscopic universe within the human cell, gives us another key to understanding the world in which we live.

That is science.

This book is a scientific chronicle written by the explorers of our generation: the "new explorers."

I was accompanying Dr. John Fitzpatrick of Chicago's Field Museum of Natural History during the final stage of his exploration of the cloud forests of the Peruvian Andes. It wasn't the actual discovery of new species of birds that struck me on that trip: it was the process, that hearkened back to the most traditional scientific efforts of the past.

When I reached him, Dr. Fitzpatrick had been living with his team of University of Chicago graduate students for two months in the rainforest in very wet conditions.

At one stage we were crossing a swollen Amazonian river at midnight. I was worried about our camera gear

piled at the rear of the dug-out canoe and shouted that a company of US Marines wouldn't attempt this crossing in the dark. Fitzgerald tried to reassure me, "We'll be fine—if we don't drift into the rapids."

There it was, a revelation. This scientist came from a world of electron microscopes, linear accelerators, and high resolution computer imaging, but at this instant he was hardly a breath away from Darwin.

The challenges haven't changed at all. Scientists still have to embrace the earth with adventure to understand it, just like their predecessors of centuries past.

Since that first adventure in the Amazon, I've been back half a dozen times, following other scientists trying to buy time for the rainforest.

I've climbed over the edge of an eagle's nest, examined ancient bones from a graveyard in Peru, participated in more than my share of neurosurgery, and watched cheetahs running free in Namibia.

· Trying to find the new explorers of our time has been a marvelous experience. And with the help of the United States Department of Energy, we've taken these adventures into classrooms to spark the imagination of young people so they too can become new explorers.

And that has been the most satisfying adventure of all. Bon voyage.

Bill Kurtis

THE USE OF LASERS HAS
revolutionized many areas of surgery.
Here, a fine argon laser beam is
being used to correct otosclerosis
in the inner ear.

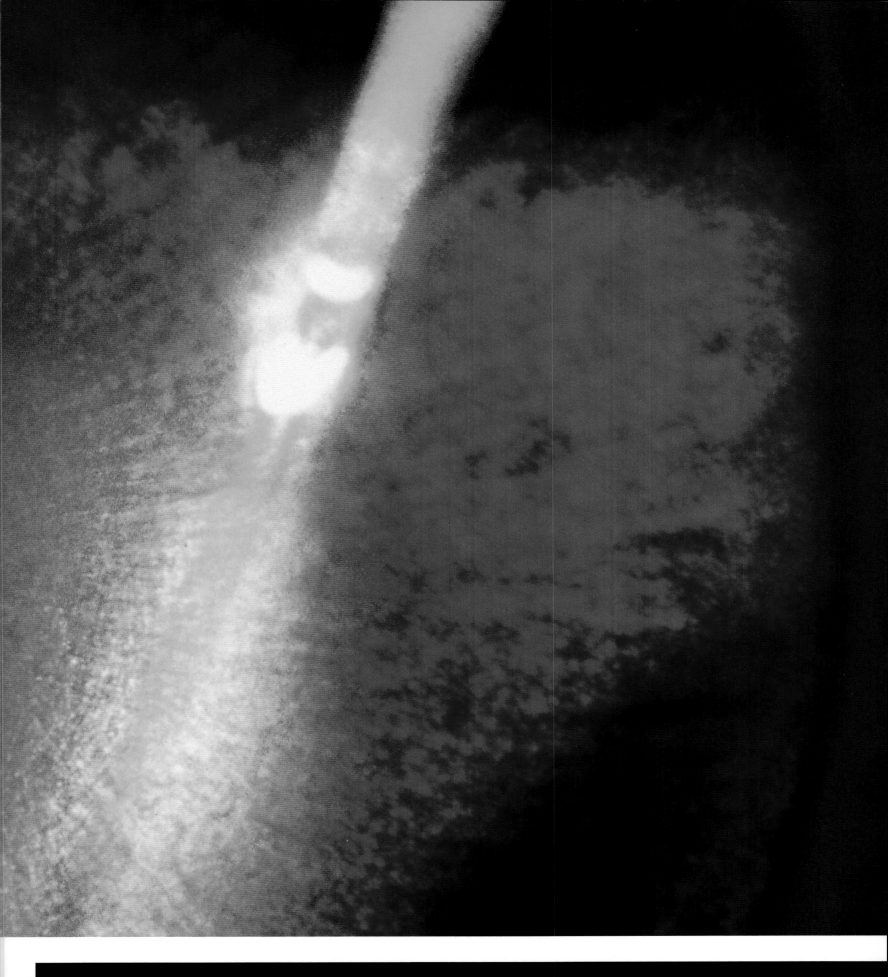

MEDICAL ADVANCES

TROPICAL RAINFORESTS, SUCH AS
*this one in the Amazon region of
Brazil, cover only 2 percent of the
earth, yet they support more animal
and plant species per acre than any
other place on the earth. These wet,
warm forests average from 20 to 86
species of tree per acre (1 acre is 0.4
hectare). North American temperate
forests, in contrast, average 4 tree
species per acre.*

➤ MANY MEDICATIONS IN USE
*have been developed from the
natural chemicals found in plants.
Some examples are morphine,
codeine, cortisone, diosgenin,
atropine, and reserpine.*

Luiz C. Marigo/Peter Arnold, Inc.

Twentieth-Century Medicine Man

SY MONTGOMERY

The dense tropical rainforest of the Amazon may hold the cures for thousands of humankind's diseases. What may be "miracle" plants to us are the same plants that local Indian tribes have relied on since ancient times to cure their infections, stop bleeding, help with childbirth, and stun or poison their enemies. But Amazon Indians' lands and lifestyles are under threat. To gather this precious knowledge before it is too late, Dr. Mark Plotkin has been trekking into the rainforest for the past ten years and living intermittently with the Indian tribes there. As Director of Plant Conservation for Conservation International, Dr. Plotkin hopes to learn from the Indian culture and explore the far-reaching possibilities of rainforest plants.

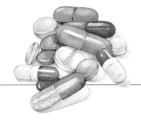

Mark J. Plotkin

DR. PLOTKIN COLLECTS A *"magical plant" from a Yanomami Indian. A member of the black pepper family, the plant is used in an exorcism ritual.*

THE AMAZON BASIN HAS THE *largest area of rainforest in the world.*

Mark J. Plotkin

ALTHOUGH MISSIONARIES HAVE *introduced Western clothes, this Tirió Indian still wears a headdress, beaded armbands with a scarlet macaw feather, and body paint.*

AMAZON RAINFOREST

COLOMBIA   VENEZUELA
ECUADOR
GUYANA
SURINAME
FRENCH GUIANA

PERU
BRAZIL
BOLIVIA

PARAGUAY
ARGENTINA
URUGUAY

CHILE
ATLANTIC
OCEAN
PACIFIC
OCEAN

In 1982 27-year-old Mark Plotkin first landed at Kwamalasamotoe village which is on the edge of the Amazon rainforest of southwest Suriname, north of Brazil. His bush pilot left him there with this goodbye: "Let me give you some advice: stay away from the women. If you don't, the men will come after you, and all their arrows have poison tips."

RICHES IN THE RAINFOREST
An early map of this part of the Amazon listed only two types of Indians: hostile and unfriendly. If this was true, it was with cause. For hundreds of years, Westerners had come here only as conquerors—of land or souls. They stole Indian land, kidnapped their women, suppressed their culture and their religion.

But Mark Plotkin was different. He had come here to learn from the Tirió about the green, wet world that had sustained them for centuries, maybe for millennia. As an ethno-botanist, whose discipline combines anthro-pology and botany, Plotkin studies the way native people use their plant resources.

16

Explorers have traditionally brought home valuable new products from their expeditions to foreign cultures: before Columbus returned from his visit to the Americas, the French had no vanilla, the Swiss had no chocolate, the Irish had no potatoes, and the Italians had no tomato sauce. These new foods all came from plants from the Americas.

Today the most valuable of new plant products may be medicines. Tropical rainforests, home to a fifth of all the world's plant species, could offer an undreamed-of pharmacopoeia of medical cures for diseases ranging from cancer to AIDS. Only 1 to 5 percent of the Amazon's estimated 80,000 plant species have ever been studied—by modern scientists, that is. But tribal peoples know them well, and the village shaman, chief medicine man, acts as tribal archivist for the people's experience.

This is why the young ethnobotanist had first come to the Amazon jungle: to apprentice himself to a witch doctor—to become, in effect, a sorcerer's apprentice. In his pursuit of tribal knowledge of plants, Plotkin crosses cultures and travels around the world—from the rainforests of the Amazon to the spiny desert of Madagascar and then back to the sophisticated medical laboratories of the National Cancer Institute and his office in Washington, DC, where he serves as Vice-President of Conservation International.

AN ALIEN IN THE JUNGLE

Dr. Plotkin began his work with the Tirió, and to them, even a decade later, he still returns. When he first arrived, they called him pananakiri—the alien. The smooth-skinned Tirió laughed at Plotkin's hairy face and chest, and asked him many questions.

Through a translator from the neighboring Wai Wai tribe, Plotkin convinced the group to allow him to stay. They showed him to a hut where he unpacked his plant press and hung up his hammock.

A woman brought in a wooden bowl filled with what appeared to be foaming gruel and offered it to him.

"To this day, the hardest part of my job is not the heat or the mosquitoes," he says. "Without question, it is drinking cassiri." Thick, warm, and sour, cassiri is made in batches by women who chew up manioc and then spit it into a tub of water. Enzymes from their saliva ferment the beer.

Plotkin drank it down, smacked his lips and said through the translator, "Delicious! Can I have some more?" The woman smiled.

CATHARANTHUS ROSEUS
Containing more than 75 alkaloids, the rosy periwinkle is a veritable medicine cabinet. It is commonly used in the treatment of leukemia and Hodgkin's disease, and tribal people in Madagascar administer extracts to lower the blood sugar level of diabetics.

FOR A TRIBAL FEAST THESE
Yanomami girls have painted their bodies and pierced their faces with decorative little sticks.

Robert Harding Picture Library

WEARING THE WESTERN
clothes that are being seen more
frequently, this Tirió Indian
holds the bark of the virola tree.
Throughout the Amazon Indian
tribes use its blood-red sap as a cure
for fungal infections of the skin.

PAPAVER SOMNIFERUM
Morphine and codeine are extracts
from this plant, more commonly
known as the opium poppy.

THE SHAMAN OF THE
Yanomami Indians communicates
with the spirit world. Plant-induced
hallucinations and dancing are part
of the religious ritual.

JAGUAR SHAMAN

For the next few days of 90°F (32°C) heat,
Plotkin hacked his way through the jungle,
following the eldest shaman. Although at least
60 years old, the elder man leapt over small
streams like a deer, and the muscles of his arms
were hardened from decades of archery. Plotkin
noticed that he never seemed to smile. With
dour dignity, the shaman pointed out the bark,
leaves, roots, fruits, stems, and flowers he
commonly used for healing.

The young man had seen few of these
plants growing wild before. Many of them,
though, were from families he recognized—
families of plants known to be rich in powerful
chemicals. Plotkin had occasion to test some of
these plant medicines on himself. The sap of the
virola tree cured fungal infections he picked up
in the jungle—ailments that modern treatments
can barely touch. Once he walked into a wasp's
nest: when a shaman applied the bark scraped
from the kurunyuh shrub to the stings the pain
stopped within three minutes.

With each new plant the shaman pointed
out, Plotkin realized he could be seeing a drug
that might ease immeasurable human suffering.
He addressed his teacher, the shaman, in terms
of deep respect. He asked deferentially how the
medicines were prepared: "Do you burn it then
grind it? Is it rubbed on as a poultice or drunk

as a tea?" The shaman answered through the
interpreter. But he never smiled.

One night, after three days of working with
the Tirió shaman, Plotkin had a dream—or was
it a vision? As he lay in his hammock, he saw an
enormous jaguar materialize from the jungle
night. It walked into his hut, directly up to him,
and stared him in the face. Plotkin woke up
trembling, covered with sweat. In the morning,
he sent a message to the shaman via an interpreter: "Tell him," he said to the Wai Wai
messenger, "that I have seen the jaguar."

The shaman replied immediately to the
message. "Yes," he said, "That was me."

It was the first time Plotkin had known
the shaman to show a smile on his face.

THE GREAT WHITE WITCH DOCTOR

The Jaguar Shaman, as Plotkin has called him
ever after, has remained one of Plotkin's two
most revered teachers.

The other is a man Plotkin calls "the great
white witch doctor"— Richard Evans Schultes,
the tall, white-haired Harvard Professor

A PROCESSION OF YANOMAMI Indians arrives for a funeral feast. Typically at such feasts they grind up the bones of an ancestor to consume with banana beer.

DURING A SNUFF-TAKING ceremony, Dr. Plotkin's face is decorated by a Yanomami Indian as a gesture of friendship and welcome.

A YANOMAMI INDIAN SCRAPES bark from a tree of the nutmeg family to use in preparing snuff. Dried, ground-up snuff is used daily and has hallucinogenic properties.

Emeritus whose research arguably founded the modern science of ethnobotany.

Richard Schultes began a botanical exploration of the Amazon half a century ago, and still, at the robust age of 78, makes annual treks to revisit Colombia. He has single-handedly collected over 25,000 botanical specimens new to science, 5,000 of which he expects will prove one day to benefit humankind.

Plotkin and Schultes met when Plotkin was a young college dropout working at Harvard as a curatorial assistant. He signed up for a night course with Schultes. One slide from the first lecture changed Plotkin's life: "These are Yukuna Indians doing the sacred Kaiyahree dance under the influence of a hallucinogenic potion," Schultes narrated, projecting an image of three men wearing bark masks and grass skirts. "The one on the left has a Harvard degree."

At that moment, says Plotkin, he knew what he was going to do with his life. But becoming an ethnobotanist, he learned from Schultes, involves much more than learning the science, and more than having an adventuresome spirit. Perhaps what is even more important is practicing the art of jungle etiquette.

JUNGLE ETIQUETTE

"Much can be accomplished if the ethnobotanical investigator treats natives as a gentleman should," Schultes tells his classes. "He must realize that, far from a superior individual, he is in many respects far inferior to the native in the native's own environment."

Behaving like a gentleman in a remote village half a world away requires social graces unlisted by Emily Post. Among the dozens of tribes Plotkin has visited since he began his career, proper etiquette sometimes required that he pick squiggling worm larvae out of bubbling pots or that he dine demurely on boiled rat with the whiskers still on. He has participated in tribal festivals and ceremonies, festooned himself with macaw feathers and anteater claws, and let himself be painted with dark blue ink for tribal festivals. (He also discovered, on his way back to the United States, that the ink does not readily wash off.)

A Forest Pharmacy

Before bark from the cinchona or "fever bark" tree was used to cure malaria, millions of people in Europe had died of what was one of the world's most deadly diseases. Bloodletting had been the treatment of choice, until a Jesuit missionary returning from Ecuador in the seventeenth century brought back the bark that became thought of as a miraculous cure. For 200 years the drug was used successfully in Europe, although knowledge of how it was prepared was limited to the Indians who collected it and the Jesuits who exported it. Then the bark was analyzed and doctors discovered the alkaloid that made it effective. They named it quinine, a name taken from the Indian word quinquina. Doctors still use quinine to treat strains of the disease which are resistant to other drugs.

DIOSCOREA VILLOSA
Cortisone is extracted from this plant, which is a member of the yam family.

Victor Englebert/Comstock

Fever bark tree is only one of many plants considered a miracle drug. It is only recently that scientists discovered that another bark, that of the Pacific yew tree, has the potential to treat a variety of cancers.

Curare, a poison preparation still used on Amazon Indian arrow tips, was sought for centuries by explorers who had heard of its legendary ability to stun or quickly kill. Today, as tubocurarine, it is used routinely in hospitals as a preoperative muscle relaxer. The antidote to curare is derived from a plant now used to treat glaucoma.

About a quarter of modern medicines contain materials of natural origin; about half of these come from plants. Penicillin hails from a mold; morphine and codeine from the opium poppy; cortisone and diosgenin, one of the active ingredients in birth control pills, were originally extracted from Mexican and Guatemalan yams. Atropine has several medicinal uses and is made from the belladonna plant. Reserpine, which is derived from a shrub used to treat snakebite, lowers blood pressure and is a powerful drug for treating hypertension.

In Madagascar tribal people used extracts from the ornamental rosy periwinkle to lower diabetics' blood sugar levels. Tested in American labs as an insulin substitute, the drug was ineffective. But it proved to be the first truly effective drug for fighting childhood leukemia, producing remission in 85 percent of cases that were formerly hopeless.

The forest pharmacy contains numerous drugs whose properties have been synthesized and are in common use today. But what plants have we yet to discover? The rainforest is disappearing at a rate of 50 million acres (more than 20 million hectares) a year.

With it go plant species that may treat currently incurable diseases.

CINCHONA CALISAYA
The bark of this South American plant contains quinine, a life-saving medicine for the treatment of malaria.

HUNTING WITH A LONG BOW, A YANOMAMI
hunter uses curare-tipped arrows. For centuries curare
was sought by explorers for its legendary ability to stun
or to quickly kill.

ATROPA BELLADONNA
Atropine, a drug used in the treatment of stomach ulcers
among other things, is made from the belladonna plant.

Robert Harding Picture Library

LEARNING FROM THE TRIBES

Tribal people are not always ready to welcome
a pananakiri, however, even if he is a gentleman. On one trip Plotkin went to look for a
particular shaman in southeastern Peru. The first
day was spent traveling in the open, under the
hot tropical sun. The second day's journey took
him upriver—until his boat hit a log and sank.
His party retrieved most of the equipment,
flagged down another boat, and spent another
day in transit. Finally he arrived in the shaman's
village, to ask the great healer to share his plant
knowledge with the faraway visitor. Roughly
translated, the witch doctor's response was:
"None of your damn business." Plotkin packed
up his plant press and headed elsewhere.

"Eliciting information from these people is
not always easy," says Plotkin. "You come to live
with them, you come to eat with them, you
have to try to learn their language. You come to
build up a relationship based on trust, friendship, and even love before they'll open up to
you and teach you the secrets of the forest."

With the help of the Jaguar Shaman and
the other men and women of the Tirió tribe,
Plotkin has collected and studied well over
1,000 of the jungle plants they use in their daily
lives. They have taught him the secrets of their
arrow poison—and its antidote. They have explained 300 different plants used for medicines.
There has been so much to learn that he has
been coming back, year after year, for more
than a decade, each time learning a little more.
No longer do they call him pananakiri. Now
he is called Jacko—brother—and the dour-faced
Jaguar Shaman greets him by tickling him until
both explode with laughter.

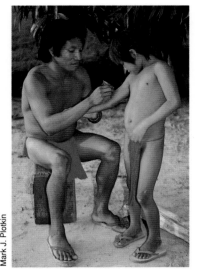

Mark J. Plotkin

A TIRIO INDIAN USES A VIROLA
leaf medicinally. There are many
species of virola trees in the
rainforest. Virola's effect and use
depend on how and when it is
collected and prepared. Indian
medicine men say it cures
infections and skin rashes.

A FISHING EXPEDITION IS AN
enjoyable excursion for all. Fish is
an important supplement to cassava,
the staple of the Yanomami Indians'
diet. The people use their knowledge
of plants to hunt fish in shallow
waters, using plant poisons to stun
the fish in the water, and then
scooping the fish into baskets.

Tropical Rainforests of the World

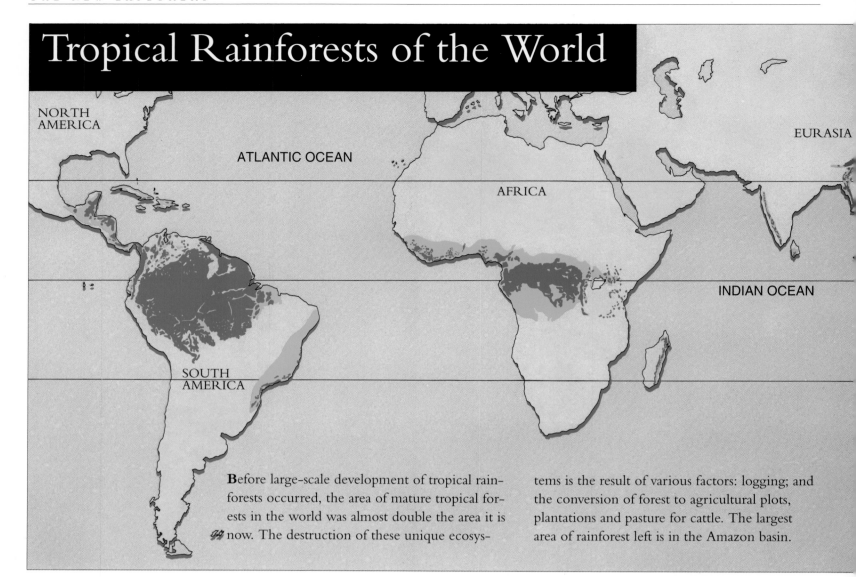

NORTH
AMERICA

ATLANTIC OCEAN

AFRICA

EURASIA

INDIAN OCEAN

SOUTH
AMERICA

Before large-scale development of tropical rainforests occurred, the area of mature tropical forests in the world was almost double the area it is now. The destruction of these unique ecosystems is the result of various factors: logging; and the conversion of forest to agricultural plots, plantations and pasture for cattle. The largest area of rainforest left is in the Amazon basin.

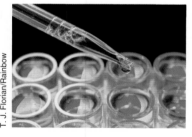

T. J. Florian/Rainbow

CELL CULTURE VIALS OF
tropical plant-derived medicines are among the many thousands of plants being studied in laboratory tests at the National Cancer Institute and in the laboratories of many large pharmaceutical companies.

➤ **AS THE RAINFOREST SHRINKS**
from forest burnings and as Western influences grow, the Indians' red breechcloths will give way to trousers and polyester dresses. Over ninety tribes have disappeared since the turn of the century.

THE SHRINKING RAINFOREST

Each year as he flies over the rainforest which surrounds the Tirió's village, Plotkin finds the tree-cloaked areas smaller and smaller. Each year he finds fewer young adults in the village. One of his young hunting buddies just left for the city to work as a night-watchman in a factory.

Worldwide, rainforests like the Tirió's are being stripped for lumber and cleared for cattle ranches and farms at the rate of 2,500 acres (1,000 hectares) a day. Rainforest species are disappearing faster than scientists can name them. And disappearing faster yet, says Plotkin, is the specialized knowledge of elderly village medicine men, like the Jaguar Shaman.

"Every time one of these medicine men dies, it is as if a library has burned down," he observes. "In fact, it's worse than that, because this is knowledge that is recorded nowhere else. When these men die, this knowledge is lost and it is lost forever."

Today Western scientists are scrambling to tap into that knowledge before it is lost. In

Kurtis Productions

1988, the US National Cancer Institute launched a five-year, $2.6 million program to scour the world's tropical rainforests, collecting plants from Asia, Africa, and South America with medical potential. "Nature contains a lot of novel and unusual molecules that the chemist at the bench may not have ever discovered," says Dr. Gordon Cragg, a scientist with the natural products branch of the Institute.

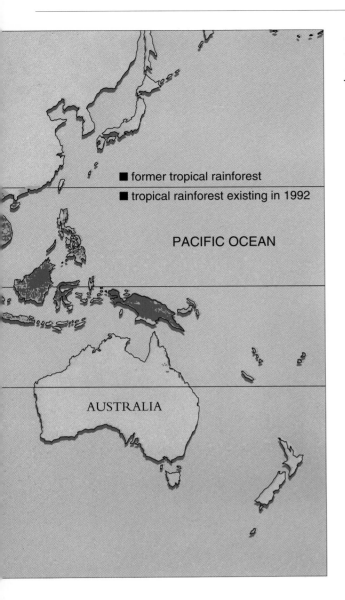

■ former tropical rainforest

■ tropical rainforest existing in 1992

PACIFIC OCEAN

AUSTRALIA

and is proving a tremendous help to the four young Tirió men who are now learning the Jaguar Shaman's trade—the first apprentices he has had since Plotkin showed up a decade ago.

Amid the doleful predictions about the future of tropical rainforests, amid ideologies that would seem to pit human culture against the survival of the natural world, Plotkin's exploration of tribal traditions offers inspiration and hope. Ethnobotany is showing the important role and potential contribution of so-called primitive peoples—who are now recognised as the real keepers of the forest.✪

CURCUMA LONGA
Commonly known as turmeric, this plant's main medicinal usage is for blood diseases and eye infections. Popular as a cooking spice, turmeric also aids digestion.

THE BURNING OF VIRGIN FORESTS *is turning the once lush Amazon into a dry desolate plain. What species may be extinguished in the conflagration ... what cures for human disease will be lost forever?*

If these products which the Indians are teaching scientists about do prove to hold the secrets of new medical cures, they will provide a powerful new economic argument for un-developed nations to preserve their dwindling rainforests from chainsaws and bulldozers—one of the conservation incentives expounded at the headquarters of Conservation International.

THE SORCERER'S APPRENTICE

But Plotkin is also doing something more. Conservation International recently initiated a "Sorcerer's Apprentice" program to employ young men and women in forest societies to learn from traditional healers and midwives. The program is already supporting tribal apprentices in Costa Rica and Suriname.

In the process of exploring the plant lore of the Tirió, Plotkin is also working to preserve the culture that produced it. Recently he presented to village elders the results of his research document on the Tirió pharmacopoeia. This work has been translated into the Tirió language

Chico Paulo/Stock Photos/DDB Stock Photo

THE INTENSE BLUE-GREEN LIGHT
*beam produced by an argon laser
pinpoints and destroys target tissue
during eye, brain, and gynecological
surgery. The narrow and uniform
light is generated by a powerful
electric current passing through an
argon gas filled tube.*

➤ THIS CROSS-SECTIONAL VIEW
*of the human head was created by
magnetic resonance imaging (MRI).*

The Laser's Edge

LEONARD J. CERULLO

As the last decade of the twentieth century begins, the neurosurgeon has an arsenal of technological marvels to work with. Of all the technological advances that have occurred in the last ten years, it is the laser that has made the most dramatic contribution to medicine and, more particularly, to brain surgery. This new technology allows doctors to penetrate deep within the brain. Dr. Leonard Cerullo, Medical Director of the Chicago NeuroSurgical Center, is one of the world's foremost neurosurgeons. He is in the front line of the war against brain disease, fighting battles with the medical world's most sophisticated technology.

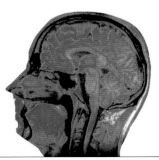

A CAT SCAN IS IN PROGRESS, *with the scanner and patient in the background and the radiographer working at the scanner's computer terminal in the foreground.*

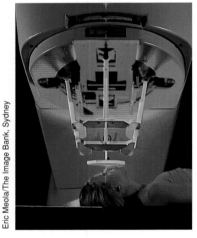

THIS CAT SCAN IS PROJECTING *low-dosage x-ray beams through the brain. Disruptions in x-ray absorption signal an abnormality.*

Hundreds of years ago the Aztecs, Incas, and other early civilizations relied on rough trepanation techniques to bore a hole in the skull when they performed brain surgery. Such techniques, with very little change, were used for brain surgery during the centuries that followed. It is only in the last two decades that science has provided surgeons with a technology that has substantially advanced the area of brain surgery. The development of laser technology has revolutionized this area of medicine and enabled neurosurgeons to perform procedures that were not previously possible.

TOOLS FOR DIAGNOSIS

Treating disorders of the brain has always posed a special difficulty for physicians. The brain is housed in such a rigid casing (the skull) and is so densely packed that any injury or disorder, such as a tumor, abscess, or blood clot, creates a buildup of pressure. For example, as a tumor expands, it compresses the nearby brain tissue and can lead to blindness, dementia, or paralysis. In some cases a tumor cannot be completely removed, yet removing some portion of it will relieve the pressure and the attendant symptoms. In other cases a tumor may have deadly potential and must be removed as quickly as time and technology allow.

Essentially there are three major obstacles to successful brain surgery. First, surgeons must precisely locate the problem. Second, they must control bleeding from the scalp, skull, and brain. And, third, they must control pressure and swelling within the brain and skull that may occur during surgery.

LOCATING THE PROBLEM

The array of diagnostic tools available today has overcome the obstacle of precisely locating the site of the problem. For the neurosurgeon, one of the main tools in diagnosing a brain problem is computerized axial tomography (CAT). Developed in the early 1970s, CAT scans ushered in a new era of sophisticated technology. Developed specifically for the study of the brain, CAT scans provide images of the brain substance itself, going beyond the capability of traditional x-rays and using less radiation. The technique uses a computer to measure the loss of power of a number of intersecting x-ray beams as they pass through the brain, and to produce clear cross-sectional images of the brain, allowing tumors to be identified and located with great precision.

Magnetic resonance imaging (MRI), which has been in use since the 1980s, provides images of the brain of even greater detail. The patient lies inside a massive cylindrical magnetic field and is exposed to bursts of magnetism followed by radio waves. MRI uses strong magnetic fields to orient molecules within the brain, and radiowaves to jolt them out of position. Sensors then measure the energy given off as they spin back into position. From this information, the computer is able to provide detailed and clear pictures of the brain, its vessels, and even the chemical composition of its cells. For the neurosurgeons and their patients, these advances mean that brain disease, the enemy, now has no place to hide.

Neurosurgeons also use angiograms as a diagnostic tool. With a television monitor to assist, the doctor threads a catheter into a brain artery. This artery is injected with iodine (which is impervious to x-rays), x-rays are taken, and the doctor is provided with a picture that shows the relationship between the artery and any disease or pathology in the brain.

CONTROLLING BLEEDING

The development in the 1960s of bipolar cautery allowed the surgeon to better control bleeding. This sophisticated electrocautery confines the heat-generating electrical current to the tips of the operating forceps, thus reducing the spreading of thermal damage to nearby tissue. With the development of the laser, even more advances have been made in this area, and the laser can also be used to coagulate tissue and stop bleeding.

The Early History of Brain Surgery

In some early cultures, such as those of the Aztecs and Incas, any diseases of the brain that had no visible wounds, that were not part of the natural order of life, were seen as coming from evil spirits. And such spiritual disorders required spiritual treatments.

Elaborate ceremonies were held to cast off evil spirits. Dances were performed, drums beaten. Incantations, amulets, charms, and all the other devices available to the local spiritual healer were employed. When these approaches didn't work their magic, the healer turned to a more direct approach to let the demons out: trepanation.

For this, the spiritual healer used a primitive tool to bore a hole in the skull. The hole was usually the size of a napkin ring. In some cases, opening the skull might release the pressure emanating from within. But the tools were extremely primitive and they might just as easily destroy the brain of the afflicted.

Trepanation was performed for centuries, perhaps by more sophisticated practitioners. It remained a standard surgical procedure for headaches, epilepsy, and unusual problems. And latter-day trepanations were not greatly different in technique or in success from those evil spirit releases practiced by the Aztecs and Incas.

Post-mortem examinations allowed surgeons in the seventeenth and eighteenth centuries to begin to under-stand the nervous system and its connection to specific areas within the brain. They learned that the back of the brain controlled vision. Later, by skillful examination of patients before and after surgery, they began to pinpoint, with variable accuracy, left versus right side processes.

A major problem of brain surgery was bleeding. No stitches could be applied to the bony surface of the skull.

And no stitches could be applied to the substance of the brain itself. The introduction of a seemingly simple bone wax in the late 1800s was the first effective control against constant oozing of blood from bone edges of the skull opening. Brain surgery was becoming routine by the early 1900s, and neurology was beginning to be a specialty in medicine.

The introduction of electrocautery in the 1920s permitted safe and effective control of bleeding from the brain's soft functional tissues. Neurologists could now direct surgeons to the site of attack and anticipate at least some measure of success. Further refine-ment was dependent on the development of new technology to help in both the location and the treatment of brain injuries and disorders.

Prado Museum, Madrid/Giraudon

DURING THE MIDDLE AGES BRAIN SURGERY AND ITS ASSOCIATION *with the release of evil spirits often required the presence of the clergy to ensure success. Jerome Bosch (1462–1516),* **Extraction de la pierre de folie.**

Mary Evans Picture Library

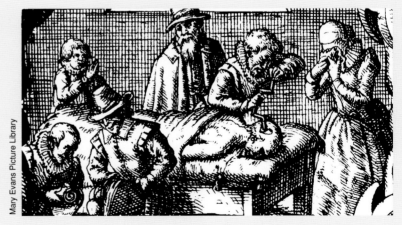

FROM PREHISTORIC TIMES, BRAIN SURGERY INVOLVED BORING A HOLE *through the skull with a sharp-edged tool. This illustration of brain surgery dates from the seventeenth century.*

A. Tsiaras/Science Source/
Photo Researchers Inc.

THE BRAIN'S ELECTRICAL
activity can be recorded by electro-
encephalography (EEG). Electrodes
are applied to the scalp or placed
against the surface of the brain
during surgery.

LASERS HAVE MEDICAL USES
other than neurosurgery. Here a
laser is used to burn through plaque
in an artery.

CONTROLLING PRESSURE AND SWELLING

Advances in anesthesiology and physiology solved many of the problems of control of intracranial pressure during surgery. Techniques such as brain mapping and continuous EEG recording enable physicians to know on a moment-to-moment basis the exact status of an anesthetized patient. By using this information neurosurgeons are able to anticipate and avoid procedures which might damage the brain.

The three major barriers to successful neurosurgery had been overcome. The stage was set for the new generation of weapons, such as the operating microscope and the laser, to be used in the battle against brain disease.

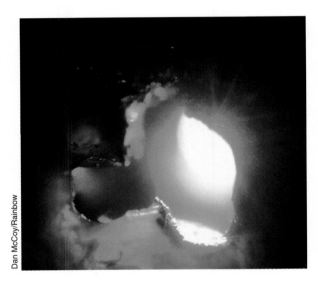

Dan McCoy/Rainbow

MICRONEUROSURGERY

When specialists in ophthalmology brought the new operating microscope to the attention of neurosurgeons, microneurosurgery was born. This new microscope allowed surgeons to work with great accuracy by illuminating living tissue, offering enhanced magnification, and the ability to use binocular vision through a deep and narrow exposure as the surgeon operated. The results of using this microscope confirmed that gentleness and precision, seemingly taken for granted, were the most important determinants of successful brain surgery.

THE DEATH RAY THAT HEALS

The laser ray was first mentioned as a "death ray" in 1898 by the writer H. G. Wells in *War of the Worlds*, his science fiction fantasy. His death ray was a beam of light that could pierce bricks or trees. From the realm of science fiction the idea of the laser ray traveled to the science lab, and as early as 1917 Albert Einstein and Nils Bohr speculated that atoms which had absorbed radiation or light could be stimulated to release that light as energy. Fifty years later this theory began to be put into practice. The energy harnessed by the intense light beam of a laser was soon able to be used for cutting through metal, scoring diamonds, or repairing the damaged tissues in the eye. For neurosurgical

AFTER USING A GAS DRILL TO
enter the skull, the surgeon must
cut through the soft protective layers
of the brain. With a microscope
operated by foot pedal, the surgeon
can control focus and magnification
while guiding the laser beam
with hand dials.

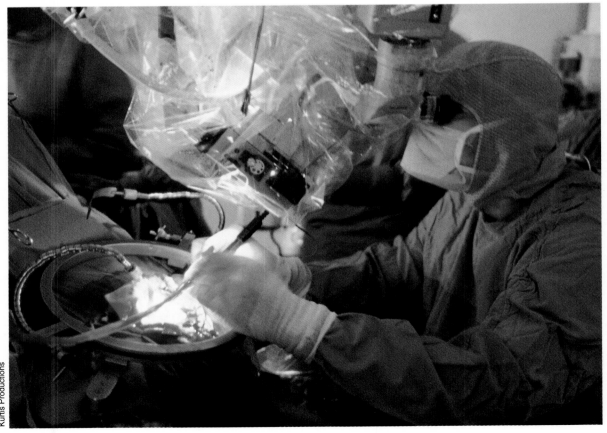

Kurtis Productions

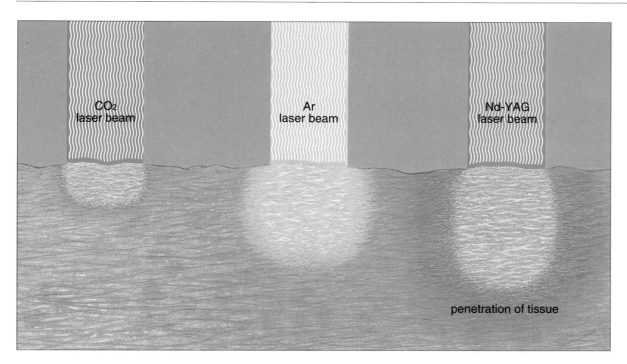

Mel Di Giacomo/Bob Masini/The Image Bank

penetration of tissue

THE DIFFERENT TYPES OF *lasers generate specific wavelengths. The different wavelengths of these three medical lasers each have different absorption activity with biological tissue. The carbon dioxide (CO_2) laser is absorbed by water and is ideal for cutting and vaporizing tissue. The Argon–ion (Ar) laser is absorbed by pigmented materials such as blood and is an excellent laser for coagulation. The Nd-YAG (neodymium yttrium–aluminum–Garnet) laser is also absorbed by pigmented materials and has a deeper thermal effect on tissue.*

use, however, early laser-generating equipment was too cumbersome, and the device was abandoned until the mid-seventies.

The laser (Light Amplification by the Stimulated Emission of Radiation) generates a specific wavelength of light. Conventional light sources, such as an electric bulb or flame, radiate their atoms randomly, in all directions, and over a wide range of wavelengths. Laser light, in contrast, is organized and its wavelengths are uniform, concentrated, and regularly spaced in a narrow wavelength frequency range. When the laser's light waves move in unison they produce a monochromatic light of enormous intensity, the power rated in watts. The power released by an electric light bulb is 100 watts. A laser can release ten billion watts. Doctors can pass the intense heating power of this wattage through optical fibers and concentrate it onto a tiny area to burn away diseased tissue and coagulate bleeding vessels.

Laser's light is so intense, so pure and, when concentrated, so hot that it can vaporize tissue in several billionths of a second. The laser's narrow beam of energy can cut through tissue with less surgical trauma than the surgeon's conventional scalpel. Essentially a bloodless scalpel, the laser has quietly revolutionized surgery.

Two decades ago neurosurgeons would have tried to remove a patient's brain tumor by pulling it with instruments or their fingers. The results of such an approach often damaged the nearby areas of the brain, which were pulled out along with the tumor. Conventional surgical tools could not reach tumors located deep

within the brain. Today, laser light, controlled by dials, aided by the microscope for precise visualization, is beamed from an optical fiber to shrink such tumors.

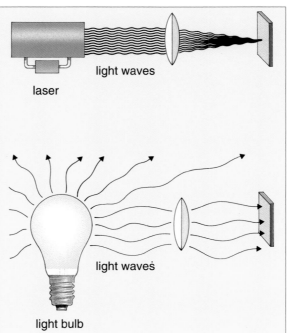

A CO_2 (CARBON DIOXIDE) LASER *beam is directed at a tumor during brain surgery. The CO_2 laser is widely used in brain surgery for its ability to vaporize tissue with minimal damage to the surrounding area. Because these light rays are invisible, a red helium–neon pilot light is added as an aiming beam.*

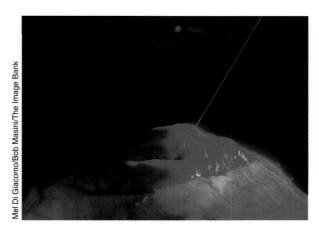

THE LIGHT PRODUCED BY AN *incandescent light bulb has no coherence or directionality. The light produced by a laser, however, is parallel, monochromatic and coherent, so it can be focused by a lens.*

Using the Laser

The neurosurgeon begins a laser surgical procedure to remove a tumor by using the laser's light to vaporize the tumor's outer cover. The laser soon reduces the cover to smoke. The laser is not only able to make such extremely delicate superficial incisions, but also it does not affect brain tissue that is only a few cell widths away.

To remove the tumor itself, the neurosurgeon must work slowly and carefully, using forceps to push the tumor away from healthy tissue, while using the laser at low energy to vaporize the tumor. For tumors that are particularly dense, the wattage of the laser must be increased. Extremely tough tumors that once would have been deemed inoperable are easy work for the laser's intense power.

When operating with a laser, the surgeon can manipulate the wavelength, exposure length (time), and output power of the laser, and the amount of tissue area to be exposed. Some wavelengths of laser can be delivered through glass "wires" or fibers. Others are bounced from mirror to mirror in order to reach a target at a difficult angle.

As accurate as the laser is, however, it is the neurosurgeon's skill that may make the difference between a healthy outcome, paralysis, or even death. And brain surgery, even with a laser, is a long procedure. The painstaking work with the laser for one tumor can take six hours or more of nonstop concentration. The laser is used both to vaporize tissue and to coagulate leaking blood vessels, so reducing the bleeding that was such a problem in the early days of brain surgery.

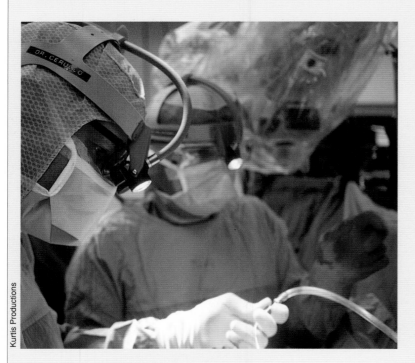

Kurtis Productions

HOW A GAS LASER WORKS

A laser produces a coherent beam of light. In a gas laser, gas atoms absorb energy from electrons moving through the gas and energy is released as light.

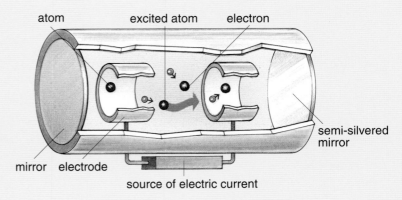

atom   excited atom   electron
semi-silvered mirror
mirror   electrode
source of electric current

1. In a gas laser, gas atoms are excited to a high-energy state by electrons in an electric current. One excited atom spontaneously releases a light ray.

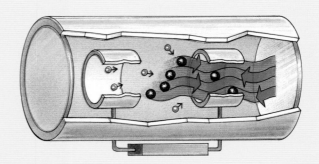

2. The light ray from the excited atom hits another gas atom causing it also to emit a light ray. The mirrors at each end of the laser reflect the light rays, causing more and more excited atoms to release light.

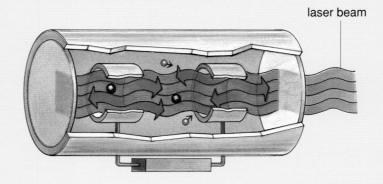

laser beam

3. All the light rays vibrate together forming a coherent light beam. This beam increases in strength as more and more light rays are emitted and it pulses through the semi-silvered mirror as laser light.

Dan McCoy/Rainbow

LASERS ARE WIDELY USED IN *other applications. This dramatic view is of a communications laser.*

NEW TECHNIQUES

Now neurosurgeons are investigating new laser types, exploring lasers that can penetrate even further to reach deeply buried blood clots. They are experimenting with different laser wavelength frequencies. And they are experimenting with combinations of chemicals and lasers. Researchers are injecting photosensitive dyes or other elements such as gold into areas of the brain where they may be retained, such as tumor sites. They then radiate the dyes within the tumor cells with a laser beam, trying to excite the chemicals and destroy the covering cells. For some disorders of the brain, unamenable to standard laser procedures, this technique of photosensitization may have important implications.

There are many frontiers left to conquer in the war against brain disease. But in a very brief space of time the laser has removed many of the obstacles to successful brain surgery and changed the lives of neurosurgery's patients, clearing away tumors, prolonging and improving life.☢

Alexander Tsiaras/Science Photo Library/The Photo Library

AN ARGON LASER BEAM IS BEING FOCUSED *through a microscope onto the brain. Typically used for photocoagulating blood vessels, the argon laser's blue-green or green light is easily absorbed by hemoglobin. Major investigations are underway to use the argon laser as a "vapor laser" in tandem with experimental photosensitive chemicals for reaching currently inaccessible locations in the brain.*

≪ **WEARING THE HEADGEAR USED FOR OPENING** *and closing procedures, Dr. Cerullo adjusts a suctioning tube during brain surgery. The headgear includes a headlight and glasses that magnify 2 to 4 times, providing a wider field of view than the operating microscope.*

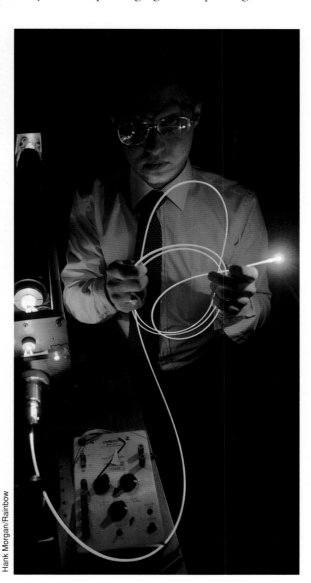

Hank Morgan/Rainbow

DR. TERRY FULLER HOLDS IN HIS *hands the fiber optic cable that transmits the carbon dioxide laser he helped develop. Dr. Fuller is head of the laser surgery research laboratory at Sinai Hospital in Detroit.*

The Invisible Blade

Imagine the precision of a laser without the need to open the skull. With the development of Gamma Knife radiosurgery (stereotactic radiosurgery), neurosurgeons can use an "invisible blade" to treat brain tumors and malformations of arteries and veins. Stereotaxis is the ability to mathematically locate any object by its height, length, and width from a given reference point. This concept allowed early navigators to cross the oceans and more recent explorers to navigate space. The same principles apply to brain surgery.

The Gamma Knife uses approximately 200 finely focused beams of gamma radiation to converge on a target in the brain. The process uses multiple beams or a single beam from multiple directions. The convergence of the ionizing radiation is intense enough to destroy without the need for open surgery and is accurate to within one-tenth of a millimeter. Tumors can be operated on without breaking the skin.

This knifeless operation is performed without general anesthesia. The sedated, awake patient is outfitted with a

DEVELOPED BY DR. LARS LEKSELL *in Stockholm, Sweden, the Gamma Knife treats conditions previously considered inoperable, such as vascular anomalies in critical areas of the brain.*

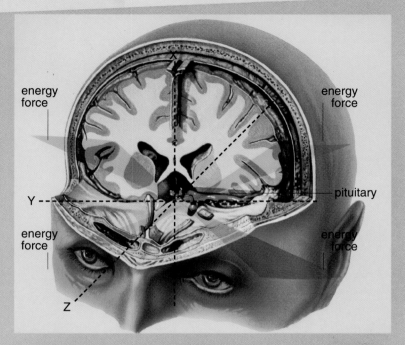

energy force

energy force

pituitary

energy force

energy force

Y

Z

STEREOTACTIC RADIOSURGERY REQUIRES THE MATHEMATICAL LOCATION *of a tumor or malformation. Here, in an operation on the pituitary, the intersection of X, Y, and Z locates the target point for the beams. The blue triangles represent energy forces focusing in from different directions.*

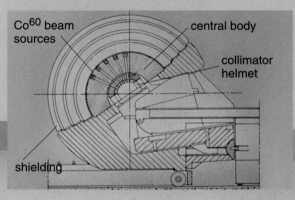

Co^{60} beam sources

central body

collimator helmet

shielding

THE SOURCE OF THE GAMMA KNIFE'S ENERGY IS RADIOACTIVE COBALT *or Co^{60}. There are approximately 200 cobalt^{60} sources arranged in a hemisphere, all of which are pointed at the target. These sources transmit from the unit through a collimator helmet worn by the patient. This helmet is fastened in position by a stereotactic frame. The gamma unit is cased in a strong shielding to prevent any radiation leakage.*

The Gamma Knife

stereotactic head frame which must be carefully adjusted to keep the head from moving. The frame also has marks which appear on angiograms and CAT scans to help determine the precise location of the problem. The 30 minutes it takes to fit the frame is often longer than it takes to perform the operation—on average 20 minutes. The frame is then attached to a helmet containing holes through which the radiation beams are emitted during the operation. Using remote control, doctors focus radiation beams through the helmet to treat the problem area. Although

pressure is felt during the operation, no pain is experienced. The patient is even free to talk during the process. The skull is left intact and the patient can leave the hospital the next day, although the healing process can take days, months, or even years.

The Gamma Knife was approved for use in the United States in 1987. Less than two dozen are available in the world. This marriage of mathematics and physiology has enabled neurosurgeons to reach the goal of eliminating traditional brain surgery.

WHERE IT ALL BEGINS:
a photomicrograph captures the moment at which the blastocyst formed from the union of sperm and ova begins its first division to form the embryo. The rapidly increasing ability of biologists to intervene in and to manipulate this process has far-reaching implications in the struggle to maintain species diversity in a world rapidly being stripped of its natural environments.

➤ FOR MILLENNIA, ANIMALS *have been maintained in captivity to serve a wide variety of purposes. In ancient Egypt, the sacred ibis was worshipped and protected as a destroyer of snakes and locust plagues, and large numbers of its mummified remains have been found in temples.*

Cincinnati Zoo

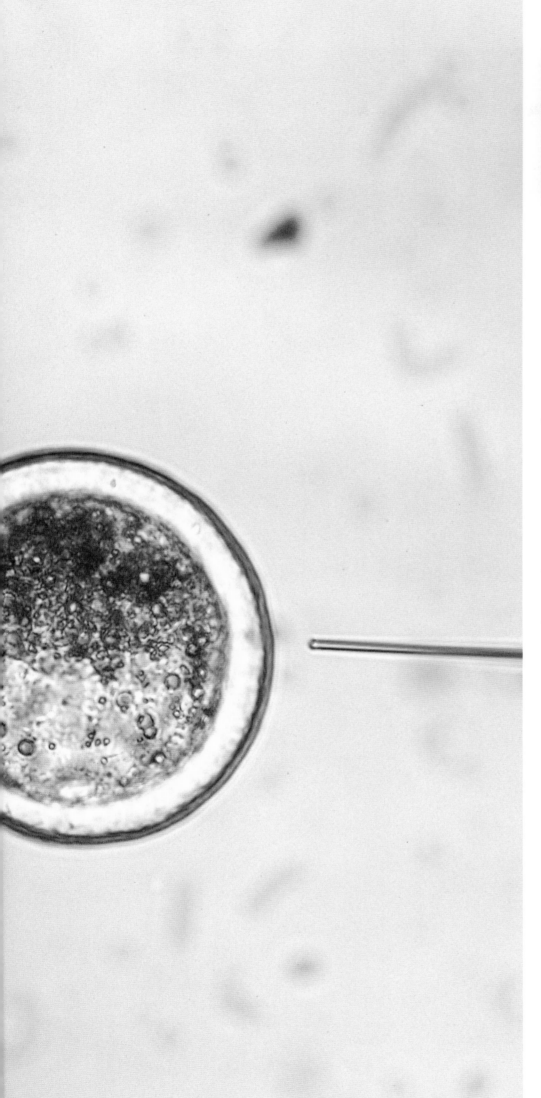

Test Tube Zoo

BETSY L. DRESSER AND
KAREN B. WACHS

As many as 100 species of plants and animals become extinct every day. Researchers predict that in the next few decades half of all the world's species may die out. As the threat to the world's wildlife grows, a team of scientists at the Cincinnati Zoo is using the latest in reproduction technology to save endangered species. Dr. Betsy Dresser and her team of scientists at the Center for Reproduction of Endangered Wildlife (CREW) are working to preserve the world's diverse animal life by applying such state of the art tools as artificial insemination, embryo transfer, *in vitro* fertilization, and surrogate parenting.

AKBAR CROSSES THE GANGES *with his imperial retinue. Greatest of the Mogul emperors, Akbar ruled India from 1556 to 1605. He was noted for his fascination with elephants, and was reputed to have maintained stables of tens of thousands of these huge beasts.*

The Victoria and Albert Museum/ Bridgeman/ Giraudon

Ronald Sheridan/Ancient Art & Architecture Collection

HUMANS HAVE ALWAYS SHOWN *a preoccupation with the very large and the very fierce in the animal world. Here a lion draws a chariot, portrayed on an Italian terracotta plaque dating from the second century A.D.*

THIS ANCIENT MOSAIC *portraying a nobleman riding a leopard illustrates the fascination wild animals held for the ruling classes of the ancient world.*

House of Masks, Delos, Greece/The Bridgeman Art Library

Although Noah could be credited as the first zookeeper and the first conservationist, historically the attitude of humans towards animals has been less benign than Noah's. To appreciate the role that today's zoos are playing, it is helpful to look back at the history of human involvement with wild animals, for the idea of a zoo or menagerie dates back to ancient times.

ROYAL MENAGERIES

The keeping and displaying of exotic animals is a tradition common to the ruling classes of the ancient civilizations of Asia, Africa, and Europe. Huge collections of wild animals were kept for royal amusement or as symbols of social status or imperial power. What may have been the first formal zoo dates to the fifteenth century B.C., when Hatshepsut, then queen of Egypt, commissioned an animal-collecting expedition. It returned with monkeys, leopards, cheetahs, and birds, and introduced the rare giraffe to the queen's palace gardens.

Generally, exotic animals were presented as gifts or tribute to kings and persons of power, and they were considered as valuable as precious metals and jewels. Animals were also acquired on military expeditions to foreign countries, either as the trophies of military victories or through trade in exchange for territory.

Human attitudes toward wild animals in ancient civilizations were an odd mix of reverence and cruelty. Egyptians considered certain animals sacred, like the lion, the baboon, and the

ibis. These animals were given royal protection. In both Egyptian and Roman civilizations, wild animals were used extensively in triumphal processions and trained to pull chariots.

Animals were later used in more violent spectacles. By the first century B.C., Rome's highest officials were staging animal hunts and increasingly bloody battles between animals in the arenas. Later, in the 1500s, Henry VIII and also Elizabeth I of England entertained visitors by staging combats between lions and tigers.

MORE THAN CURIOSITIES

The first effort to acquire scientific knowledge of animals came perhaps in 1100 B.C., when the Garden of Intelligence was created by the ruling Chinese emperor. It contained examples of every animal to be found within the bounds of the then Chinese empire, and is thought to have been established for educational purposes.

In the fourth century B.C., Aristotle kept a private "zoo." From his study of living animals, he prepared an encyclopedia which classified and described over 300 species.

With a few exceptions, the idea of keeping animals for scientific study and education did not begin in earnest until the nineteenth century. At that time interest in animals came on the heels of a number of new theories of animal physiology and relationships. These included Linnaeus' revolutionary systematic classification of animals and plants and Cuvier's studies in comparative animal anatomy and animal habits.

THE FIRST MODERN ZOOS

Louis XIV of France is often credited with planning the first real "zoo" at Versailles in the seventeenth century. However, this zoo did not become "public" until after the French Revolution, which began in 1789.

The word "zoo" itself was first coined as a colloquial expression for the Zoological Society of London. The open-to-the-public Zoological Society of London was established in 1826. Soon after, the idea of city zoos maintained with public funds took hold, and public zoos were built in many European and American cities.

At first, most zoos were content to merely exhibit wildlife and to provide educational displays. When the captive animals died, they were simply replaced with new wild caught specimens. But by the 1960s, the impact of the human population explosion, pollution, poaching, and over-hunting was taking its toll. Zoos found that it was becoming difficult or impossible to replenish their animal collections from the wild.

Zoos then began to take on a new role as stewards and conservators. These new stewards

THE ROMANS WERE FOND OF spectacles in which large numbers of gladiators fought to the death with wild beasts in an arena. This ivory carving is from Constantinople (now Istanbul), established as the eastern capital of the Roman Empire by Emperor Constantine in A.D.330.

LOUIS XIV OF FRANCE WAS determined to make his palace at Versailles the showcase of all things regal. Part of the palace grounds was given over to his private zoo, portrayed in this drawing.

ZEBRAS AT HOME UNDER THE *slopes of Mount Kilimanjaro, Kenya. Modern zoos have an increasingly important role to play in animal conservation as wild places like this rapidly disappear.*

Australian Picture Library/Vincent Serventy

THE TYPICAL NINETEENTH-*century zoo displayed a preference for the largest and most exotic of animals. There was little concern for housing them in enclosures appropriate to their various lifestyles, and captive breeding programs were all but non-existent.*

Ann Ronan Picture Library

Dan McCoy/Rainbow

BULL SEMEN IS LOWERED INTO *frozen nitrogen. Stored at a temperature of -321°F (-196°C), its viability can be maintained indefinitely.*

began to realize how little was actually known about the genetics, reproductive physiology, and requirements of wild animals. Zoo professionals really began to tackle the problem, and the quality of wild animal care rapidly improved.

A MASTERPLAN FOR SPECIES SURVIVAL

In 1980, the American Association of Zoological Parks and Aquariums (AAZPA), named conservation as its highest priority. Zoos realized that if they were to keep wild animals alive in captivity for long periods of time they required a new, coordinated, scientific approach to conservation, and so the Species Survival Plan (SSP) was created in 1981. It was a plan devised by AAZPA that aimed even further than saving endangered captive populations: zoos also saw that they were becoming survival centers for animals vanishing in the wild.

The SSP selects endangered species considered "sustainable" in the future and prepares a breeding strategy for each species. By breeding animals which are genetically sound, zoos hope to reinforce captive populations that are weak and on the verge of extinction. They also can reintroduce these animals in areas where the wild population has dwindled, become genetically depressed, or totally disappeared. Ten years after its creation the SSP was managing cooperative captive breeding programs for 62 different species of animals.

The captive care of each species is another major concern of the SSP, and it promotes research in this area as well.

THE FROZEN ZOO

In addition to preserving living populations of wild animals, an SSP goal is to maintain representatives of the world's endangered wildlife in "frozen zoos." There, scientists can preserve the valuable genetic material—the eggs, embryos, tissue, and semen—of endangered species in liquid nitrogen freezers, thereby preserving a species' genetic diversity in a limited amount of space. As might be expected, there is limited room in zoos for the many offspring necessary to continue genetically sound family lines. Frozen germ plasm (gametes and embryos) also allows shipping frozen sperm or embryos between distant zoos rather than risking the often difficult transport of animals designated for breeding. This option of artificial breeding also can assist animals who are physically or psychologically incompatible for mating but whose breeding is necessary for the species' future.

In Vitro Fertilization

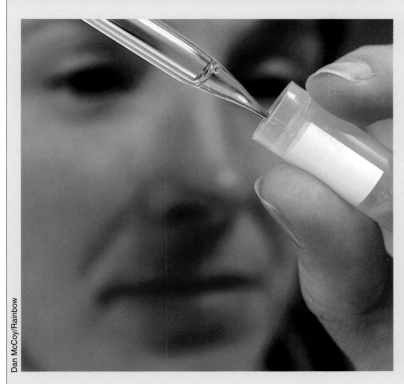

Dan McCoy/Rainbow

A REPRODUCTIVE PHYSIOLOGIST WORKS WITH AN UNFERTILIZED
horned oryx egg. The oryx is a large African antelope.

Perhaps the most revolutionary technique in reproductive science, *in vitro* fertilization (IVF), also known as "test tube fertilization," has successfully allowed previously infertile couples to produce healthy babies. Researchers hope they can do for endangered wildlife what they have done for humans. To date much of the pioneering work with IVF has been done with endangered cats, such as the Indian desert cat, ocelot, and serval, and with primates, such as the baboon. Dr. Betsy Dresser and her team at CREW have been worldwide leaders in this research.

IVF eliminates many of the problems wildlife researchers have encountered with artificial insemination, a technique used for decades for farm livestock. With artificial insemination, sperm is collected from a genetically desirable male and then placed in a fertile female. However, knowledge of the female's reproductive cycle is critical, and pregnancy often does not occur, resulting in unnecessary stress to the animal and a loss of valuble time and genetic material.

IVF, in contrast, creates a pregnancy outside the body, in the laboratory. The process begins by collecting sperm from a male. The sperm is kept warm and sterile in a petri dish or test tube. Meanwhile a female has been injected with hormones to stimulate ovarian activity. Eggs are extracted from the female's ovaries with an apparatus which applies a gentle suction action. To begin an immediate fertilization, the eggs are put together with some of the sperm collected earlier.

Success now depends on keeping the eggs and sperm alive and healthy. Nutrients help keep them alive outside their natural environment. Fertilization will occur when a sperm cell penetrates an egg on its own or when researchers use a needle puncture technique to assist in penetrating the egg membrane.

Within 24 hours, researchers can watch the fertilized cells begin dividing to become an embryo. The cells can continue to mature, uninterrupted, until they are placed into a surrogate. It takes two or three more days before the embryo, the size of a speck of dust, is ready for transfer into a surrogate, which has been given a hormone injection to prepare its body to accept the embryo. Or the embryo may be placed in a liquid nitrogen tank and stored for future transfer.

After the transfer into the surrogate's uterus, proof of success is still months away. The researchers must wait out the gestation period. At any time the surrogate mother may shed the embryo, leaving researchers to review their techniques and begin the process again. Much of their review work involves intense study of the surrogate's reproductive cycle and a continual refining of the culture process to find the optimal time for transfers.

Cincinnati Zoo

IVF EMBRYOS ARE TRANSFERRED INTO THE UTERUS OF AN
anesthetized Indian desert cat, which is an endangered species.

Transcontinental Embryo Transfer

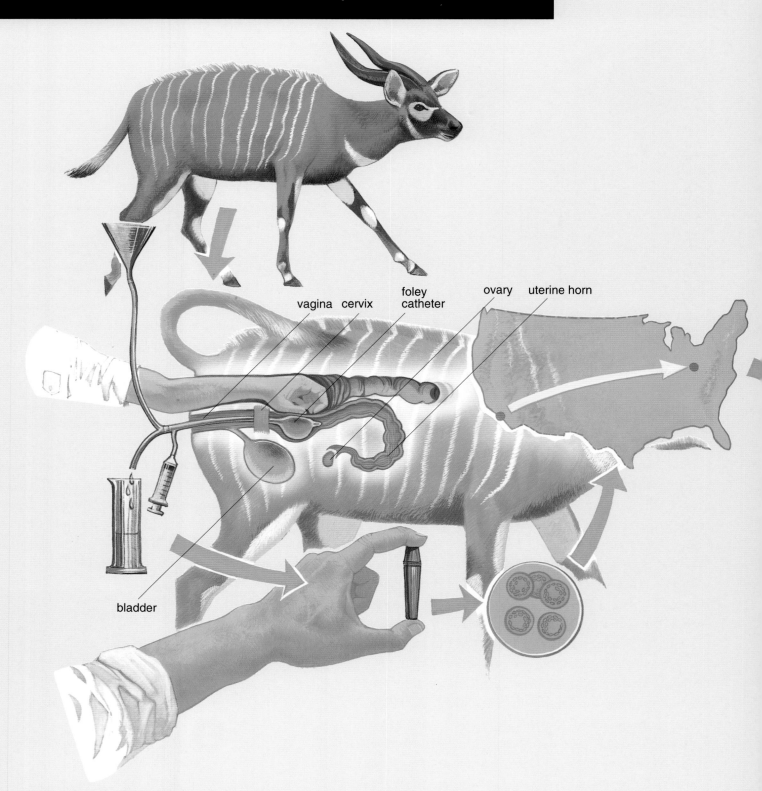

Less than 1,000 bongos exist in the wild today and only 70 live in captivity in North American zoos. The largest herd is at the Los Angeles Zoo. CREW, in cooperation with the Los Angeles Zoo, began a program in 1983 to increase the numbers of the bongo species.

In August 1983 a female bongo from the Los Angeles Zoo herd was selected as a donor for an experimental interspecies and intraspecies embryo transfer. She was injected with hormones to cause her to superovulate and was then bred naturally with a male bongo from the same herd. Meanwhile at the Cincinnati Zoo, 4 eland females and 1 bongo female were chosen to receive the embryos.

Two of the five embryos "took" and were carried to term by the surrogates—one of the elands and the bongo.

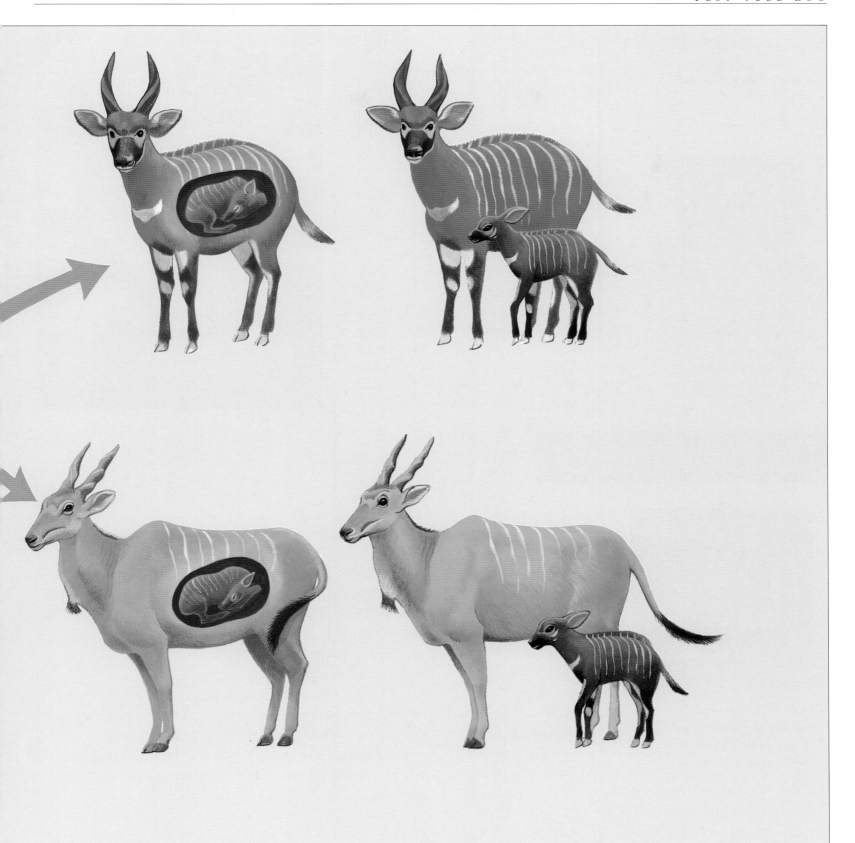

Non-surgical embryo recovery is a modification of the technique used in the commercial cattle industry. It involves the removal of free-floating microscopic embryos approximately seven days after fertilization, before they attach themselves to the female's uterine wall.

To remove the embryo the researcher's arm is inserted into the lower rectal passage of the animal which lies directly above the reproductive tract. The ovaries are examined first, before a foley catheter is passed through the cervix and up into the uterine horn.

A specially prepared saline solution is then flushed through the catheter and the uterus, then back out into the collection vessel, so that the embryos are transferred from the mother's body to the collection vessel.

➤ DR. DRESSER CHECKS A TANK *of liquid nitrogen in her "frozen zoo", containing the cryogenic samples of animal reproductive material at CREW.*

Cincinnati Zoo

A VETERINARY TEAM WORKS ON *an eland antelope during a non-surgical embryo collection procedure. Dr. Dresser's pioneering work in finding non-surgical methods of embryo transfer has attracted interest in zoos around the world.*

For years the domestic livestock industry has successfully and routinely used artificial reproduction techniques like embryo transfer, artificial insemination, and cryopreservation. However, to apply the same techniques to wild animals is a far more complicated and challenging task. For each new species they work with, researchers must start fresh, using an approach based on trial and error. They operate with the added pressure of knowing that their experiments are using the limited genetic materials of endangered animals.

The Center for Reproduction of Endangered Wildlife (CREW), at the Cincinnati Zoo and Botanical Garden, has been pioneering research in this exotic animal territory. CREW's director, Dr. Betsy Dresser, a reproductive physiologist, heads a team dedicated to preserving endangered species using the newest techniques in reproduction science. At the heart of their research facility lies CREW's Frozen Zoo and

Steve Feist

Out of the Test Tube

Steve Feist

PLANTS AS WELL AS ANIMALS CAN *be propagated using cryogenic techniques, and are potential candidates for the "frozen zoo" approach.*

The concept of using "universal surrogates" to incubate the embryos of rare and endangered species has now proven itself. Ideally, surrogates are either domestic animals or wild animals which are non-endangered and plentiful, but they must be closely related to the donor species in order for the pregnancy to be successfully completed. So far the eland antelope has proven a suitable surrogate for the bongo antelope, the Holstein cow for the Asian gaur, and the horse for the zebra. Dr. Dresser's team at CREW is in the early stages of fact-finding research with the rhino, and the white rhino is looking like a promising surrogate candidate for embryos of other rhino species.

CREW is hoping that the domestic cat will turn out to be a suitable surrogate for several species of small, endangered exotic cats. Because many exotic cats do not breed readily in captivity and have not responded well to artificial insemination, CREW has focused much of its

cat research on the development of *in vitro* fertilization techniques. With this technique, sperm and ova are collected separately and put together in a test tube so that fertilization occurs outside the body, or *in vitro*. In 1989, a domestic cat surrogate gave birth to an endangered Indian desert cat using these techniques. The Indian desert cat kitten was not only the world's first exotic cat conceived *in vitro*, but also the first cat of any kind to be born as the result of an interspecies embryo transfer.

This was one of the more fortunate cat species. For others, the research process goes more slowly. Finding the appropriate reproduction technology for each animal species takes time, in a world that is fast losing its wildlife and its wildlife habitat. Researchers must learn the intricacies of each animal's reproductive cycle and anatomy. Yet reproduction technology may be the most important conservation tool modern zoos possess. As technology continues to progress, many zoos of the future may indeed turn out to be frozen zoos and test tube zoos, holding animals waiting for space to breed.

A MALE INDIAN DESERT *cat with his surrogate mother, an ordinary domestic cat.*

Ron Austing/Cincinnati Zoo

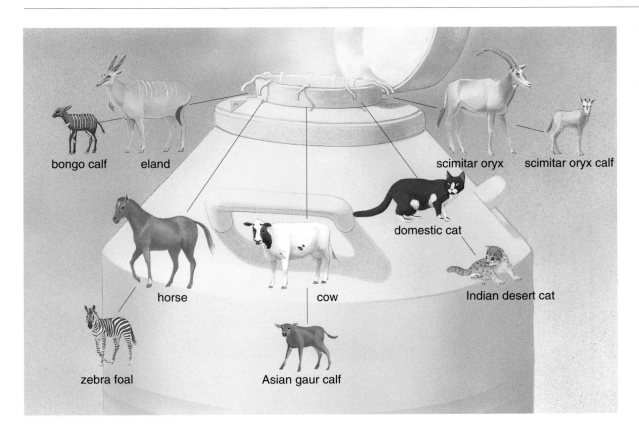

bongo calf   eland   scimitar oryx   scimitar oryx calf

horse   cow   domestic cat

Indian desert cat

zebra foal   Asian gaur calf

THE SUCCESS OF MANY SPECIES *transfers and frozen embryo transplants gives hope for the survival of endangered exotic species.*

Garden—tanks of liquid nitrogen within which lie the reproductive cells of dozens of different species of animals and plants. At temperatures of −321°F (−196°C), the genetic samples can be maintained in a state of suspended animation indefinitely. Later, the embryos can be thawed and "brought to life" by transplanting them into other animals which act as surrogate mothers.

CREW gained international attention in the early 1980s for its work in embryo transfers. 1983 marked the first successful nonsurgical embryo transfer in an exotic species: the eland, a shy, twisted-horned antelope, largest of all the antelope species. Dr. Dresser placed an eland embryo into a surrogate of the same species and a healthy eland calf was born. Shortly thereafter, Dr. Dresser used the same technique for an interspecies transfer. This time an eland was a surrogate for the development and birth of a healthy bongo calf—the bongo is a rare, spiral-horned antelope, the most colorful of the antelope species and smaller than the eland.

The progress at CREW was soon marked by another success, an eland to eland embryo transfer, using an embryo which had been frozen for 18 months before being transferred. The concept of the "Frozen Zoo" became more than just a pipe dream.

The researchers at CREW continue to pioneer new surgical and also nonsurgical procedures, procedures which vary greatly from species to species. Countless variables can occur during the collecting, culturing, freezing, thawing, and transferring of an embryo and the techniques are still far from consistent. But the new explorers in this field are working with both a sense of hope based on past successes and also a sense of urgency, racing to perfect each of the various techniques before many more species are lost forever.✪

Cincinnati Zoo

Cincinnati Zoo

TWO PATHWAYS TO THE SAME *result: a healthy bongo calf. In one case (upper) an eland served as a surrogate mother for a transfer of an embryo of another species, while in another (lower), a bongo gave birth to a calf not her own as a result of an embryo transfer.*

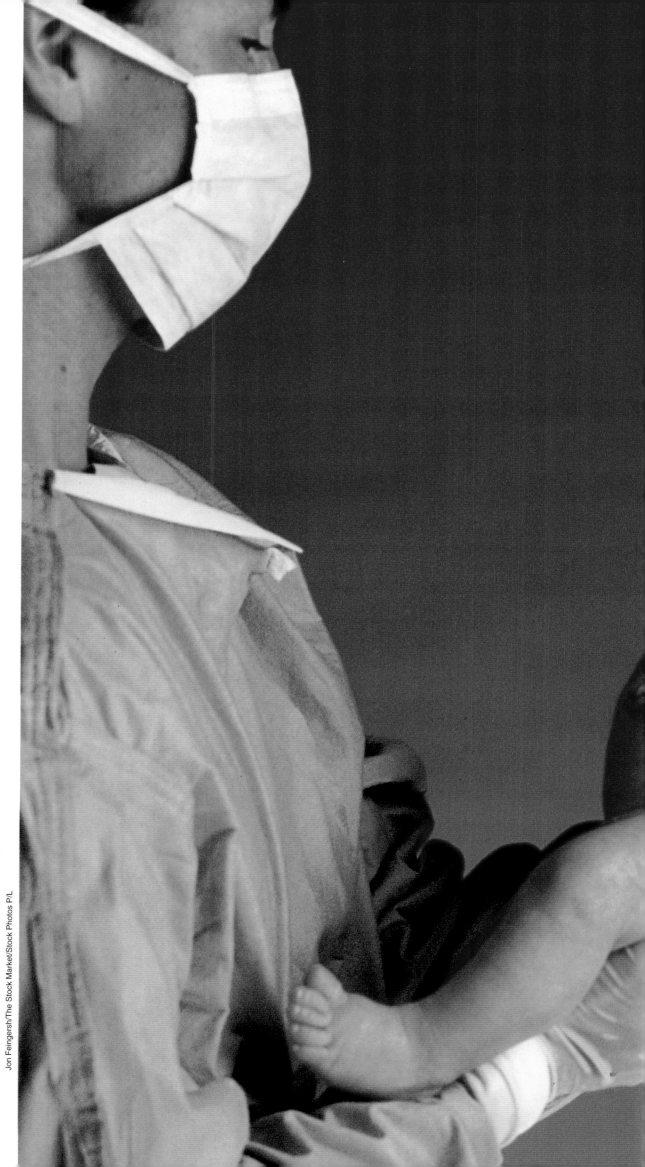

A HAPPY, HEALTHY, BOUNCING *baby is how most people picture a new addition to the family. However, a small proportion of babies are born with some disease or abnormality, or prematurely. Until recently, little could be done for such infants, but within the past two decades or so, dramatic advancements in neonatology have allowed many of them to survive and to develop into normal healthy babies.*

➤ A COMPUTER COLOR-ENHANCED *image of a human fetus. A vital ally in the neonatal care of babies has been the rapid development of sophisticated non-invasive methods of examining the fetus while still in the womb.*

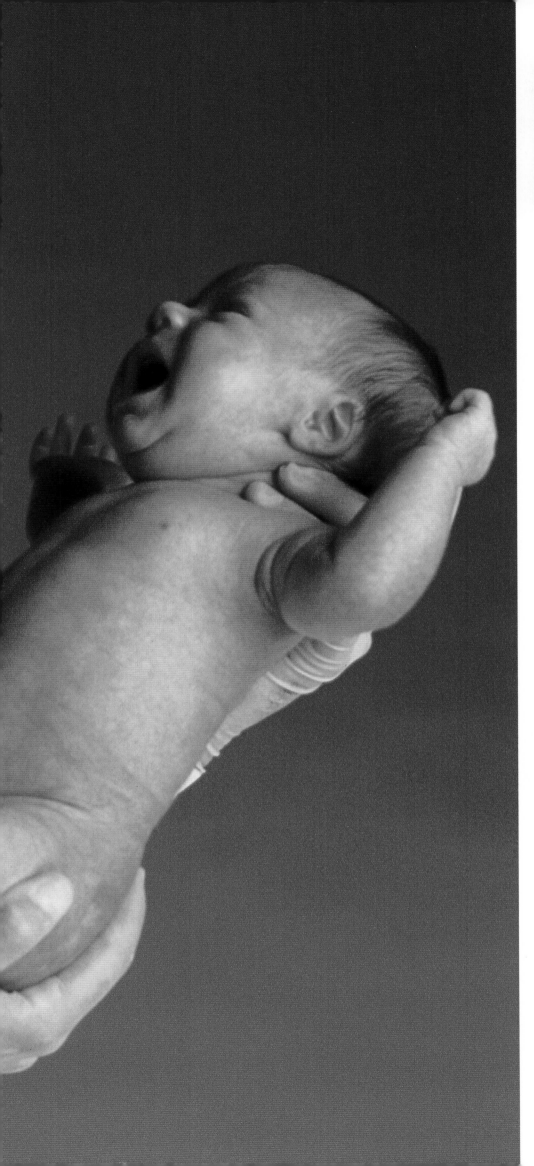

Miracle Babies

MARLETA REYNOLDS

Neonatology, the care of premature and critically ill newborn infants, has been called the newest field in medicine. It is only two decades old as a pediatric subspecialty. Since its founding in the mid-1970s, it has evolved with awesome speed. Breakthroughs in neonatal care have increased the infant survival rate beyond anything our grandparents dreamed of. Today not only do many of these newborns survive, they grow up to live healthy, normal, vital lives. Dr. Marleta Reynolds is a specialist pediatric surgeon. As a result of Dr. Reynolds' work, and the work of her colleagues, children who otherwise might have faced certain death are given a second chance.

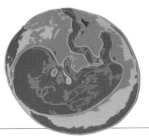

A HEALTHY BABY IS ALERT, CAN *breathe normally, regulate its own internal body temperature, and respond to its surroundings. However, some babies are born with problems that mean they do not have these capabilities.*

Jenny Mills

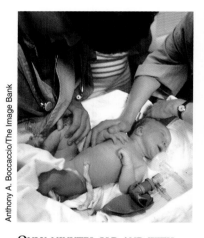

Anthony A. Boccaccio/The Image Bank

ONLY MINUTES OLD AND WITH *umbilical cord still intact, a newborn baby is quickly examined by the delivery team before being given to the mother.*

A FETUS LIES CUSHIONED IN THE *amniotic sac, nature's own humidicrib. The fetus is connected through the umbilicus to the placenta and the mother's own life-support systems.*

Only this afternoon life had seemed sweet to this new mother. Her thoughts throughout much of the day had been about the child she was carrying.

Now she is lying in an unfamiliar room. Outside, in the corridor, her husband is talking with her doctor. Later she will say that she thought she could recognize her husband's voice. But this is doubtful because at the time she was sedated. Still it is understandable that more than anything else she would want to know what her husband and the doctor are discussing. However she is exhausted, and she falls back into a heavy sleep.

Outside in the corridor the doctor's voice, although calm and soft, is anything but casual. The best thing to do now, the doctor is advising the husband, is to return to his wife who will be waking up momentarily.

In the doctor's opinion, things have not gone well. The young woman had started labor, but monitors had shown that the baby's fetal

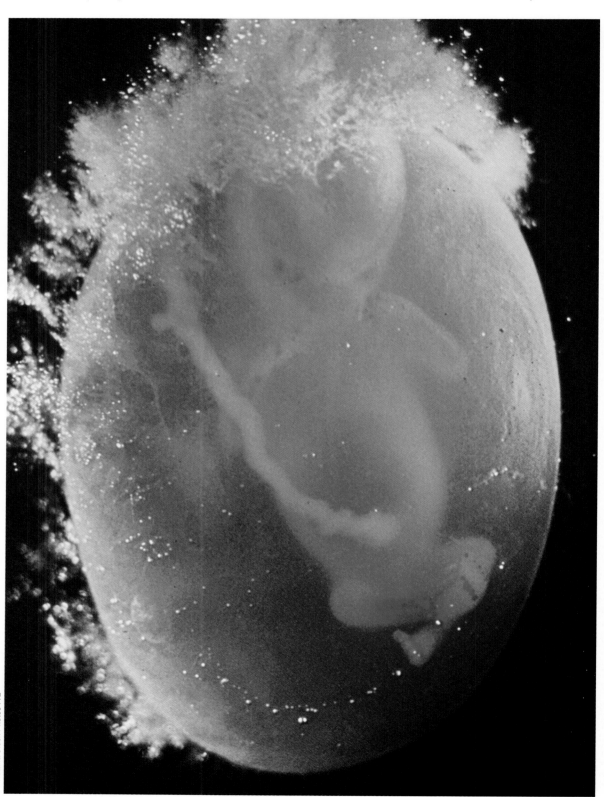

Phototake/Stock Photos P/L

heart rate was poor, making immediate surgical delivery necessary. Minutes after the baby boy had been delivered he had begun sucking in his chest and abdomen, an action that told the doctor he was struggling to breathe.

In order to force oxygen into the baby's lungs, a tube was inserted into his mouth and down between his vocal cords. A second tube, through which blood and nutrients could be passed, was gently threaded into the artery at the end of the baby's umbilical cord until it reached a position near the baby's heart. And a telephone call was made to another hospital—one with a neonatal intensive care unit.

PERSISTENT FETAL CIRCULATION

The doctor suspects that the baby's breathing is rapid and labored because the baby has been born with a congenital diaphragmatic hernia. This is a defect that allows the intestines to shift into his chest and restrict the growth of his lungs.

The lungs of a baby with this condition are hypoplastic, which means smaller than normal. In infants with hypoplastic lungs the small blood vessels that bring blood to the lungs tend to squeeze shut. The result is that the infant is deprived of oxygen.

Feeling himself suffocating, he responds by breathing harder. Unfortunately this doesn't help. The blood, unable to flow in a normal way, begins to mimic the pathways it used when the infant was still in the womb. This condition is called "persistent fetal circulation." If it cannot be reversed, the baby will not survive.

EMERGENCY EVACUATION

The diagnosis is preliminary. But it is enough for the doctor to have asked for an emergency evacuation to a neonatal intensive care unit where a pediatric surgeon like Dr. Marleta Reynolds can evaluate the infant's condition and repair the diaphragm. Already the infant's skin is turning blue from the lack of oxygen.

The hospital corridor suddenly fills with the rush of footsteps. A helicopter is about to land on the hospital roof and the doctor and his team are taking the infant to meet it.

Time is of the essence. The helicopter never shuts off. To be heard the doctor must shout above the pitch of its whirring blades. The transport team has drilled over and over again for just this sort of mission. The baby is transferred into the helicopter. The nurse inside immediately begins evaluating the baby's condition.

NORMAL CIRCULATION AFTER BIRTH

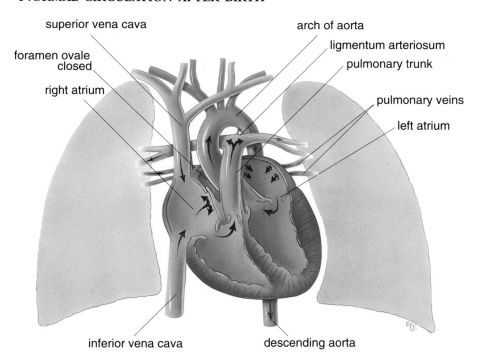

■ high oxygen saturation of blood   ■ low oxygen saturation of blood

MOST BABIES ARE BORN WITH NORMAL BLOOD CIRCULATION AND STRONG LUNGS. *In normal circulation the oxygenated blood circulates from the heart throughout the body and deoxygenated blood returns to the heart.*

PERSISTENT FETAL CIRCULATION

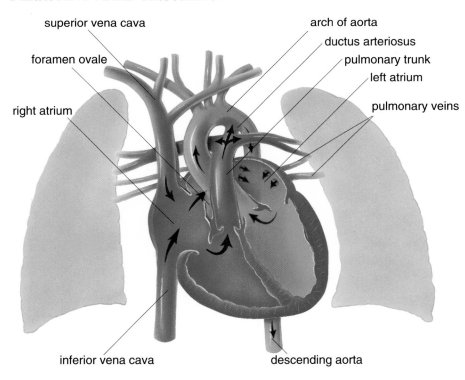

■ high oxygen saturation of blood   ■ low oxygen saturation of blood

IN A BABY WITH PERSISTENT FETAL CIRCULATION THE BLOOD FLOWS AWAY FROM THE *lungs, mimicking the pathways it took during circulation in the fetus. This is caused by the small blood vessels in the hypoplastic lungs which squeeze shut, so that the blood's normal pathway is blocked and the baby is deprived of adequate oxygen.*

A DOCTOR USES A STETHOSCOPE *to check for any anomalies in a newborn infant's respiration and heart beat.*

During the fifty-five minutes it takes to get to the neonatal intensive care unit the transport team continues to pursue the life-sustaining measures that commenced in the delivery room. One member of the team sees to it that the infant receives oxygen. Another uses the radio to advise the waiting pediatric surgeon on the infant's condition. A third continuously monitors the infant's vital signs.

THE INTENSIVE CARE UNIT

At the neonatal intensive care unit a team of specialists has already assembled and is preparing for the baby's arrival. What they know is that they will be receiving a newborn in severe respiratory distress. Assuming the preliminary

diagnosis of congenital diaphragmatic hernia is correct, they suspect that the infant is suffering from pulmonary hypoplasia.

In its severest form pulmonary hypoplasia may present in the first hours of life. In severe hypoplasia the only way to prevent death is to put the infant on an artificial life support system.

In this infant's case he began developing symptoms of pulmonary hypoplasia in the delivery room. So the team plans for the worst. When the infant arrives his skin is blue from lack of oxygen and he has no blood pressure. A neonatologist is standing by to help resuscitate the baby. It is clear to the team that his only chance for survival is an artificial life support system. The surgeon makes an urgent telephone call to the parents to let them know the team's evaluation and to obtain their consent.

Time is crucial. If the baby's heart stops, he will not be able to be placed on life support. Yet despite this urgency the baby must first undergo a series of diagnostic tests to confirm that he meets the requirements.

A pediatric neuroradiologist performs an ultrasound of the baby's head to see if there has been bleeding into the brain. In this case he can find no signs of bleeding, so the team is reasonably sure that the baby has suffered no apparent brain damage. A pediatric cardiologist performs an echocardiogram that lets the team

---

THIS NEWBORN BABY'S *diaphragm did not form properly in the womb and his stomach, spleen, liver, and intestines have herniated into his chest. Due to the hernia the normal growth of his left lung is retarded and hypoplastic (smaller than usual). His heart has been pushed into the opposite side and his blood flow is affected. He may develop persistent fetal circulation.*

➤ **AFTER THE BABY'S CONDITION** *is stabilized, a straightforward operation is performed to repair the hole in the diaphragm. An incision is made in the abdomen and the herniated organs are returned to the abdomen. The hole is closed with suture or prosthetic material.*

CONGENITAL DIAPHRAGMATIC HERNIA

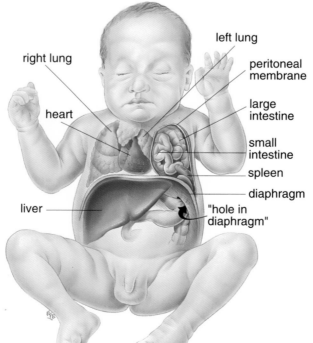

right lung
left lung
peritoneal membrane
heart
large intestine
small intestine
spleen
diaphragm
liver
"hole in diaphragm"

CONGENITAL HERNIA REPAIR

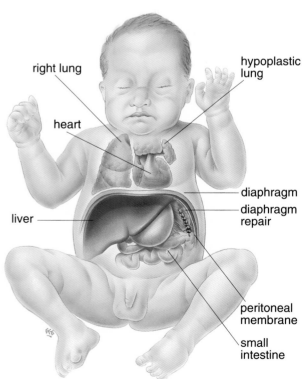

right lung
hypoplastic lung
heart
diaphragm
diaphragm repair
liver
peritoneal membrane
small intestine

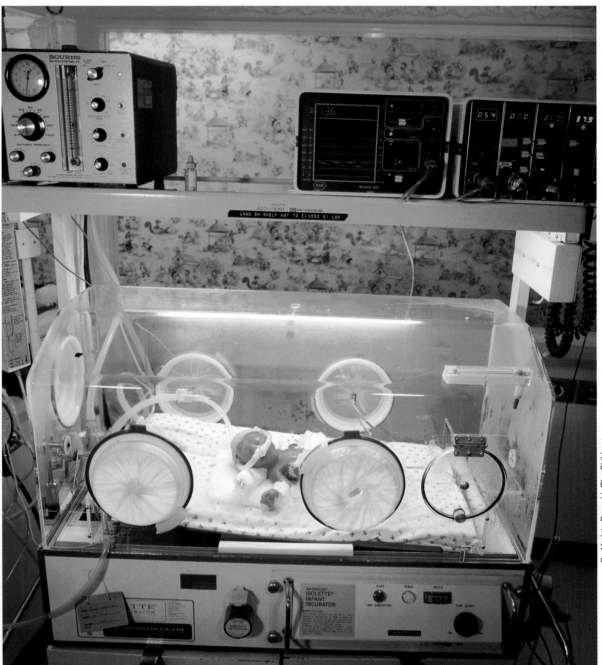

S. Fraser/Princess Mary Hospital/Science P/L/The Photo Library, Sydney

ONLY 12 HOURS OLD AND BORN *13 weeks premature, a tiny baby lies in a hospital incubator. The incubator enables doctors to maintain an environment of optimum temperature, humidity, and oxygen concentration while therapy gently coaxes the baby's own internal life-support systems into proper function.*

A DELICATE OPERATION TO *repair a congenital diaphragmatic hernia. This condition allows the intestines to shift into the chest and restrict the growth of the lungs, causing respiratory distress.*

members glimpse the baby's beating heart. He can find no signs of congenital heart disease or other cardiac conditions.

Nurses, respiratory therapists, and other specialists complete the team. X-rays show that although the baby's lungs are small, they are probably big enough to support him if he can make it through this crisis.

In a matter of minutes the team has determined that the baby's condition is potentially reversible. But without assistance from an artificial life support system the baby's chances of surviving are less than one in ten. With life support, the odds improve considerably. Depending on the underlying condition, the chances of survival of babies given life support ranges from 60 percent to 90 percent.

ARTIFICIAL LIFE SUPPORT

Even while the baby is being tested, he has been placed on the operating table and simultaneously prepped for surgery. As soon as the team has established that he meets all the criteria, a generous dose of narcotic is administered, along with a second medication to ensure that the baby will not move during the operation, and Dr. Reynolds makes the first small incision.

The life support system on which the baby is to be placed is called Extracorporeal Membrane Oxygenation, or ECMO. ECMO is a heart–lung bypass system in which a machine is substituted for the baby's heart and lungs. The goal is to give the baby's real heart and lungs an opportunity to rest and recover. Each baby is evaluated on an individual basis.

A CRITICALLY ILL BABY ON *ECMO (Extracorporeal Membrane Oxygenation), a heart-lung bypass system in which machinery substitutes for the infant's own vital organs. Monitors and catheters of various kinds deliver medication and gather data on blood pressure, temperature, and other vital signs.*

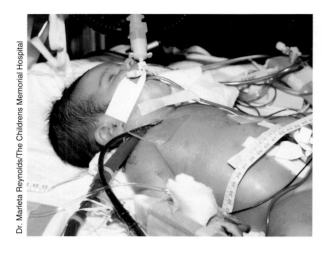

Dr. Marieta Reynolds/The Childrens Memorial Hospital

BABIES WITH SEVERE LUNG *hypoplasia and persistent fetal circulation may need the assistance of ECMO (Extracorporeal Membrane Oxygenation). This machine does the work of the baby's heart and lungs, allowing these vital organs a chance to strengthen.*

Some babies have their diaphragmatic hernia repaired before going on the life support system. The most critically ill babies are placed on ECMO before the repair is done.

Dr. Reynolds inserts two small catheters into the baby's neck, one in the right internal jugular vein and the other in the right common carotid artery. The first catheter, the one inserted into the jugular vein, is passed all the way down the vein and into the first chamber of the

heart. The other, the one inserted in the artery, is passed into the aortic arch where blood will be returned to the baby's body.

Once these tubes are in place and connected to the circuit, the ECMO machine is turned on. Gravity drains blood from the baby through the tube in the jugular vein. The ECMO machine then pumps this blood through a membrane oxygenator, which washes out the carbon dioxide and simultaneously permeates it with oxygen. Finally the machine reheats the freshly oxygenated blood and pumps it back into the baby by means of the tube in the carotid artery. When the baby's condition stabilizes, the diaphragmatic hernia will be surgically repaired.

POTENTIAL COMPLICATIONS

Although the ECMO machine itself may seem simple, the complications that can occur while the infant is on it are anything but simple. The biggest risk the infant faces comes from the drug heparin, which is used to prevent the blood from clotting. Heparin ensures that the blood

EXTRACORPOREAL MEMBRANE OXYGENATION (ECMO) CIRCUIT

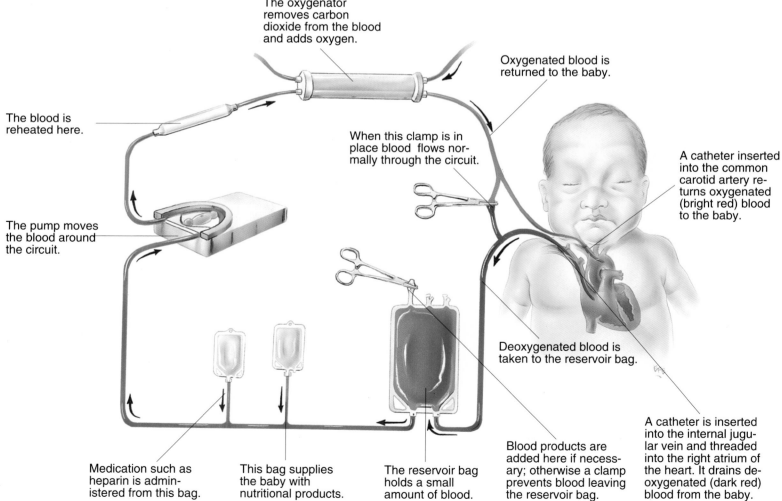

The oxygenator removes carbon dioxide from the blood and adds oxygen.

Oxygenated blood is returned to the baby.

The blood is reheated here.

When this clamp is in place blood flows normally through the circuit.

A catheter inserted into the common carotid artery returns oxygenated (bright red) blood to the baby.

The pump moves the blood around the circuit.

Deoxygenated blood is taken to the reservoir bag.

Medication such as heparin is administered from this bag.

This bag supplies the baby with nutritional products.

The reservoir bag holds a small amount of blood.

Blood products are added here if necessary; otherwise a clamp prevents blood leaving the reservoir bag.

A catheter is inserted into the internal jugular vein and threaded into the right atrium of the heart. It drains deoxygenated (dark red) blood from the baby.

Neonatal Care: A Developing Science

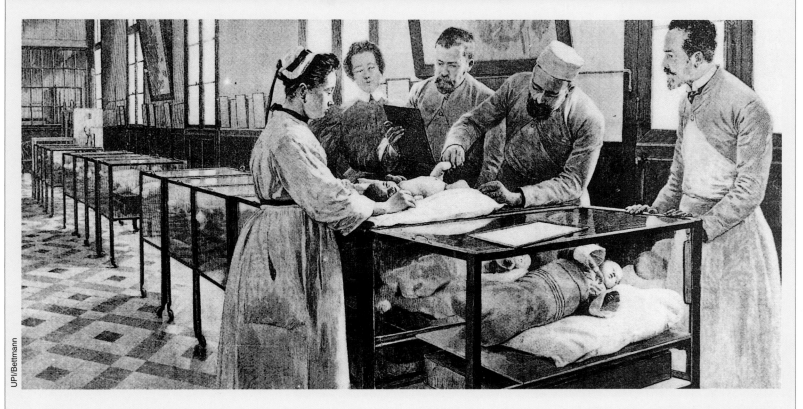

UPI/Bettmann

Today neonatal intensive care units are so numerous that it is hard to believe that just twenty-five years ago there was little hope for babies who were born too soon, too small, or with congenital problems that threaten survival.

The ancient Greek medical authority Hippocrates himself proclaimed that no infant born before the seventh month could survive. It was not until the end of the nineteenth century, some twenty-three centuries later, that physicians began to challenge this myth.

A celebrated French obstetrician by the name of Tarnier was disturbed by his inability to treat premature newborns. On a visit to the Paris Zoo in 1878 he had the idea for a warm-air incubator, which he and his associate, Pierre Budin, installed at the Paris Maternité Hospital. The French government honored the two physicians "for saving a battalion from the slaughterhouse of infancy."

Pierre Budin went on to devote a lifetime to the care and study of premature infants. Today Budin himself is celebrated as the father of premature care.

INFANT INCUBATORS WITH LIVING INFANTS

At the turn of the century there still was so little hope of saving premature infants that Martin Couney, one of Budin's pupils, was able to persuade doctors and parents to send these babies to his Kinderbrutanstalt or child

INVENTOR OF AN EARLY VERSION OF THE HUMIDICRIB, DR. TARNIER *examines his tiny patients in a Paris maternity hospital.*

hatchery. To raise money for his research, Couney took his collection of incubators and premature infants on a kind of road show throughout Europe.

In 1901 he came to the Pan-American Exposition in Buffalo, New York. For the next thirty-nine years Couney exhibited premature infants at fairs, expositions, and amusement parks throughout the United States.

Although Couney was criticized for giving premature infants the status of a carnival freak show, the money that the general public paid to gawk at these "prodigies of nature" for most of them meant the difference between life and death. It was this money that enabled Couney to support and train his team of nurses and to continue his research into the care of premature newborn infants.

In his day Couney's premature baby shows were a great success. He became a leading specialist in neonatology. Wherever he exhibited he lectured about early childcare techniques. Doctors and parents gave him their premature infants as he was better able to care for them. In Chicago he met and greatly influenced Julian Hess who later became one of the leading authorities on premature care. Records show that Martin Couney cared for over 5,000 babies during his lifetime.

THE BIRTH CRISIS YEARS BEHIND *her, an ECMO graduate smiles at the camera. Regular attendance at out-patient clinics will ensure that any lingering complications are dealt with effectively.*

flows smoothly. But it also places the baby at risk for dangerous external bleeding from incisions or puncture sites and internal bleeding into the brain and other organs.

Of the babies placed on ECMO, some 7 to 20 percent may later have problems related to their brain. Some of these problems are the result of the baby's critical condition before going onto ECMO. Others may be related to the loss of the carotid artery and jugular vein or to the prolonged use of artificial life support systems. The problems range from treatable seizures, to developmental delay and mild to severe mental retardation.

Complications of artificial life support may arise in almost every organ system. The heart may develop irregular beats or have compromised function because of the inadequate oxygen delivery to the heart muscle before ECMO support. The kidneys can be adversely affected by low blood pressure that often exists before

ECMO is started. It may be necessary for an additional dialysis apparatus to be added to the ECMO circuit if the baby's kidneys should fail temporarily. Most of the complications can be anticipated and treated.

Depending on the severity of an infant's condition and how quickly the lungs recover, ECMO may be needed for as little as three days or as long as three weeks. During this time, the neonatal team maintains a round-the-clock vigil.

A nurse, trained in the care of a baby on ECMO, is in constant attendance. In addition, an ECMO specialist sits by the pump to manage the complex machine and make adjustments. Respiratory therapists also assist with the care directed at improving the baby's lungs. Physical therapists position the baby and perform physical exercise to reduce the stiffness the baby suffers from restricted motion.

The team of doctors, nurses, therapists, specialists, and social workers help educate the

Neonatal Care in the 1990s

Advances in the care of premature infants—especially of the critically ill newborn—have put the subspeciality of neonatology at the cutting edge of medical science.

Transport teams are trained to move the babies from community hospitals to neonatal intensive care centers in a matter of minutes. Electronic monitoring devices identify problems before they become life-threatening emergencies. Probes on the baby's skin constantly regulate the infant's temperature and vital signs. For example, a probe is connected to the specially designed bed. If the baby's temperature drifts outside a specified range, heating units within the bed are activated.

Heart rate and rhythm also are monitored with a separate set of electric "leads" which are applied to the baby's skin. Tiny blood pressure cuffs are wrapped around the extremities, and another machine will record the blood pressure at preset intervals. The pulse oximeter, the newest in non-invasive monitoring devices, is applied on a finger or toe. Light is transmitted through the skin and absorbed by the blood. The meter detects the absorption of oxygen and translates it into a saturation reading.

Every seriously ill newborn is monitored with these devices. Artificial organ and life support systems such as ventilators, dialysis machines, and ECMO assist in supporting babies temporarily.

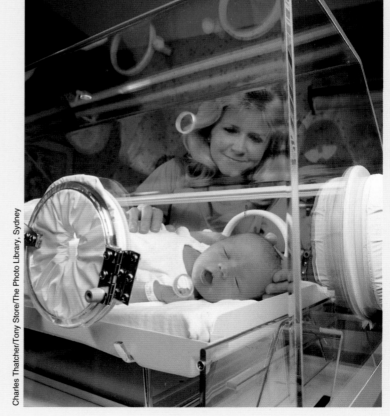

KEPT AT ARMS-LENGTH BY A BARRIER OF HI-TECH GEAR, A MOTHER *caresses her baby. Notwithstanding the specialist medical teams and their sophisticated apparatus, the bond between mother and child remains a crucial element of support as the tiny infant struggles to survive.*

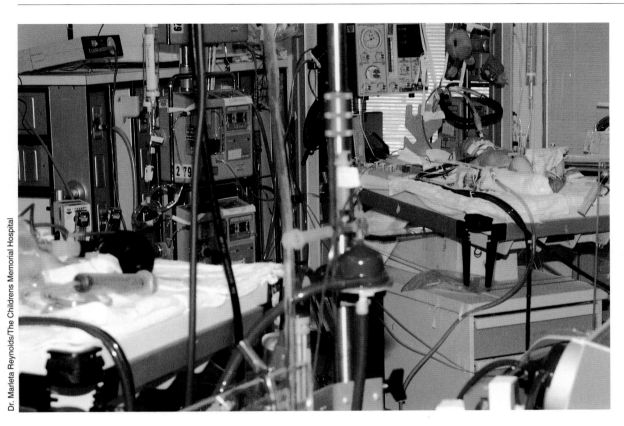

Dr. Marieta Reynolds/The Childrens Memorial Hospital

family, answer their questions, and try to relieve some of their anxiety.

Every day an ultrasound of the head is done and a pediatric neuroradiologist reviews the result. Serious bleeding into the brain would force the team to discontinue ECMO. Daily x-rays of the chest are obtained to monitor improvement of the lungs and to identify possible complications. Repeated physical examinations help detect improvement. As the baby's lungs improve, the required amount of ECMO support decreases.

THE "WEANING" PROCESS

The baby will be disconnected from the machine when there is physical and laboratory evidence that he can breathe on his own with minimal ventilator support. To test the baby's lungs the machine is temporarily stopped for between 15 minutes and an hour. If the baby cannot maintain adequate oxygen concentrations in the blood, the machine is then restarted and another trial will be attempted in 24 to 48 hours. If the baby passes the test, the ECMO support will be discontinued.

The decision to remove the baby from support is difficult because premature removal may result in a return to "persistent fetal circulation." But time spent on ECMO that is not necessary may result in serious complications. ECMO support is not usually reinstituted once the catheters have been removed.

The baby's lungs continue to improve over the next several days and weeks and the baby is then weaned from the ventilator and oxygen therapy. The physical therapy is continued after ECMO. Before being discharged from the hospital, the baby's hearing is tested and a special x-ray scan of his head is performed to check for previously undiagnosed problems. A developmental specialist examines the baby before discharge and at regularly scheduled intervals as an outpatient. Hearing tests are repeated at yearly intervals because these babies are at risk for hearing impairment.

Some babies are discharged with supplemental oxygen and alternative methods of feeding. The parents are trained to care for their infants before they take them home.

The majority of babies placed on ECMO survive. Follow-up studies have shown that most will grow and develop normally. Frequent outpatient visits and examinations can identify children who may be having problems. Early intervention programs help to allow these children to achieve their maximum potential. The parents of these children are encouraged to treat their ECMO babies as normal children.

The baby whose story began this article is now more than six months old. He has made a good recovery, and is normal and healthy. Due to the work of Dr. Reynolds and the rest of the team, this baby and others like him have the chance to survive and live normal lives.✪

Dr. Marieta Reynolds/The Childrens Memorial Hospital

THE MAJORITY OF INFANTS *requiring ECMO make a good recovery, going on to become normal healthy children.*

William L. Fash

RUINS AT COPAN, ONE OF THE
major centers of the Maya empire.
The remaining stones and their
glyphs are the key to understanding
the lost Maya civilization.

54

GREAT MYSTERIES

THIS AERIAL PHOTOGRAPH *shows a giant spiral that two thousand years ago was etched into rocky desert near the Peruvian coast. Who drew this spiral, and why, are questions that scholars have been trying to answer for over fifty years.*

➤ A NAZCA VASE, DECORATED *with fox figures. Like other American Indian people, Nazca potters did not use a potter's wheel. Their pottery was hand coiled, smoothed down to a thickness of about $\frac{1}{8}$ inch (3 millimeters), and fired at 203°F (95°C).*

Tony Morrison/South American Pictures

The Mystery of the Lines

PHYLLIS BURTON PITLUGA

The little South American town of Nazca is a six-hour drive down the coast from Lima, Peru. Two thousand years ago, in the rocky desert just north of Nazca, a forgotten people etched into the surface of the land enormous drawings the size of football fields, and lines straight as arrows that go on for 20 miles (32 kilometers). Maria Reiche is recognized worldwide as a leading authority on these lines. Phyllis Pitluga, Senior Astronomer at the Adler Planetarium in Chicago, collaborated with Reiche over the last decade. Working with Reiche's maps and her own measurements of hundreds of lines, Pitluga has proposed an ingenious solution to the mystery of the lines.

Tony Morrison/South American Pictures

WHY DID THE NAZCA PEOPLE *draw the figures so large? The tuber plant drawing could almost fill a football field.*

MARIA REICHE STUDIES A FIGURE *that is strikingly similar to one of the huge Nazca drawings. Perhaps Nazca architects used such stone carvings as blueprints for drawing the larger figures.*

THIS HUGE DRAWING OF A *monkey is near a double spiral (in the upper third of the photograph). Two thousand years ago this spiral was carved into the sand with meticulous precision, following established mathematical rules.*

Two thousand years ago the Roman general Octavian Caesar concluded over 150 years of civil strife within the Roman Empire and had made himself the undisputed master of Europe. Yet at the same time, in another part of the world on another continent, other people had different ambitions. Unlike Caesar, they did not leave any written history that might reveal their intentions. The evidence of their existence is carved on the desert plain itself, in the gigantic figures and lines still visible there.

Who were these people? How did they draw these incredible figures? And for what purpose did they draw them?

FIGURES, DESIGNS, STRAIGHT LINES

The lines fall into three tidy categories: representational figures, geometric designs, and straight lines extending to the desert horizon. The 27 representational figures studied by Pitluga depict birds, whales, seaweeds, a spider, a monkey, a fox, and an iguana. Triangles, rectangles, and zigzagging and oscillating lines make up the geometric designs. Long straight lines, some as long as 20 miles (32 kilometers), have been drawn next to and through the figures and the geometric designs.

The first question that leaps to the mind about the Nazca lines is their size. Why would anyone make such huge drawings? Most of the animal and plant figures are so large that each would fill an entire football field. Indeed the scale on which they have been drawn is so

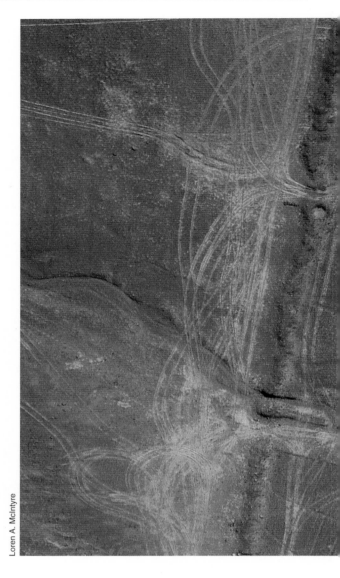

mammoth that to anyone standing on the flat plain of the pampa these figures are nearly invisible. The only way they can be seen distinctly is to view them from an airplane.

The second question is how were these colossal lines and figures drawn? Today, were you to draw a straight line on such a scale, you would use a surveyor's tool. But from what we are able to tell, 2,000 years ago the Nazca Indians did not have anything like the equivalent of a surveyor's tool. Yet their lines are unwaveringly straight for 20 miles (32 kilometers).

The figures of animals and plants present an even more puzzling mystery. These figures are of the same themes, although stylistically different, as much smaller figures that the Nazca people painted on ceramics from the same period. In all likelihood the figures found on the pottery held the same symbolic meaning as their much larger counterparts. So by logical inference the huge animal and plant figures are mirror images drawn to scale—a mammoth, almost inconceivable scale! How could these people have made such sophisticated drawings?

THE DESERT DRAWING OF A spider spans 140 feet (43 meters). At the time this figure was etched into the sand it aligned with the stars of the constellation of Orion. Notice the lines drawn through it and next to it, and the stretched right foot.

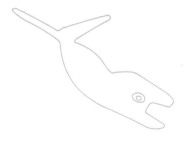

THIS AERIAL PHOTOGRAPH OF the hummingbird drawing gives an idea of the scale on which the Nazca figures are drawn. Some are so mammoth that to anyone standing on the flat plain of the pampa the designs appear only as random lines.

THE ORIGIN AND MEANING OF THE LINES

Why carve patterns and lines into a dark, stone-strewn desert surface? Why draw on such a colossal scale? Why make them all but invisible to anyone at eye level? Without surveying instruments or the aid of a written language, how were they made? How could such realistically animated shapes be scratched into a rocky surface? What tools did these artists use? And did their drawings have any functional or symbolic purpose?

Speculations abound. Some theorists suspect that the figures and lines may have a religious significance. This, they argue, accounts for the colossal scale. The drawings were never meant to be seen at eye level by ordinary sight. Instead their creators intended them to be seen by mountain gods, who, finding pleasure in the giant images, would bestow wisdom, knowledge, and joy on the people who drew them.

Others think that the lines may have had a ceremonial significance. For example, they may have been used in ritual dancing. Still others see the shapes as expressions of art. This, they argue,

is why you see similar images painted on the ceramics which have been found in the ancient graves of the Nazca people.

Perhaps the most intriguing suggestion—certainly the most publicized—compares the long rectangles in the Nazca desert to airfields. Could the lines have been used by ancient astronauts who traveled to the planet earth for reasons we will never know?

While the idea of ancient astronauts stirs the imagination and attracts the curious, it offends serious researchers who recognize that the surface is neither flat nor firm and so an unlikely landing place. Phyllis Pitluga, our new explorer, sees the lines as a kind of light that shines back into the darkness of a forgotten time. To her these desert shapes make visible a vanished people who built a civilization much more advanced than we thought possible.

A LONGSTANDING LEGACY

Amazingly these superficial etchings have survived for some 2,000 years. Longevity, however, is perhaps the easiest thing to explain

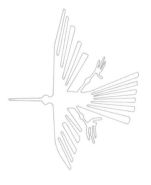

MANY OF THE DESIGNS DRAWN onto the desert, such as the killer whale and the condor bird, can also be found on Nazca pottery.

MARIA REICHE ATTEMPTS TO *obtain a better perspective of the remarkable lines in the desert. This photograph was taken in 1946.*

about the lines. The coast of Peru has a climate and soil perfectly suited for preserving massive shapes etched into its surface. A tableland of rock, sand, and clay, it is a desert environment so dry that it rarely rains, and even then the rainfall usually consists of only a few drops that evaporate as soon as they fall. Lack of rainfall was important in ensuring that something of the Nazca people and their culture would survive indefinitely in their drawings.

Desert winds, on the other hand, might have erased them centuries ago, except that the pampa is blanketed with iron-rich surface rocks that are too heavy for the wind to carry off. Even the clay underneath the blanket of surface rock is a crusty unchangeable surface.

Initially, because the lines were carved into this gypsum-based soil, they were white, and glowed at sunrise and sunset, and contrasted against the dark iron oxide in the rocks. But over the centuries the wind blew tiny dark stones into the carved out hollows of the lines. Gradually this caused the drawings to darken.

Today, when seen from an airplane, the figures and lines look much darker than they would have 2,000 years ago.

LEARNING ABOUT THE LINES

In 1939 Paul Kosok, historian-archaeologist from Long Island University in New York, came across the Nazca drawings while searching for ancient aqueducts. Almost immediately he began the first systematic survey.

In that same year, Maria Reiche began assisting Kosok in Lima. At the December solstice in 1941, she traveled to Nazca to see the drawings for herself. A German mathematician living in Peru, she instantly found herself with many more questions than answers about these remarkable carvings. She became Kosok's lifelong collaborator. When he died in the mid-1940s Reiche continued by herself the work they had begun together.

The first task was to survey and map the sites. In the next four decades, Reiche tirelessly mapped both the 10 square mile (26 square kilometer) complex next to Peru's Ingenio Valley and the multitude of smaller centers that border it. She worked mostly on foot and alone. Her tools were a simple tape measure and hand-held sextant, a pencil, and a notebook. During the night, in a tiny room she had taken down in the valley below the complex, Reiche transferred the measurements onto charts. Occasionally she plotted the curved furrows that revealed a figure.

Maria Reiche thought that if she could discover how the figures were drawn, it might reveal why they were drawn. Gradually this idea emerged as the basic premise behind her work.

As she completed more charts she began experimenting with techniques that could be used to create these huge drawings. Her mathematical training led her to explore units of measurement and geometric constructions. Trying with lengths for a unit of measurement, she discovered that many of the geometric designs could be replicated using multiples of 39.5 centimeters ($15\frac{1}{2}$ inches).

THE DOUBLE SPIRAL

As the inherent mathematical properties of spirals have been known for millennia, it was only natural that an ancient geometric figure near the edge of the pampa—a huge double spiral—would be one of the first figures Maria Reiche chose to analyze.

PERU

Lima

Nazca region

PACIFIC OCEAN

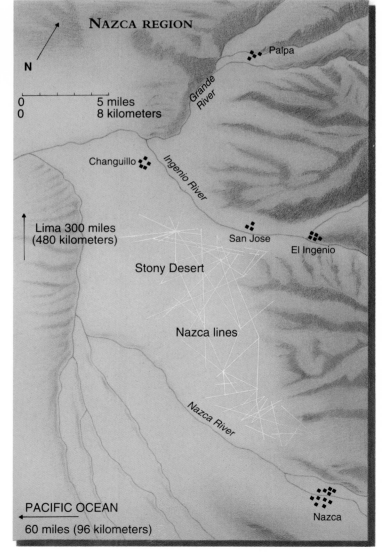

NAZCA REGION

N

0   5 miles
0   8 kilometers

Grande River

Palpa

Changuillo

Ingenio River

Lima 300 miles (480 kilometers)

San Jose

El Ingenio

Stony Desert

Nazca lines

Nazca River

PACIFIC OCEAN

60 miles (96 kilometers)

Nazca

Loren McIntyre

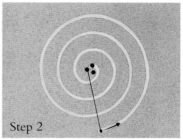

Step 1

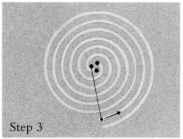

Step 2

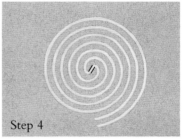

Step 3

Step 4

SPIRAL CONSTRUCTION BEGAN *with (1) the positioning of three posts, one with a long cord attatched. A spiral was inscribed (2), marking the path of someone walking around the three posts, keeping the line taut. A second spiral was marked (3) in the same way, with a shorter cord. Last, the inner ends of the spiral were joined (4).*

There were long months of trial and error while Reiche explored various techniques that the ancient Nazca people might have used to create this huge design on the desert. Finally she located the starting points that she had been looking for. These were three points on the desert surface. Each was 395 centimeters (12 feet 11½ inches) apart, a distance which is ten times 39.5 centimeters (15½ inches), the basic unit by which all the lines can be divided.

At each location Reiche drove a post into the ground. Next she tied a long cord to one of the posts and stretched it out over the desert to the edge of the spiral. Keeping the cord pulled taut and walking round and round the three posts, she demonstrated that she was drawn into the center following the same spiralling pathway that had been scratched into the desert surface two thousand years ago.

Certainly such simple posts and cords were available to the Nazcans. So they could have used this method to create the huge double spiral, making the second, inside spiral by shortening the cord to start halfway between the two outer curves of the first spiral.

Maria Reiche had demonstrated that the lines most likely were drawn with meticulous precision. It seemed clear that the drawings were intended to calculate something. But what?

Reiche realized that many of the straight lines pointed to where the sun rose or set at the June and December solstices—the longest and shortest days of the year. Other lines aimed toward the rising and setting of the moon at its northernmost and southernmost extremes on the horizon. Reiche suspected that the Nazca people had used the lines to keep track of seasonal changes.

Phyllis Pitluga

MARIA REICHE AND TEOFILO *Guia at work setting up their surveying equipment. The measurements they made were transferred onto Reiche's meticulous charts.*

New Year's Dawn

A Nazca astronomer-priest may have observed the dawn rising of the stars of the flower (the Pleiades and Hyades) announcing the beginning of a new year (mid-May in A.D. 201).

MARIA REICHE SPENT 40 YEARS *surveying and mapping the representational figures, geometric designs, and straight lines etched on the desert by the Nazca people.*

➤ **A NAZCA MALE DRESSED IN** *headband, poncho, tunic, and skirt.*

During the decades that she had mapped and studied the Nazca drawings, Reiche had become one of the world's foremost authorities on them. By 1983, nearly blind from glaucoma and suffering restricted mobility due to unidentified Parkinson's disease, this remarkable woman was greatly in need of assistance.

It was at about this time that she received a telephone call from Phyllis Burton Pitluga, Senior Astronomer at the Adler Planetarium in Chicago. Pitluga had been teaching world ancient astronomy, and was visiting Peru to learn about Inca astronomy at first hand. Only that morning Pitluga had flown over the pampa on a sightseeing trip and gazed upon the drawings for the first time. She was so inspired by her first view of them that when she landed she immediately telephoned Maria Reiche and invited her to lunch. Almost instantly the two women became friends. Shortly after that Reiche asked Pitluga to become her collaborator.

AN ASTRONOMICAL OBSERVATORY

Could the huge figures and lines be parts and pieces of an ancient astronomical observatory? Pitluga was the first to recognize

that the lines originate at mounds of stones near large plazas and extend to the desert horizon. In fact, of all the ancient structures in the world conjectured to be astronomical observatories the Nazca Lines provide the most precise, least ambiguous sight lines. Two thousand years ago a Nazca astronomer might have gazed down one of these lines to that point where the line ended. And there, where the sky met the ground, the astronomer might have seen the sun, moon, and stars rise or set, and by those observations known what time of the year it was and whether crops should be planted.

THE CONSTELLATIONS

Pitluga knew from having read the reports of early Spanish explorers that the native Peruvians, called Incas at that time, had an agricultural and ceremonial calendar based on the rising and setting of celestial objects along the horizon. Could it be, she wondered, that the figures and lines were somehow oriented to the constellations? Could observers look down the line and across the figure to see the pattern as a constellation rising or setting in the sky?

streets. On the desert the trick was to place the tripod of the telescope so that it oriented dead north. Inasmuch as there were no reference marks, this was tedious work. The position of the sun had to be measured every time the telescope was repositioned.

For each line Pitluga recorded measurements in three different locations about 300 feet (90 meters) apart. An assistant, Teofilo Guia of Nazca, held a numbered pole upright in the line's center, a point midway between the border of stones that outlined either side of the line. The team worked in the morning for greater accuracy. Later in the day the air above the dark rocks would become hot and would make objects in the distance appear wavy and distort the readings from the theodolite.

They followed the same procedure for each line that crossed the spider. The lines all begin at one spot and extend past the spider to the western horizon. Once Pitluga knew where on the horizon the lines pointed, they began checking to see which stars would have set at the ends of these lines some 2,000 years ago.

When she finished her measurements and analysis, she could see that 2,000 years ago on that Peruvian plain the figure of the spider aligned with the stars of the constellation that we call Orion. Thus it is quite possible that the Nazca drawings were intentionally aimed toward the constellations, and their symbolism would be akin to the Greek mythological representations of the constellations that the Western world uses.

Steve Carr

PHYLLIS PITLUGA USED A *theodolite to take sun sightings. For every measurement three separate sightings were made.*

Pitluga formulated these questions into a working hypothesis and set out to test it. She began with the drawing of a 140 foot (43 meter) spider. She had to determine where on the horizon the spider and the lines drawn through it and next to it were pointing.

To do this a special kind of a telescope called a theodolite was used, an instrument that modern surveyors use when surveying city

James D. Nations/DDB Stock Photo

ONE OF THE MYSTERIOUS NAZCA *triangles. If you look closely you can see long, straight lines beside it. Some of these lines continue for 20 miles (32 kilometers).*

Nazca Graveyards

BILL KURTIS EXAMINES *a bleached skull from a Nazca graveyard.*

It is impossible to look out across the Peruvian pampa at the giant figures that were etched into its surface so long ago and not wonder about the people who drew them. Who were these people? What were their dreams, their ambitions? How did they live? What did they believe in? How did they see themselves?

We may never know. Centuries of desert winds have raked Peru's coastal tableland. They have scoured its surface of almost every remnant of this once imposing civilization. All that is left, besides the strange giant figures, are the graveyards. Yet these, too, are disappearing.

TOURISTS AND COLLECTORS

The convenience and speed of modern travel have transformed once distant and exotic lands into vacation playgrounds. By the 1980s scores of visitors were journeying to Nazca and driving out onto the pampa to see the ancient markings. Inadvertently many sightseers drove across the markings themselves. For the first time in 2,000 years this ancient astronomical observatory was in danger of being destroyed. This threat forced Maria Reiche to take time away from her work to successfully lobby the Peruvian government to pass protective legislation aimed at keeping tourists from obliterating this remarkable legacy.

THOUSANDS OF ANCIENT NAZCA GRAVES HAVE BEEN LOOTED *leaving the people's remains scattered across the graveyard.*

NAZCA ARTISTS NOT ONLY WORKED IN CERAMICS BUT ALSO PRODUCED *wonderfully crafted garments, such as this intricate feather mantle.*

Reiche, however, was not so lucky with the Nazca graveyards. Among the affluent nations of Europe, Asia, and North America, collecting antique arts and crafts has been fashionable for over a century. Indeed the appetite among collectors for such artifacts seems insatiable. In the little town of Nazca, for example, it has created a strong market in the fine weaving and ceramics that the ancient Nazca people buried with their dead. As a consequence, their graveyards are looted almost nightly.

NAZCA GRAVES

The dry climate of the desert, which was essential in preserving the lines and figures, also protected the graves of the Nazca dead. In fact, most of what we know about this ancient people comes from their graves.

For example, most scholars agree that the Nazca people must have had a strong belief in an afterlife, for they buried their dead with special preparations and in a manner that was designed to preserve the corpse. They wrapped the mummies in their finest weaving and fixed them in seated positions in the tombs. Moreover the Nazca people interred other exquisite weaving and polychrome pottery with their dead, for use in the afterlife, or as gifts for the gods.

To see the bones of these people scattered amidst the plundered graveyards is heartbreaking. The graveyards themselves now look like bomb craters. If archaeologists had only had an opportunity to document the contents of each of these graves, we might have known much more about this ancient and remarkable people.

THE GYRATING EARTH

However, there are several lines that were drawn across the spider figure. Why did the Nazca people decide to add these lines?

Pitluga argues that the Nazcans were forced to add these lines because over the years the stars themselves appeared to drift northward. For example, the Nazca people first drew a line aimed at the setting of the bright star Rigel, which is found in the constellation Orion. At the same time they etched the figure of the spider into the desert, touching its left knee to the line. They made the width of the figure match the apparent size of the included stars as seen from the beginning of the line.

After a couple of hundred years, however, they noticed the stars setting further to the northwest. So they cut a new line across the spider that aimed at the new position of the star Rigel. Several centuries later Rigel was setting even further to the northwest, so they began tracking the stars Betelgeuse and Bellatrix on the right side of the spider, and stretched the right "foot" of the spider to meet these newest lines.

Today we know that the earth gyrates in a 26,000-year cycle. Because of this we can't see what the Nazcans saw 2,000 years ago. In another 24,000 years, however, the figures and sky will match once again.

APPLIED MATHEMATICS

From watching the skies the Nazcans would have known, just as we know today, that the stars of the spider would set some time during each twenty-four hours. In any year, however, there would be only a few mornings when the spider's stars set at dawn. A week earlier or a week later the stars would not be visible against the lines. For only a few days in December did the stars arrive above the spider as they were reflecting the glow of the dawn's light. To the Nazcans this could have been a sign that soon their desert rivers would fill with water as the rain began to fall in the distant Andes. It could signify that it was time to plant seeds so that they would be ready for the precious water which was to come.

The effort expended by the people of Nazca in etching these lines into the rocky ground of the desert would have been well worthwhile. If they and their descendants could have been able to predict the passing of the seasons, this accuracy would play an important part in their daily lives, particularly in the success of their crops and, presumably, their relationships with their gods.✪

SPIDER–ORION CORRELATION

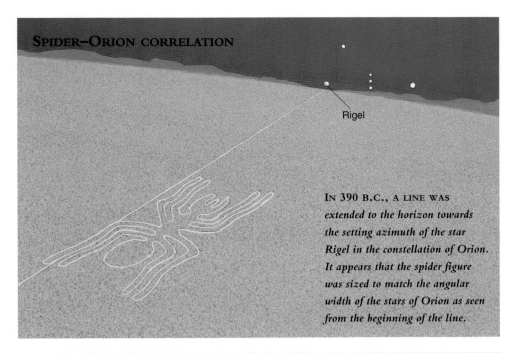

Rigel

IN 390 B.C., A LINE WAS extended to the horizon towards the setting azimuth of the star Rigel in the constellation of Orion. It appears that the spider figure was sized to match the angular width of the stars of Orion as seen from the beginning of the line.

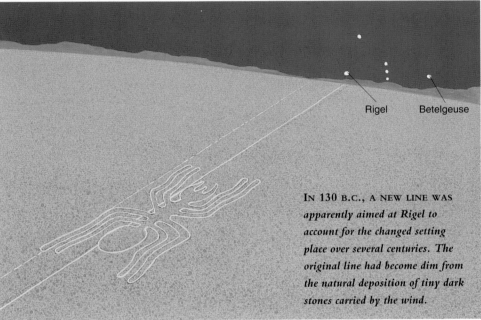

Rigel   Betelgeuse

IN 130 B.C., A NEW LINE WAS apparently aimed at Rigel to account for the changed setting place over several centuries. The original line had become dim from the natural deposition of tiny dark stones carried by the wind.

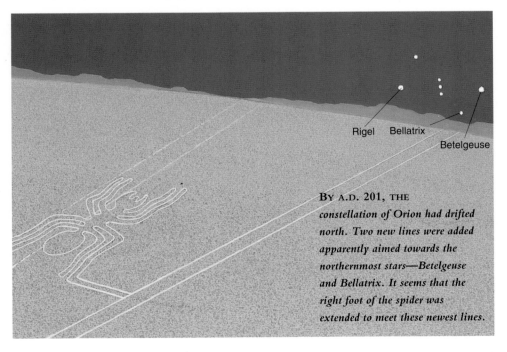

Rigel   Bellatrix   Betelgeuse

BY A.D. 201, THE constellation of Orion had drifted north. Two new lines were added apparently aimed towards the northernmost stars—Betelgeuse and Bellatrix. It seems that the right foot of the spider was extended to meet these newest lines.

THESE BRILLIANT BLUE AND *yellow shapes are magnified vanillin crystals from malt, photographed with a polarizer and a tint. By providing a window into a previously invisible world, the light microscope makes it possible to identify an amazing variety of materials by analyzing the size, shape, and position of minute particles.*

➤EARLY MICROSCOPES WERE *made in many different shapes and sizes. This one was produced in Paris in 1751.*

M. I. Walker/Photo Researchers Inc.

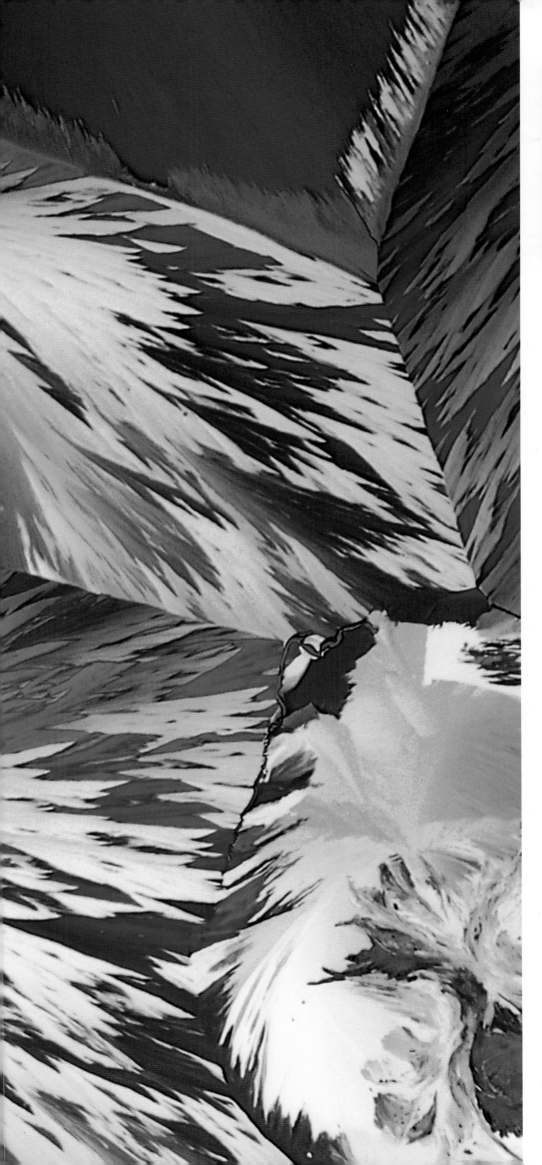

The Lens Never Lies

WALTER C. MCCRONE

I n Plato's *The Republic* Socrates defines "the idea of good" as "that which imparts truth to the known and the power of knowing to the knower." In a later section of *The Republic*, it becomes clear that Socrates is talking about light. Over three hundred years ago Anton van Leeuwenhoek discovered a way to bring this light to objects that are so small they cannot be seen by ordinary sight. At the McCrone Research Institute in Chicago, Illinois, Walter C. McCrone and his colleagues use light microscopes to shed light into a darkness the human eye cannot hope to penetrate.

Musée National Des Techniques/Lauros Giraudon

For six centuries a piece of modest cloth some 3 feet (almost 1 meter) wide and 14 feet (4.3 meters) in length has captured the imagination of millions of people. The cloth itself is of little importance. But what is important—what is everything to those who would believe in this cloth—is the unforgettable image that is imprinted on it.

The shroud is an amazingly detailed image of a cruelly beaten man. To some people the shroud images are blood, sweat, and tears. To others they suggest a painted image. To some it is an artist's inspired concept of Christ's Passsion. To others it is a contact print of a man, front and back.

Over the centuries many people have believed exactly this. For those who believe in the authenticity of the cloth and in Christianity, these reddish brown stains are nothing less than the dried blood of the Messiah.

Throughout the Christian world this cloth has become known and venerated as the Shroud

THIS SIXTEENTH CENTURY *painting by Clovio Giulio depicts La "Sindone" or the "shroud" of Jesus, which shows two images, front and back, of a naked, crucified man. The shroud became one of the most famous religious relics of all time, although its authenticity has been often questioned.*

Walter McCrone

DR. WALTER MCCRONE IS *pictured with one of his favorite microscopes, the Nikon SKe polarized light microscope, at the McCrone Research Institute.*

Galleria Sabauda, Torino/SCALA

The Art of Forgery

Forgery is an extremely difficult and intricate affair. A forger not only must produce a likeness that corresponds to what people expect the actual object to have looked like, but also must compose it exclusively from materials that were available and can be dated to the era when the original object was supposedly produced.

For example, to counterfeit an image painted by Rembrandt a forger must use not only materials available to Rembrandt in the early 1600s but also materials that are datable to that period. To measure the authenticity of an object such as a painting or the Shroud of Turin, scientists look for the mistakes a forger almost has to make—the use of pigments and other materials unavailable at the time of the alleged artist.

The Louvre, Paris/Walter McCrone

AS A STUDENT THE ARTIST Edouard Manet copied this painting of the Infanta Margarita by Velasquez. To verify it was Manet's work and not a modern forgery, Dr. McCrone used the light microscope to date and identify pigment samples from the Infanta and Manet's other paintings of the time.

of Turin. Visitors from many nations come to the Cathedral in Turin just to peer at the famed shroud above its altar.

THE AUTHENTICITY OF THE SHROUD

Although the Church has never claimed that the shroud is the actual burial cloth of Jesus, many accept its authenticity. The image on the cloth matches the Gospel's description of the marks that might have been found on Christ's body—scourge marks, blood from the crown of thorns, marks on the hands, and a spear wound in the right side. Still there were those who questioned the shroud's authenticity. For centuries, however, there seemed to be no way to disprove that it was the true burial shroud.

It is particularly ironic that in an attempt to establish the shroud's authenticity science turned to a tool as old-fashioned as the light microscope, an instrument invented four hundred years ago. In spite of the existence of dozens of twentieth-century scientific instruments such as electron and ion microscopes, x-ray diffractometers, laser raman microprobes, and infrared spectrometers, only the light microscope was able to shed any light on the truth of the shroud's image. For only with its aid was Dr. McCrone able to identify the materials in the shroud.

The image on the shroud was composed of a reddish brown stain, considered by many viewers to be very similar in appearance to dried blood. If this could be identified as a body-fluid image there would be few non-believers left.

Samples of image substance needed for microscopy were obtained by the forensic technique of taping the surface. A clear one-sided sticky tape like 3-M MagicTape is ideal and is used to lift fingerprints or suspicious dust from any surface by crime-scene investigators.

In October 1978 thirty-two tape samples were taken from body- and blood-image areas as well as several image-free areas. These were examined by Dr. McCrone over the next two years. He looked for frankincense and myrrh (frequently used in burial procedures at the time of Christ's death), blood, and other body fluids.

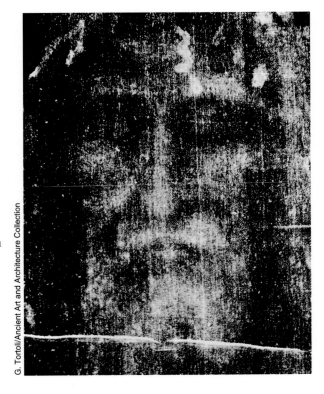

G. Tortoli/Ancient Art and Architecture Collection

A PHOTOGRAPHIC NEGATIVE OF the face on the shroud revealed surprising details, such as forehead bloodstains which appeared consistent with a crown of thorns. Scholars of the time became convinced the shroud was authentic.

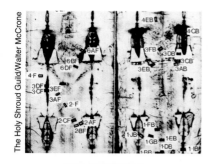

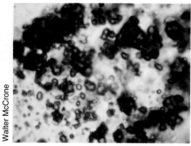

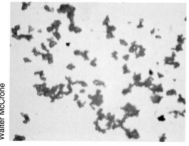

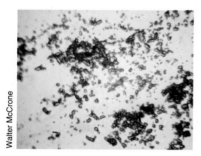

TOP, VIEWS OF THE TWO HALVES *of the Turin Shroud show the locations of the sticky-tape samples. Below are magnified red ochre particles from the shroud; vermilion pigment used by the shroud artist; and vermilion pigment produced by a modern method (bottom).*

EXAMINING THE STICKY TAPES

The first examination of the sticky tapes showed the only red material present on the body-image area tapes was red ochre, a time-honored paint pigment used since the days of cave wall artists. Microchemical tests for blood and body fluids were negative. Finally, under the light microscope Dr. McCrone saw that the tiny red ochre pigment particles were bound to the linen fibers of the shroud by collagen tempera. This was sufficient evidence to say that the shroud was definitely painted by an artist.

A few weeks later, another red pigment, vermilion, was identified in a blood-image area. This second pigment, apparently added only to the blood-image areas, was a form of vermilion only available after A.D. 800. Collagen tempera, red ochre, and vermilion were in common use in Europe during the Middle Ages. An artist working at that time would have turned naturally to those materials.

A BRILLIANT FORGERY

Dr. McCrone concluded from his tests that the shroud had been painted by an artist just before 1356. In fact, he was so sure of his conclusion that he said the shroud probably had been painted in the year 1355. This was one year before the shroud first appeared in history as a revered relic in a newly established church in Lirey, France. Dr. McCrone's conclusion was supported by Pierre d'Arcis, Bishop of Troyes, who in a letter to Pope Clement VII in 1389 stated that his predecessor (Henri of Poitiers, then Bishop of Troyes) had "discovered the fraud, and how said cloth had been cunningly painted, the truth being attested by the artist who had painted it."

Carbon dating would have corroborated this conclusion. Unfortunately in 1978, when these tests were undertaken, carbon dating required an impossibly large sample of the shroud, so it was not done. In October, 1988, however, a new carbon dating procedure requiring much less material yielded results from three independent laboratories agreeing on a date of 1325 plus or minus 65 years. These results were very gratifying to Dr. McCrone. As he later remarked, "They are only off by 30 years."

THE LIGHT MICROSCOPE

Dr. McCrone's investigation of the Shroud of Turin shows that the light microscope is still a serviceable tool for shedding light into the world of the infinitesimal—a secret world, obscure to our naked eye, yet a domain of undeniable importance, for in it are sheltered many of the great mysteries of art, religion, archaeology, and crime.

Although more modern instruments are available to Dr. McCrone, he feels that the light microscope can be used to more quickly solve many difficult problems, some of which cannot be solved by the newer techniques.

To understand the light microscope it is necessary only to grasp that it is an extension of our eyes. Envisage the world we live in, the everyday objects of this world—the building in which you make your home, or the cars that pass you as you walk down a city sidewalk, or something as simple as a box kite, or as familiar as a telephone, or as tiny as an ant or a hole in a needle. Now consider the tens of millions of objects that are smaller than the hole in this needle, objects that in our everyday lives we find hard to see, or don't even know are there. For example, consider a single cotton fiber, or a red blood cell, or a chromosome, or a titanium white pigment particle.

The light microscope extends our vision. By magnifying otherwise invisible objects, it makes it possible for us to identify the things that surround us which we cannot see with our unextended, normal vision. But more importantly the light microscope allows us to study and learn about these things, about their condition, their source, and their method of production. In other words, we do microscopically precisely what we have done all our lives macroscopically. We study and learn about the world we live in.

A SINGLE-LENS MICROSCOPE

A magnifying glass, later known as a simple microscope, has been available for many centuries. Roger Bacon (1214–1294) was the first to use such a microscope as a scientific instrument. It remained, however, for Anton van Leeuwenhoek (1632–1723) to refine the simple microscope to its highest possible state with a magnification approaching 300× and a resolution of 1 to 2 microns.

A spectacle maker, Zacharias Jansan, is credited with production of the first compound microscope about 1600. However, the images produced by this two-lens (objective and eyepiece) instrument were much less clear than those produced by the simple microscope; the

How the Microscope Has Changed the World of Science

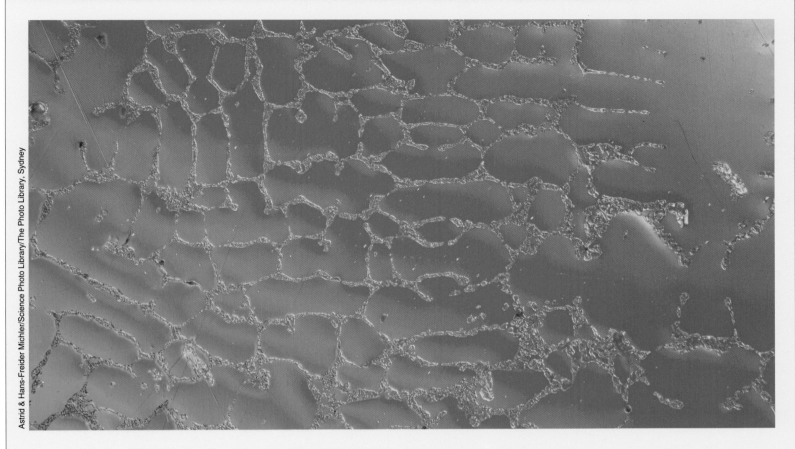

Astrid & Hans-Freider Michler/Science Photo Library/The Photo Library, Sydney

In every field from medicine to metallography the microscope has paved the way for great advances.

Centuries ago, scientists peering through a new device, which they had named a microscope, were able at last to confirm the idea that blood circulated through the body. And later, using similar devices, other scientists were able to show the relationship between disease and bacteria.

By showing the internal structure of metals and alloys, the microscope has led the way to the development of stronger and lighter alloys. Other improvements in almost all areas of technology have helped us produce better drugs, ceramics, polymers, insulation, food products, paints, and textiles.

CNRI/Science Photo Library/The Photo Library, Sydney

THIS LIGHT MICROGRAPH SHOWS A GREATLY MAGNIFIED THIN *section of aluminum alloy containing 40 percent copper. This ability to show internal structural detail is one of the most useful attributes of the light microscope.*

The microscope helps the pathologist to check tissues for cancer, the oil prospector to look for oil, the forensic scientist to solve crimes, the art conservator to unmask a forged painting, and the textile fiber manufacturer to produce a cloth strong enough to stop a bullet.

The list could go on almost endlessly. Few fields of human endeavor exist that have not been directly affected by the microscope.

THE MOST COMMON BACTERIAL INHABITANT OF THE *mouth and throat,* **Streptococcus viridans,** *is shown in a typical paired formation, magnified by the transmission electron microscope (TEM). This bacteria may cause human infections including tooth decay, endocarditis, and abdominal abscesses.*

Ann Ronan Picture Library

THIS COMPOUND MICROSCOPE *from about 1874 uses the sun as a light source. A separate lens focuses the sun onto the microscope's stage.*

eyepiece greatly enlarged the image formed by the objective but it also enlarged the faults inherent in each of the two lenses.

Less than a hundred years later, Anton van Leeuwenhoek and his single-lens simple microscope forever changed the scientific world. His observations, at magnifications as high as 280×, revealed red blood cells in circulating blood, bacteria, spermatozoa, protozoa, and hundreds of other objects only discernible when greatly enlarged. From 1673 on, over almost fifty years, he sent letter-reports to the Royal Society in London, directly affecting and accelerating scientific interest and progress in chemistry, biology, and medicine.

LIGHT MICROSCOPE

THE LIGHT MICROSCOPE *magnifies objects invisible to the naked eye. As well as being used for identification, the image can give extra infomation about the minute particles it magnifies.*

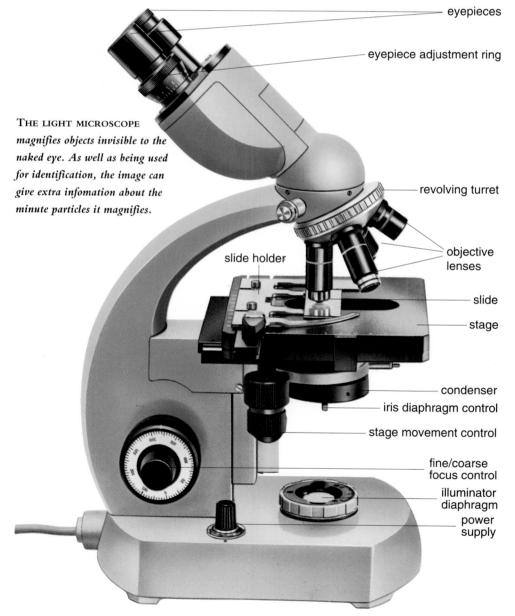

- eyepieces
- eyepiece adjustment ring
- revolving turret
- slide holder
- objective lenses
- slide
- stage
- condenser
- iris diaphragm control
- stage movement control
- fine/coarse focus control
- illuminator diaphragm
- power supply

THE COMPOUND MICROSCOPE

Van Leeuwenhoek's microscopes so adequately served the scientific needs of the day that development of the compound microscope was postponed decade by decade. Only during the 1820s did improvements in glass making and lens design make possible a compound microscope superior in performance to the simple microscope. These improvements, due to greatly increased magnification and much clearer images, resulted in a quantum leap into modern light microscopy.

The corrected design of the two-lens compound microscope soon made possible many other improvements in illumination, visibility, and resolution of tiny detail, as did the use of polarized light, fluorescence, reflected light, and darkfield. New methods of preparing specimens for microscopical study of materials such as metals, minerals, and crystals enabled better analysis of these materials. With these improvements a light microscopist became able to identify most microscopic substances on sight, just as all of us identify larger objects without a microscope. In addition, a microscopist could characterize minute objects more completely and more quantitatively.

This makes the identification much more certain and more useful. The quality of a paint pigment as well as how and when it was first produced can be ascertained. Likewise, the evidence of heat treatment and the physical properties of an alloy are apparent microscopically. In fact no other instrument can make such meaningful observations.

THE POWER OF THE LIGHT MICROSCOPE

The scientific value of the light microscope as a microanalytical tool is not based on its magnifying power. In fact, it is most often used today at 100 to 200×—the same range that was achieved by van Leeuwenhoek over three hundred years ago. Although today's light microscope is capable of useful magnifications 10 to 20× higher than van Leeuwenhoek could command, its real power lies in its precise focusing and resolving functions.

As a scientific instrument it provides the microscopist with the ability to measure important physical properties of tiny individual particles (for example, dimensions, spectral absorption patterns, color, refractive indices, dispersion of index, reflectivity, melting points, and phase transition temperatures).

Light Path from Object to Retina for Simple Light Microscope

retina

lens

light path

eye

magnifier lens

object

image

Light rays from an object are bent by the magnifier lens to an extent determined by its curvature, forming a larger image beyond the object.

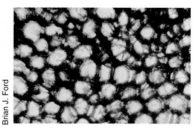

Brian J. Ford

USING A SHAVING RAZOR, VAN *Leeuwenhoek cut this thin section of cork and sent it to the Royal Society of London in 1675. This unique photomicrograph was made using one of van Leeuwenhoek's own microscopes.*

Electron microscopes make visible objects thousands of times smaller than the light microscope can even see, much less resolve. Although they also operate in the same size range as the light microscope, these costly electronic instruments do not allow characterization and identification of tiny objects with the facility of their relatively inexpensive cousin, the light microscope.

This is not to deny the value of electron microscopes. But when it comes to identifying pigments in a Raphael or a Picasso painting, samples from the moon, or trace evidence in a crime lab (fibers, drugs, glass, explosives, soil minerals or dust in general), the light microscope has no peer.

THE ATLANTA MURDERS

One of the worst mass-murderers in history was at work in Atlanta, Georgia, during 1979 to 1981. Working with the police was Larry Peterson, a light microscopist of the Georgia Bureau of Investigation Crime Lab. By identifying the fibers found on the victims Peterson had built up a particle-by-particle picture of the suspect—his home, his cars, his dog, locations he frequented, and many other things. Whenever police thought they had found a suspect, they always checked him against Peterson's particle evidence.

One such suspect was Wayne Williams. Williams had been observed in his car around the time and place one victim was dumped off a bridge into the Chattahoochee River. The splash alerted police who were staked out nearby, and

Williams was apprehended as he left the scene. Unfortunately no one had seen Williams on the bridge. To make matters even worse, at first the police could not find a body and therefore could not be sure that a body had been thrown into the river. Two days later, however, the corpse of Nathaniel Cater, the twenty-eighth victim, came to the surface. It was clear that Cater's body had made the splash that police had heard two nights before.

From a search of Wayne Williams' apartment and cars, police gathered bits of fiber that not only matched the particle-by-particle description which Larry Peterson had built up of the suspect, but also fibers taken from the victim's clothing. The District Attorney, however, was not convinced and it looked as if Williams would remain free.

Dr. Larry Howard, Larry Peterson's boss and at the time the Director of the Forensic Services Division of the Georgia Bureau of Investigation, called the McCrone Research Institute. Dr. McCrone and other microscopists went to Atlanta to examine Larry Peterson's data and slides. The individual members of the team completed their separate examinations and came to a unanimous conclusion. The particle evidence corroborating Wayne Williams' guilt was overwhelmingly compelling.

The District Attorney charged Williams with the murders of Jimmy Ray Payne and Nathaniel Cater, two of the victims. Williams is now serving time in the penitentiary. In Williams' case the microscopical evidence was absolutely convincing.

UPI/Bettman

Larry Peterson/Georgia Bureau of Investigation

TOP, WAYNE WILLIAMS, MUSIC *promoter and photographer and suspect in 28 Atlanta murders, is handcuffed and led to court. Above are the unusual synthetic green fibers (greatly magnified) from Williams' bedroom rug, found on at least 18 of the victims.*

The Light Microscope versus the Electron Microscope

A light microscope enlarges the image of a tiny object to a size large enough to identify the object at sight. It also uses polarized light, filters, and ultraviolet or infrared light to reveal additional properties of tiny particles. In this way light microscopes can be used to identify the chemical properties inherent in tiny particles.

The basic idea of the microscope is the use of two lenses to form a magnified image. One, the objective lens, projects an enlarged image which is further enlarged by the ocular lens which functions much like a hand magnifier. As this lens combination is moved closer to an object, it produces a fully detailed image which is impossible to see with the unaided eye. Most microscopists use a

Gary Laughlin/McCrone Research Institute

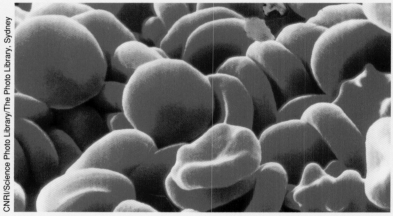

CNRI/Science Photo Library/The Photo Library, Sydney

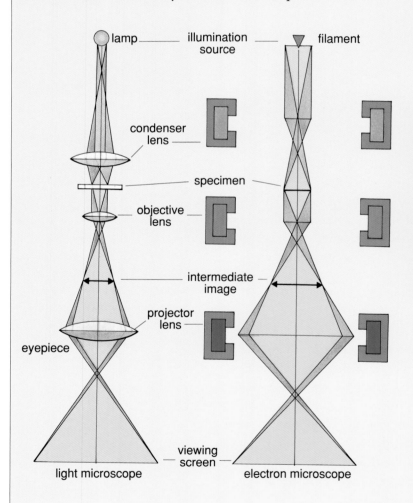

lamp — illumination source — filament

condenser lens

specimen

objective lens

intermediate image

projector lens

eyepiece

viewing screen

light microscope — electron microscope

BOTH LIGHT AND ELECTRON MICROSCOPES REQUIRE A SOURCE OF *illumination which is focused onto the specimen by the condenser lens. An intermediate magnified image is formed by the objective lens. This image is magnified further onto a viewing screen by the projector lens.*

magnification of 100× (a 10× objective with a 10× ocular) for most observations. This is the same magnification that Anton van Leeuwenhoek used over 300 years ago.

Electron microscopes, on the other hand, magnify objects by means of electrons and electromagnetic lenses. The obvious difference between the light and electron microscope is the magnification range, generally less than 2,500× for the light microscope but up to 1,000 times 2,500× for the electron microscope.

There are, however, other important differences. Electron microscopes show only the surfaces or a silhouette of the object viewed. The light microscope, on the other hand, penetrates the object to reveal inner detail and physical properties characteristic of chemical composition.

THE VINLAND MAP

In 1965 an apparently ancient map surfaced at Yale University. The map, allegedly drawn long before the voyage of Christopher Columbus in 1492, showed part of North America labeled as "Vinland," a territory Vikings are believed to have discovered in the eleventh century.

But scholars at Yale had serious misgivings about such an important document suddenly surfacing after centuries of total obscurity. Adding to their misgivings was the lack of any reference to the map in any document. The map had appeared out of nowhere. Again Dr. McCrone was asked to investigate.

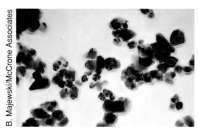

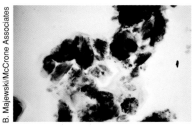

Samples of the ink were taken from twenty-nine locations on the map and examined by light microscopy. The examination showed that whoever had drawn the map had used two inks—a black ink line carefully registered over an earlier yellow ink line. The only possible purpose of the yellow ink was to simulate the yellow stain that always develops along black ink lines after a century or more.

The light microscope showed instead of a stain, a pigment-laden ink. The pigment, titanium white, did not exist before 1917 and was not produced commercially until 1920. At that date titanium white was "off-white" or yellow, and made an excellent yellow ink. The presence of an ink rather than a natural stain, and the presence of a modern pigment in that ink, was convincing evidence for scientists and scholars.

TRUTH INVISIBLE MADE VISIBLE

The Turin Shroud, mass-murderer Wayne Williams, and the Vinland Map—in each example some minute particles, invisible to the naked eye, were where they shouldn't have been. In the case of the Shroud of Turin these were paint pigments. In Wayne Williams' case they were fibers found in his apartment, in his car, and on the murder victims. And the forger who counterfeited the Vinland Map used ink pigments that did not exist before 1917.

In each instance Dr. McCrone was able to use the light microscope to shed light into the world of the infinitesimal. As a consequence, to use the words Socrates uses in Plato's *The Republic*, this instrument was able to impart "truth to the known and the power of knowing to the knower." No tool other than the light microscope could have shed so much light after so much darkness.

TOP, THE VINLAND MAP WAS A *map of the world alleged to have been made in 1440. Middle, a sample of titanium white pigment, as seen in the map. Bottom, titanium white, as ground mineral. Both samples show the anatase crystal form, unknown before 1917.*

ABOVE, CRYSTALS OF WHITING (CALCITE), *magnified by electron microscope, were identified as a man-made chemically precipitated product made after the nineteenth century. Left, artificially colored electron microscope photographs of human red blood cells (erythrocytes) that carry oxygen from the lungs to the tissues. Under pressure they appear star-shaped, as seen in the lower right-hand corner. Pictured below is a section of scirrhous (very hard and fibrous) carcinoma of the thyroid gland, magnified by the light microscope.*

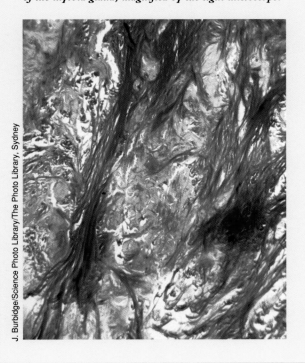

THE CLASSIC MAYA CIVILIZATION *flourished between 200 B.C. and A.D. 900, holding sway over an empire covering much of what is now Yucatan and the surrounding regions of southern Mexico, Guatemala and Honduras. Remnants of their culture, such as this site at Copan, still survived when the Spanish conquistadores arrived, but the intricate symbolism of Maya hieroglyphs has resisted decipherment until very recently.*

➤ "GRIM AND MYSTERIOUS" *are typical of the words early archaeologists applied to such enigmatic fragments as this small jade figure from Copan, one of the largest and most important of Maya cities.*

William L. Fash

Voices in the Stone

LINDA SCHELE

Deep in the jungle of Honduras, in the ancient Maya city of Copan, an international team attempts to solve the largest archaeological puzzle in the world. They are studying the stone carvings, the inscriptions, and the art the Maya left behind, deciphering the symbols of a civilization that flourished for a thousand years and then disappeared. Dr. Linda Schele, a member of this team, has spent two decades unlocking the secrets of Maya writing and has written three books on the Maya.

William L. Fash

SHADED BY A COLORFUL *parasol, Yax Pac and his family and retinue watch a ritual ballgame in a temple complex packed with thousands of spectators. Known as pitz, this ball game was more than a sport, and figured prominently in the ceremonial and religious life of the Maya aristocracy. Yax Pac was the last of the great kings of Copan, and with his death in A.D. 820 his city collapsed into ruin and never regained its former glory. This painting by H. Tom Hall brings the scene to life.*

H. Tom Hall, © 1989 National Geographic Society

Kurtis Productions

IN THE RUINS OF PALENQUE, *Linda Schele studies an array of the hieroglyphic carvings she and her colleagues have spent decades in their attempts to decipher.*

Linda Schele began a lifetime's adventure when she went on a holiday trip to see the ancient ruins of Mexico with her husband in 1970. She walked into a wondrous city whose power and beauty changed the direction of her life forever: the fabled Maya ruins of Palenque.

In 1970, the study of the hieroglyphic writing (called epigraphy) of the Maya had entered an important phase. Yuri Knorosov had shown how the ancient Maya spelled their words with syllables and word signs, while Heinrich Berlin and Tatiana Proskouriakoff had proven to almost everyone's satisfaction that the contents of the elegant inscriptions were Maya history. It was known that the stone voices spoke of the kings and their nobles—their births, marriages, deaths, their wars, their triumphs, and their defeats. However, the public and many archaeologists had not yet absorbed the implications of this brilliant work.

The accepted picture of the ancient Maya was very limited. The people were seen as peasant farmers who lived placid lives tending their corn fields, assembling once or twice a year in the great ceremonial centers they had built to house anonymous astronomer-priests whose only occupation was to follow and record the stately procession of time and the stars through eternity. People thought the Maya were fascinated with time, perhaps because their complex and highly functional calendar was deciphered long before other material was.

BREAKTHROUGH AT PALENQUE

Dr. Schele's first years of study were spent at Palenque, where Robert Rands and Merle Greene Robertson shared their expertise and work with her. Robertson, famous for the rubbings and photographs of Maya monuments she has spent a lifetime making, opened her

William L. Fash

house, her friends, and her world to Schele. In the next three years Schele learned the fine art of collaboration with Robertson and the many archaeologists and art historians who worked with her. Schele began to learn the art of research working with Robertson.

In December 1973, at a conference known as the First Round Table held at Merle Robertson's house at Palenque, Schele met Peter Mathews, a 22-year old Australian, and Floyd Lounsbury, a famous anthropologist and linguist who taught at Yale University. On the very last afternoon of the conference, Mathews and Schele, with Lounsbury's advice and help, identified the names, dates, and histories of seven men who had ruled the kingdom or been

A TYPICAL COPAN WALL, WITH *carved sculpture and intricate hieroglyphics. The Maya developed an extremely sophisticated calendar, and events symbolized in such carvings can be dated with extraordinary precision, even though the event itself may remain undeciphered.*

Carl Frank/Photo Researchers Inc.

WESTERNMOST OUTPOST OF THE *Maya empire, the huge city of Palenque in Chiapas, Mexico, overlooked the floodplain of the Usumacinta River. Its ceremonial buildings included a unique four-story tower.*

MANY MAYA HIEROGLYPHS, LIKE *these at Palenque, still resist precise translation, but a major breakthrough came when it was discovered that their message lies partly in the sequence in which the symbols appear, as well as in their content.*

MAYA WRITING

Maya glyphs are either logographs (word-signs) or syllables.

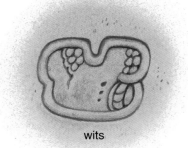

wits

THIS GLYPH IS THE LOGOGRAPH *for "wits" or in English, "hill". The symbol resembles supernatural mountain spirits portrayed throughout Maya art.*

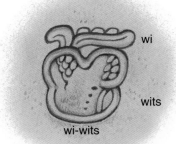

wi

wits

wi-wits

SOMETIMES ATTACHED TO THE *logograph "wits" is the syllable sign "wi". It plays a purely phonetic role and offers no added meaning.*

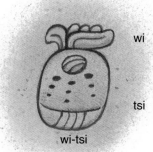

wi

tsi

wi-tsi

INSTEAD OF WRITING "WITS", *scribes sometimes combined two syllables "wi" and "tsi" to portray the same meaning.*

THIS PHOTOGRAPH SHOWS THE *modern site of Copan from a nearby hill.*

very high in the government during the last two hundred years of Palenque's history.

That amazing afternoon and the discovery of that history proved to be a turning point for Schele on a personal level and for Maya studies at a more general level. After spending the previous two years reading everything published on Maya writing, she had given up on the glyphs (the characters in the writing system) in frustration and confusion, as many others had before her. In that one extraordinary afternoon, she came to know that they could be deciphered and that the history they preserved would be read and known once again.

In a series of mini-conferences David Kelley, Robertson, Lounsbury, Mathews, and Schele worked out an approach that combined Knorosov's phonetics with Proskouriakoff's history and added a third element called syntax. Led by Lounsbury, they reasoned that the glyphs reflected the word order of spoken language. In English, for example, most simple sentences start with a subject followed by a verb. In all the Maya languages that are still spoken, as well as in earlier forms recorded from 1540 onward, the verb comes first and then the subject. English

speakers say "Kate slept" and "John hit Bob." The Maya said "slept Kate" and "hit Bob, John." The team deduced from Proskouriakoff's work and their own studies that the same word order was used in the ancient inscriptions. Thus, even if they did not know how to read a particular glyph, they could tell whether it was a verb or a subject by where it fell in a sentence. Using this approach, they were able to paraphrase the contents of Palenque's inscriptions. It was enough to begin reconstructing history and understanding some of what the ancient Maya had intended to say.

Gradually, over the years, people from many different disciplines and approaches joined the study of the glyphs. Some were archaeologists; others were linguists, art historians, and anthropologists. Many more were gifted amateurs who were just interested in the fascinating world of the ancient Maya. As more and more people joined the enterprise, the rate of deciphering accelerated. As a result of the combined efforts of these new explorers, 80 to 90 percent of the ancient inscriptions can now be understood at the general level of the "paraphrase." Researchers know how 50 to 60 percent of the signs were pronounced in the ancient languages, but with some texts, such as the well-studied tablets from the Group of the Cross or the Tablet of the 96 Glyphs at Palenque, the original sound values and the interpretation of as much as 95 percent of the text are now known.

THE CHALLENGE OF COPAN

It was in this exciting environment of discovery that Linda Schele first met Bill Fash and his wife,

Proskouriakoff Reconstruction/William L. Fash

acropolis

western court

ballcourt

Copan
stairs

temple II

north plaza

great plaza

Barbara. In 1985, Schele went to the University of Illinois as a visiting scholar, and Bill Fash came down from De Kalb to hear some of her lectures. He and Barbara wanted to start a project at Copan, the extraordinary site in Honduras.

Very little was then known about Copan's inscriptions or the history of its kings. The archaeologist Sylvanus Morley had published a volume on the inscriptions in 1920, but he had concentrated almost exclusively on their dates. In 1962 David Kelley published a glyphic history of Quirigua, a nearby site in Guatemala, and identified the first king known in modern times: 18 Rabbit. Another important milestone was Berthold Riese's proof in the early 1980s that Altar Q was a dynastic list of Copan's kings rather than an astronomer's conference. Riese's realization that the sixteen figures represented the kings of Copan seated on their name glyphs in the order of their accessions proved to be the most vital clue to Copan's history. But so far the glyphs at Copan had not been successfully analyzed because they focused on different kinds of events and used many more phonetic signs than the glyphs at Palenque.

The archaeology of Copan, on the other hand, had been studied in detail. Major excavations by the Peabody Museum of Harvard University had taken place at the turn of the century; the Carnegie Institution had sponsored a decade of excavation in the 1930s; and the Instituto Hondureno de Antropologia had sponsored extensive studies in the 1970s. The end result was an unusually full and detailed archaeological picture of the Copan valley, especially during the last two hundred years of the Classic period (A.D. 300 to 900).

Bill Fash had participated in many of the excavations of the 1970s, while Barbara had become a skilled technical artist, drawing the inscriptions and sculptures that were already known and those found during the excavations. They wanted to return to Copan to save the thousands of pieces of sculpture that lay around the ruins in huge piles, neglected and in profound danger of being lost forever. Bill Fash wanted Schele to help him do at Copan what had been done for Palenque—to bring the history alive and restore the ancient kings to modern consciousness. He wanted even more to create a team of scholars who would bring many disciplines and approaches to bear on the puzzle of Copan's archaeology and its history.

Of course, Schele agreed. How could she say no to working in the only Maya site that she thought rivaled Palenque in beauty?

THE TEAM

Over the years Fash assembled a truly remarkable team of people. He had already recruited Rudi Larios, an archaeologist from Guatemala with more experience in

THE LAYOUT AND ARRANGEMENT *of the temples and other major structures can be seen in this reconstruction.*

William L. Fash

FROM SCATTERED BROKEN *fragments, laboriously fitted together like pieces in a jigsaw puzzle, an enigmatic Maya statue gradually takes shape.*

81

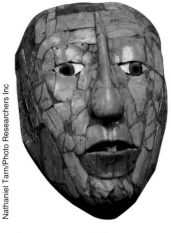

Nathaniel Tarn/Photo Researchers Inc

AROUND A.D. 750, THE GREAT
*king Pacal had his architects build
the famous Temple of Inscriptions in
his royal city of Palenque, and his
tomb was hollowed deep within its
foundations. The tomb was
discovered in 1952, and its
excavation yielded a wealth of Maya
artifacts like this jade mosaic mask
of a nobleman.*

ARCHAEOLOGISTS QUIETLY AT
*work in the sun-dappled glades of
Copan. Teams of scholars have
labored for decades over these ruins,
patiently piecing together tens of
thousands of fragments and working
to unravel the Maya epigraphy.*

William L. Fash

reconstructing and consolidating excavated
buildings than anyone else in the field. Barbara
Fash took charge of fitting the thousands of
sculptural fragments back together again and
understanding the sculptural programs that once
decorated the temples and residences of the city.
The epigraphers David Stuart, Nikolai Grube,
and Floyd Lounsbury all came to Copan to
make their own critical contributions to the
history being reconstructed.

In the early years, the team was small and
was often helped by groups of Earthwatchers,
people who contributed their time, labor,
and money to help in the enormous job of
cataloging, photographing, and storing the
sculpture that was lying around the site as
well as the new material that Fash and his
teams were excavating.

THE PAST BROUGHT ALIVE

He and Barbara focused first on understanding
the sculpture of the ballcourt. Using information from many different Maya sites they
were able to reconstruct the birds that had once
graced the ballcourt side buildings.

Later, Fash turned his attention to Structure
26, an extraordinary building graced with the
longest inscriptions surviving from the pre-
Columbian world. Consisting of over 2,500
glyphs arranged in 1,200 glyph blocks on
70 or more stairs, this extraordinary inscription
recorded the entire history of the dynasty from
the reign of its founder, Yax-K'uk'-Mo', until
the stair was dedicated in A.D. 755 by the
fifteenth king in the dynasty. In 1986, Schele
and Stuart used the information on these stairs

Stewart Aitchison /DDB Stock Photo

to identify the accession dates of the ninth,
tenth, eleventh, twelfth, fourteenth, and
fifteenth successors of the dynasty.

While tunneling through the many earlier
versions of the building that lay under the final
version, Fash and his team found a very early
stela, one of the upright stone slabs that the
Maya used to record their inscriptions. The text
recorded a day in the year 435 and the name of
the founder of the ruling dynasty, but unlike
later texts, this one was carved shortly after the
recorded date, instead of centuries later. For the
epigraphers, this was a wonderful find, for it
confirmed the existence of the early kings
recorded in later histories. The history recorded
real people and events. Most important of all,
Grube and Schele used this stela and a step that
had once sat in front of it to identify the third
and fourth successors. Grube also found the
seventh successor, whom Schele had identified
several years earlier, in the inscriptions of
Caracol, a huge site in Belize. Not only were
they finding local kings, but Grube and Schele
were also discovering a little about their roles in
the interkingdom politics of the times.

By 1989, the project had expanded to
include the entire acropolis, the huge 100 foot

THE BALLGAME WAS AN *important ceremonial and social occasion for the citizens of Copan, and thousands of people gathered around the ballcourt to watch this athletic spectacle. Rulers such as Yax Pac (763–820) viewed the contest from a temple terrace.*

(33 meter) deep structure that had resulted from four hundred years of continuous building and rebuilding by the ancient peoples. Dr. Robert Sharer, of the University of Pennsylvania, was invited to join the team. Ricardo Agurcia, a Honduran archaeologist, became co-director of the Copan Acropolis Archaeological Project, as the work had become known, and finally Fash asked E. Wyllys Andrews V, of the Middle American Research Institution, to join the project. These teams are tunneling deep into the acropolis to unravel the mystery of the history of this huge multi-layered structure. Using an extraordinary array of scientific techniques, they are discovering the buried levels, revealing the shapes of the buildings, finding burials and offerings, and dating their findings using a variety of methods. The city is truly coming to life again under their hands.

A PERSONAL VIEW

Linda Schele describes her time at Copan in these words:

"For me, the years of working at Copan have been a wonderful dream. Not only have I spent months of each year in one of the most beautiful places in North America, but I have worked with some of the finest archaeologists, architects, art historians, anthropologists, and epigraphers in the field. Even more exciting has been the adventure of finding once again the people who built the city and ruled it—the founder Yax-K'uk'-Mo' and his seventeen successors as well as the men and women who served them in all kinds of roles and offices.

"I spend my life studying the images and texts left by the people of Copan, trying to glean meaning from their patterns, sharing and debating my understanding with others who share the adventure of archaeology with me.

"In 1985, I had the privilege of hearing the great anthropologist Claude Levi-Strauss give a lecture on the art of non-Western societies like the Maya. He said that there are many people who spend their lives studying the messages these people created in the works of their minds and hands. With great persistence and luck, some of us succeed in deciphering these messages—and find they were not meant for us. But in the end, this is the miracle of the work I do . . . for although the messages of the ancient Maya were not meant for us, they are a window into a magic, wondrous world in which the ancient Maya lived."◉

William L. Fash

A STONE CARVING PORTRAYS THE *God of Scribes, an important deity in a culture whose writing was almost exclusively devoted to recording the lineages and the exploits of the kings and gods.*

The Maya Way of Life

THE MAYA WORLD

GULF OF MEXICO

Yucatan Peninsula

■ Mexico City

MEXICO

▲ Palenque

Tikal ■

BELIZE

■ Belmopan

CARIBBEAN SEA

■ Seibal

GUATEMALA

▲ Copan

HONDURAS

■ Guatemala

Tegucigalpa ■

PACIFIC OCEAN

EL SALVADOR
■
San Salvador

NICARAGUA

The Maya civilization stretched the length and width of the Yucatan peninsula, from the Pacific Ocean to the Gulf of Mexico, and included all or part of the modern states of Belize, Honduras, Guatemala, El Salvador, and Mexico. The region was divided into small kingdoms, each with its capital. Most had one or more sacred precincts consisting of pyramid-temples arranged around plazas. Here the Maya carved images of their rulers on tall stones called stelae by today's researchers. These stelae recorded the actions of those who ruled the cities, towns, and villages that dotted the Maya landscape. Although scholars now understand that rival Maya cities feuded with each other, a great deal of trade appears to have been carried on between the Maya towns, although there were no beasts of burden. The Maya grew corn, chili, beans, chocolate, squash, tomatoes, avocados, and many other fruits and vegetables.

William L. Fash

We also know from the images they left behind on stelae, murals, and pots that the Maya wore elaborately woven garments and headdresses. The women wore necklaces and earrings and face paint. Pottery was decorated with all kinds of images: from mythology, historical events, underwater scenes, gods, and ancestors.

The great courtyards in the towns were the sites for religious ceremonies led by nobles, who conducted these ceremonies wearing elaborate featherwork capes, headdresses crowned with the figures of birds and fish, brightly colored robes, and leggings of jaguar hide. Many of the stone buildings, which were elaborately carved and painted in bright colors, were dedicated to the great kings and ancestors.

IN COMPLEX SYMBOLS, THE MAYA CARVED THE EXPLOITS *and ancestry of their kings onto stone columns like this one, known to archaeologists as Copan Stela A.*

The Maya believed that their dead ancestors inhabited an "other world" and remained vital influences in their lives, along with gods, spirits, nawals, and many other spiritual forces. If one prayed with the ancestors, brought them food, and honored them, then they would help their descendants and protect their souls.

Much has been written about the Maya preoccupation with the calendar and astronomy. Their priests carefully observed the movements of the sun and moon and calculated the motions of the heavenly bodies. Their religious ceremonies were coordinated with the movements of the planets, linking their mythology to their astronomy. At the completion of time cycles their rulers practiced ritual bloodlettings. People of all social levels engaged in bloodletting or cleansing by piercing their tongues and bodies in a special religious ceremony.

A ritual ballgame (pitz) was also part of Maya ceremonies. All that is known of this is that the players fielded the ball on heavy leather padding wrapped around their hips and on a wooden yoke tied around their waists. The ballgame was part of the fundamental myth of creation that underlay Maya social and religious beliefs.

William L. Fash

THE ART OF MAYA EXPRESSION IN THEIR CARVINGS AND SCULPTURES *had reached an extraordinary level of sophistication, as revealed in these ceramic figures found in the tomb of the Copan Royal Scribes.*

EVEN MORE THAN IN MOST CULTURES, MAYA HEIROGLYPHS ARE *preoccupied with mythology and the exploits of Maya kings. Little is known of the details of everyday life in the cities and surrounding villages, except that, like peasants everywhere, they fished, grew squash, corn, and beans, and washed their clothes in nearby rivers and streams. This painting is by H. Tom Hall.*

H. Tom Hall, © 1989 National Geographic Society

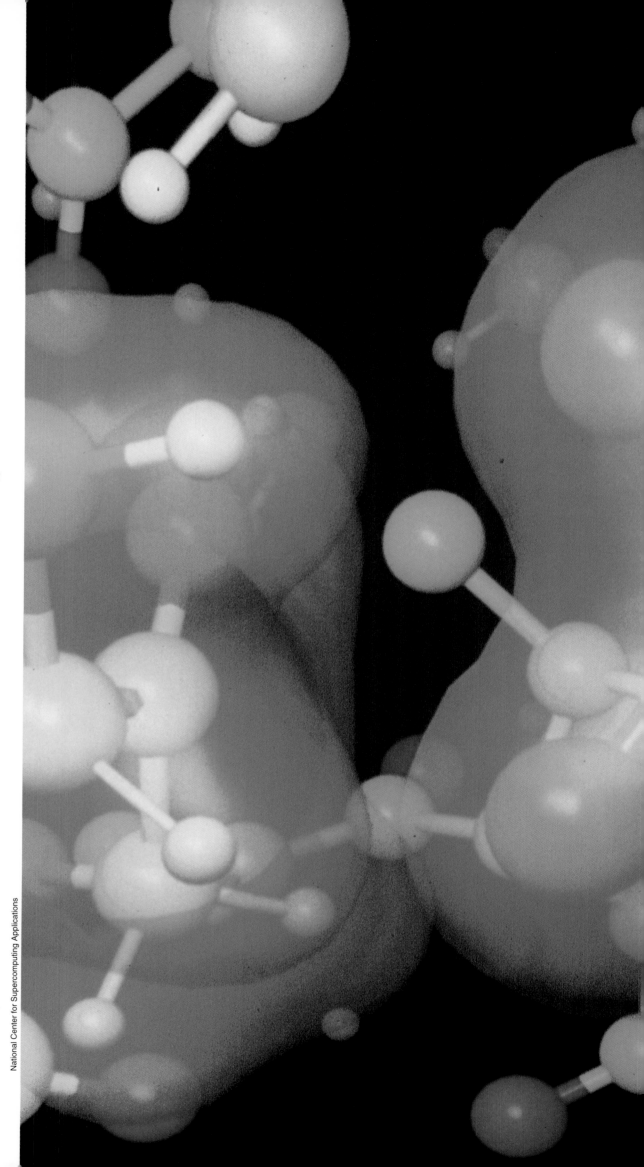

THE BEHAVIOR OF MANY
complex, dynamic systems, such
as the molecular structure of the
chemical compound modeled here,
is far too intricate for the human
intellect to grasp unaided. But
computers can make all the relevant
calculations and use the results to
construct a full-color image displayed
on a video screen. The result is a
comprehensible model of the system
under study. Now modern super-
computers are fast enough to take
the process one step further, tracking
changes in the model as its com-
ponent variables change through
time, and updating the image fast
enough to produce a smooth,
motion-picture effect.

➢ A SUPERCOMPUTER MODELS
the space mapped out by all possible
configurations of a complex molecule
as it "wiggles" through its repertoire
of energy states. By simulating the
molecular dynamics of particular
drug candidates, researchers were
better able to judge their potential
effectiveness as asthma drugs.

National Center for Supercomputing Applications

The New Language of Science

LARRY L. SMARR

Comparing the stand-alone computer that sits on your desk to a supercomputer is like comparing a bicycle to a jet airplane. Performing billions of calculations each second, super-computers transform bafflingly complex data into brilliantly colored patterns. These incredible machines seem to be making videos wherein art merges with science. But to probe deeper into the structural form of the mosaic-like shapes they create is to discover a whole new language. As our new explorers learn to decipher this complex idiom, they are exploring new worlds. Larry Smarr is the Director of the National Center for Supercomputing Applications, at the University of Illinois at Urbana-Champaign.

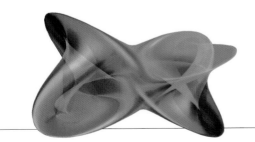

National Center for Supercomputing Applications

Try and think without language. What kind of progress could you hope to make? You would have your senses. You could look at the world about you. You could touch it, smell it, even taste it if you wanted. But without using language how could you hope to describe it?

Abstract relations, space, matter, intellect, art, music, our notions of affection and loyalty, all the things that we know and that we can explain to ourselves are inseparable from the languages we speak.

LANGUAGE AND SCIENCE

Often we cannot learn something new until we have a new language to show it to us. And this is no truer anywhere than in science. Isaac Newton, for example, sought to know more about what he called "the phenomena of motions." He wanted to understand how physical energy and the different forces around us operate. But before he could do this, he had to invent a new mathematical language, which he called the calculus.

All sciences have their own language. From this perspective the history of science is really a history of languages. It is a history of inventing new languages to find and explain new ideas.

Logic was the first great language of science. Aristotle himself claimed to have discovered it. After Aristotle there were the great languages of mathematics—geometry, algebra, the calculus. With the burgeoning of scientific thinking in the late eighteenth century still other languages flourished. Chemistry, biology, genetics, physics, geology, paleontology—each discipline began to develop its own language. And coincidentally, as these languages aided scientists in making new discoveries, the languages themselves matured. Early in this century Sigmund Freud pioneered another of the great scientific languages—the language of psychoanalysis. Much more than his theories about the id, ego, and superego, or oedipal complexes, or castration anxieties, or penis envy, Freud's great achievement as a scientist was to shed light into a new world. He literally made this world visible to us, for through his new language he gave us the means to be conscious of our unconscious.

In a sense this defines the ultimate goal of science—to push into the frontiers of knowledge, into unexplored territories, to show us what is new, what we haven't seen, what we don't yet know.

AN AERIAL VIEW OF THE SAN *Andreas fault in southern California, notorious site of earthquake activity. Computer simulations can be used to analyze the complex stresses involved as tectonic plates grind against each other.*

NASA

THE WORLD OF SUPERCOMPUTERS

Now new explorers are inventing another scientific language. And this language, just in its infancy, promises to shed light into worlds few of us are even aware exist.

These are worlds of enormously complex activity in which things come together and change into other things. Consider, for example, the process by which air pressure, heat, water content, and wind velocity come together to produce a severe thunderstorm, or the process by which an inevitable buildup of strain in the earth's crust produces an earthquake.

Such physical processes are bafflingly intricate and mysterious. For hundreds of years they have eluded even the best minds. They are just too complex to yield their secrets to the traditional scientific methods of experiment, observation, and theory.

Nevertheless, for centuries we have been accumulating mathematical equations about them. The solutions to these equations represent all that goes on in nature. Unfortunately these solutions emerge as billions of numbers so complex that they are virtually indecipherable.

THE PATTERNS CREATED BY A *violent thunderstorm can be seen from space. Today's supercomputers can simulate severe storms, revealing their complex inner processes.*

Enter the supercomputer, a machine powerful enough to approach the mathematical complexity of nature itself. Able to make billions of calculations a second, supercomputers have given us a way to comprehend billions of numbers. We simply program these super calculators to transform numbers into a still image, and thousands of still images into a video. The result: visual descriptions of complexity. These descriptions are called scientific visualization. Just as microscopes allow us to look at things that are too small to observe directly with the naked eye, and telescopes allow us to look at things that are too distant, so scientific visualization allows us to look at phenomena that are too complex to comprehend directly.

With the means to visualize complexity, interdisciplinary teams comprising scientists, computer experts, and artists are on their way to solving frontier problems in chemistry, pollution, earthquakes, severe storms, and astrophysics. Together, such teams can design new drugs, study the environment, and model cosmological phenomena. The combination of massive computing power and scientific

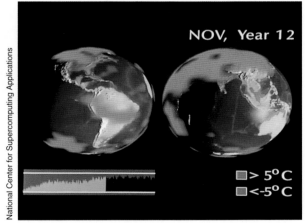

National Center for Supercomputing Applications

NOV, Year 1 2

☐ > 5°C
☐ <-5°C

SUPERCOMPUTERS CAN BE USED *to study the environment. Beginning a calculation assuming greenhouse gases have doubled, a computer tracks the effects of global warming caused by the failure of the earth's protective ozone layer. The model shows that, though temperatures will rise, it is unlikely that they will do so evenly: at year 12 from origin, red indicates predicted regions 5°C (9°F) above starting values, blue indicates regions 5°C (9°F) below starting values.*

visualization is literally creating a new language of science, one which is also more accessible to a broad public audience.

RENAISSANCE TEAMS

Until the early 1980s the United States government limited access to supercomputers almost exclusively to scientists simulating nuclear explosions and designing nuclear weapons. Researchers who wanted to use them had to apply for special security clearances and sometimes travel great distances to the few

THE RAPID PACE OF
interconnection between super-
computers, huge databases, and tens
of thousands of personal computers
is resulting in the construction of
what specialists are beginning to call
a "knowledge space." This national
network is shown here in a map of
the links between major computing
centers in the United States.

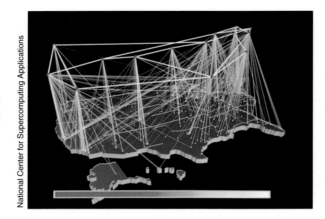

National Center for Supercomputing Applications

national laboratories where these precious national resources were kept under tight guard.

Today, however, anyone with a personal computer in a university can reach out across the national network and run a problem on a supercomputer. This synthesis of the easy-to-use personal computer, the national information network, and remote supercomputers, has created a new national infrastructure: one which could have the same sort of impact as previous national infrastructures such as the highway system, airline system, or electrical power grid.

In 1985 the National Science Foundation (NSF), an agency of the United States government, created a number of national super-computer centers. Larry Smarr is director of the National Center for Supercomputing Applications (NCSA), located at the University of Illinois at Urbana-Champaign (UIUC). At the NCSA two hundred staff members support thousands of researchers not only in the United States but around the world.

These centers provide access to a wide range of supercomputers on which researchers are busily developing new software tools for visualization and collaboration. Because the centers are located in major research universities, a great deal of interdisciplinary work emerges.

One of the most exciting consequences of this interdisciplinary work has been the development of what Professor Donna Cox, a computer artist, terms "renaissance teams." These are small teams of research scientists, computer scientists, artists, and computer professionals who develop new visualizations of natural phenomena.

They call themselves "renaissance teams" because, as Professor Cox explains, "Renaissance artists believed that the visual study of nature could in fact reveal the hidden laws of nature." Using supercomputers, the teams produce video animations of complex processes. The animations represent not only frontier scientific research, but new visual icons for our culture.

A VISUALIZATION CREATED BY A
"renaissance team." This simulation
shows why airports forbid planes to
land or take off through a thunder-
storm located overhead. Here the
rotation rate of the air flow in the
storm can be seen. The orange
ribbons show the abrupt changes
in direction which can occur. Such
disturbances could cause passenger
discomfort and, in extreme cases, risk
the safety of plane and passengers.

National Center for Supercomputing Applications

Personal Computer vs Supercomputers

Computers blossomed with the development of the integrated circuit in 1964. This breakthrough allowed millions of resistors, transistors, and other interconnecting components and their circuitry to be etched onto a tiny wafer of material, like the microprocessing chip shown here.

The personal computer emerged during the 1970s. These computers are capable of a huge range of word-processing and routine calculation chores. Each of these only requires one microprocessing chip.

With the continuing development of computers have come the supercomputers. The one shown here is the CM–5. Cooled in baths of liquid nitrogen, these sophisticated machines are capable of billions of calculations per second. Such a supercomputer can contain hundreds of microprocessing chips which will work together to analyze extremely complex material. Other supercomputers that will be at least 1,000 times faster are already on the drawingboard. These will have thousands of microprocessing chips.

In some places today's personal computers can already be networked electronically with remote supercomputers.

microprocessing chip

personal computer

supercomputer CM–5

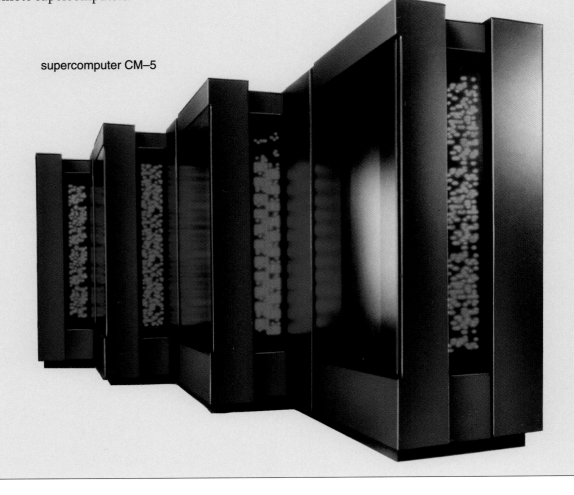

a board of microprocessing chips

Scientific Visualization

National Center for Supercomputing Applications

Imagine living three hundred years ago and looking for the first time through van Leeuwenhoek's new invention, the microscope. You would have seen shapes invisible to your naked eye. What would you have made of these shapes?

This is the position scientists find themselves in today when they look at the colorful, energized, mosaic-like shapes generated by supercomputers. Like those early microscopists, they know where the shapes come from. But they are only just beginning to learn what they signify.

A SUPERCOMPUTING MODEL

Greg McRae is a professor at Massachusetts Institute of Technology. Several years ago he began work on an elaborate model of air pollutants in the Los Angeles basin. The result was a visualization of the emissions of nitrous oxides and hydrocarbons both from the automobiles traveling the Los Angeles freeway system and from fixed point emission sites such as power plants.

In this visualization Dr. McRae computed 50 to 100 chemical reactions at each point in the atmosphere. He also included a full model of the wind patterns and topography of the basin. Topography is important because of the role it plays in trapping pollution in the foothills of the surrounding mountains.

◁ TRAFFIC ON A FREEWAY IN LOS ANGELES. CARS ARE A MAJOR SOURCE *of air pollution, emitting hydrocarbons, nitrous oxides, and carbon monoxide, all of which are toxic. The modeling power of the supercomputer offers enormous potential in helping to analyze such complex interactions.*

SMOG OVER A CITY CYCLES THROUGH A RANGE OF STATES AS SUNLIGHT *reacts on the pollutants generated by traffic and industry. The process fluctuates with local topography and changing weather parameters. This visualization and others like it convinced public officials in Los Angeles of the need to strengthen air pollution regulations.*

Running simulations on the Cray Y-MP super-computer at the Pittsburgh Supercomputer Center, Dr. McRae worked with the NCSA visualization team to create a stunning color animation of the twenty-four hour cycle of air pollution in the city. In this visualization, morning rush-hour traffic can be seen generating large amounts of pollutants, which the sun "cooks" into a high concentration of ozone during the day. Ozone is a pollutant that can cause severe respiratory distress in people. At night, the ozone is scavenged by the nitrous oxides produced from the automobiles near the ground, but maintains a high level above the city. The next morning, the cycle repeats itself.

In itself, Dr. McRae's calculation is a great research achievement. But with the stunning visualizations generated on the Cray supercomputer, it became more. It helped win one of the toughest air pollution battles in the United States. It convinced public officials in Los Angeles of the need to strengthen air pollution regulations. It also helped strengthen the National Clean Air Act.

Today Dr. McRae is in Mexico City helping to develop a similar computational tool to aid in that city's battle against air pollution.

"Artists are very important to scientific visualization," Donna Cox says, "because we are the visual experts of the culture. We know about form, we know about geometry. We know how to take these techniques and apply them to the numbers to make images that reveal information."

SCIENTIFIC VISUALIZATION IN PRACTICE

But the value of visualization is not just esthetic. It also has its practical uses. For instance, in quests to discover new drugs pharmaceutical companies such as Eli Lilly and Company may have to sort through over ten thousand chemical compounds to find one which becomes an approved drug. This time-consuming experimental method is now being augmented by supercomputers and graphics workstations.

David Herren, a research chemist at Lilly, worked with the NCSA visualization team to study the differences in a class of molecules called leukotrienes. Leukotrienes may help reduce the discomfort of asthma sufferers. Each variant of the leukotriene molecule has a slightly different shape and interacts in a different way in the body. By using the supercomputer to simulate the molecular dynamics of each drug candidate, Herren was better able to understand the potential interaction of the drug.

However, more than an animation of wiggling atoms was required, as that does not provide a quantitative picture of the effective area touched by each part of the molecule. NCSA staff developed a novel visualization approach that summed up all the points in space that the wiggling molecule occupied during the simulation. By offering a much clearer picture of the molecular dynamics of the drug, such images give reasearchers a better way to test the potential effectiveness of each molecule as a drug candidate.

Using scientific visualization in this way, the NCSA staff and David Herren virtually created a chemistry laboratory in which to test potential drug candidates. While supercomputers cannot replace an actual chemistry laboratory, they can cut a year or two off the time needed to design a drug by pointing researchers towards the most promising compounds.

Another group of researchers are using scientific visualization to help them learn about the weather. On any given day, there are about twenty thousand thunderstorms in the earth's atmosphere. The largest of these are capable of producing damaging winds, hail, and occasionally tornadoes. Each year extensive property damage occurs and lives are lost.

Although there is not much that can be done to prevent such storms, early warning of their path could be very important. Robert Wilhelmson, Research Scientist at NCSA and Professor of Atmospheric Science at IUIC, has been using supercomputers to simulate severe storms for over a decade. The equations governing air flow, solar radiation, and the various states of water can be solved to reveal the inner secrets of these powerhouses of nature. The answers are measured in tens of billions of numbers, representing the air pressure, temperature, water content, and wind velocity at each point in space for each moment in time during the evolution of the storm.

Wilhelmson worked for a year with the NCSA visualization team to produce a series of animations from the numerical output of the supercomputer. Researchers viewing these animations find themselves with a new language that describes the complex processes by which small storms develop into great tempests.

A YOUNG GIRL USES AN INHALER *to control an asthma attack. The modeling power of the supercomputer can help scientists to weed out unsuitable drugs, perhaps saving years of trial and error.*

A SUPERCOMPUTER JUGGLES *billions of numbers, each plotting a variable such as temperature or air velocity, within a grid of altitude and distances north–south and east–west, to generate this model of a thunderstorm. A semi-transparent blue shell envelops the space within which water is liquid (rain, sleet, or hail); orange represents upward moving parcels of air, blue those parcels moving downward, while yellow ribbons trace major air currents. The simulation can be run at almost any convenient speed, but numbers on the screen count off "real" intervals, roughly an hour apart in the frames selected here.*

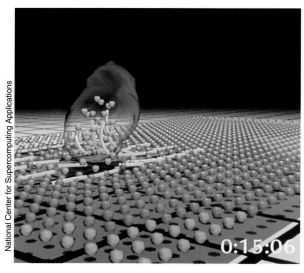

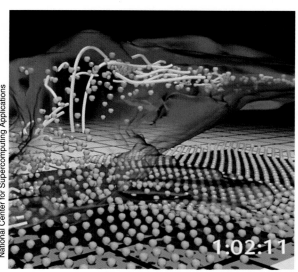

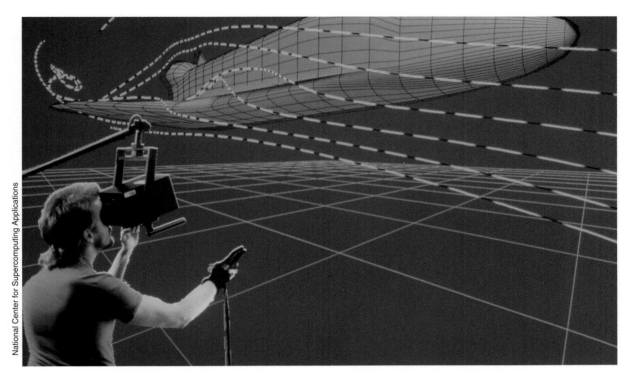

National Center for Supercomputing Applications

SUPERCOMPUTERS OPEN UP the world of virtual reality. In this development, a two-way link is established between computer and user. In constructing its models, the computer takes into account the current viewpoint and perspective of the observer, detecting every movement and instantly recalculating the model to suit: the observer becomes in effect an explorer, able to move around and even through the model.

THE FUTURE

All of the previous examples have been carried out on single supercomputers. This approach, however, is quickly changing as the national information network continues its rapid growth. In the place of the single supercomputer of the 1980s, national supercomputing centers in the 1990s are establishing "gardens of supercomputer architecture." These include vector multi-processors, massively parallel processors, and clusters of high performance workstations.

Just as modern personal computers have multiple computers inside them for computation, graphics, and input/output, at the top end of this technology a new computer is beginning to emerge which might be called a "meta-computer." A "metacomputer" is really a variety of supercomputer architectures hooked together electronically by the network with the desktop computer. In the future we will move from a model of "one person—one computer" to "many people—many computers."

The national, and ultimately international, metacomputer that emerges will not only harness vast amounts of computer power but will also access what is beginning to be referred to as knowledge space—multimedia digital libraries that will contain a large proportion of the accumulation of knowledge.

Advanced software will make accessing this information as simple as today's electrical distribution system makes using electrical appliances. In fact, it is likely that the keyboard will go the way of the buggy whip. In its place

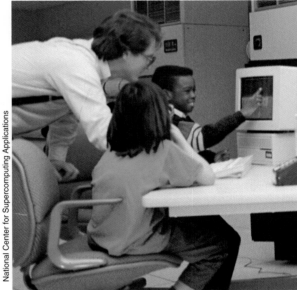

National Center for Supercomputing Applications

will be two-way voice communication with the computer network, as well as large-screen, high-definition television displays.

As fantastic as this seems, all of the technological components to make this possible are currently being researched at centers like NCSA as well as by private computer and communications companies. Not only will these developments have a major impact on research but they will also alter our entire education system. Already today, some grade school students are using personal computers networked to supercomputers to create virtual science laboratories in which they can investigate a wide range of phenomena. By the time these children have become adults, new technologies such as virtual reality will have become commonplace. ✪

INCREASINGLY, THE AWESOME power of the supercomputer lies within reach of ordinary personal computer users. This teacher coaches his students in the protocols of linking and communicating with these sophisticated machines.

95

A COMBINATION ZOOM AND TIME *exposure of a ferris wheel at an entertainment park after dark symbolizes the wealth of opportunities for investigation of the physical properties of matter and energy in familiar everyday objects.*

➤ A SIMPLE WATERSLIDE CAN BE *used to demonstrate such concepts as potential and kinetic energy, fluid and solid states, and the effects of centripetal force.*

Rock and Roll Physics

JAMES L. HICKS AND
CHRISTOPHER JOHN
CHIAVERINA

No one disputes the importance of physics. It has been called the fundamental science of the natural world. Indeed it has fathered many of the other sciences. Given a discipline of such importance, one might think that students every-where would rush to study it. Yet traditionally students rank physics among the most grueling courses in their curriculum and avoid it whenever they can. Jim Hicks and Chris Chiaverina, physics teachers at Illinois' Barrington High School and New Trier High School respectively, think that they have found the secret that could revolutionize the study of physics. Judging from the students lining up to get into their classes, they may very well have succeeded.

Tony Stone Worldwide/The Photo Library, Sydney

A SIMPLE PHYSICS EXPERIMENT: *if a beam of ordinary white light is focused through a prism, it emerges on the other side as a spectrum of different colours, thereby demonstrating that ordinary light is made up of a variety of colors.*

A YOUNG ADMIRER OF THE *wonders of holography. Holograms are constructed by lasers, which are devices that exploit the properties of light at very narrow bandwidths.*

Boring lectures being delivered in stolid monotones, endless films with muffled sound tracks, endless memorization, monotonous reiterations of tedious definitions and axioms, long hours in airless laboratories observing balls roll off tables, or steel bearings clank together, or miniaturized wave motion in little pans of water, and your grade point average always at risk—this was the typical high school physics class to many students.

Physics was something to be feared and dreaded. It was remote and mysterious and irrelevant. And the only reason students signed up for it was that college admissions committees obliged them to take it.

Yet, for all this, many students were dimly aware that physics was an important subject because it deals with the material world that is part of everyone's life. Many were also aware that to study physics was to look at the world through the eyes of a scientist: to gain an understanding of how scientists think; the kind of questions they ask; and the methods they use as they go about searching for answers. Physics forces people to think critically and analytically. And this means using logic and mathematics.

P. Plailly/Science Photo Library/The Photo Library, Sydney

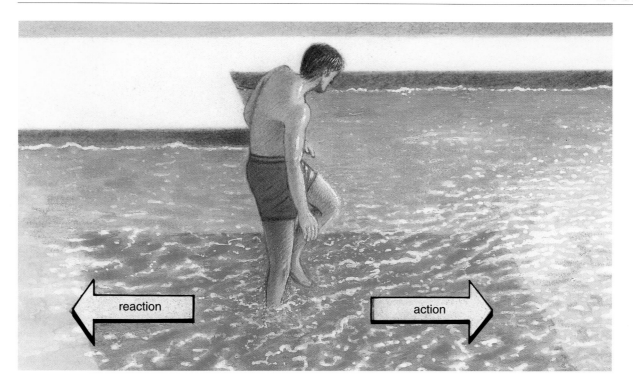

Chris Chiaverina

WHEN A PERSON'S FOOT PUSHES on the mat, action force is created; the mat then pushes back on the person's foot causing reaction force. The action force causes the mat to move to the right; the reaction force causes the person to move to the left.

THE TYPICAL HIGH SCHOOL PHYSICS CLASS

So for most students, physics was a hard subject. It demanded stretching and flexing of minds. It could be frustrating. Often it was tedious. But mostly it was just pure torture, although perhaps sometimes, in unguarded moments, some of the students may have wondered if there wasn't a real pot of riches inside all this tedium.

The typical high school physics class had the instructor standing in front of the class with a blackboard behind. The instructor delivered a lecture and students frantically tried to copy into their notebooks details of everything important that was being said.

When there wasn't a lecture, the students were quizzed. These little tests gave them the opportunity to show the instructor how much progress they were making. This meant that students were judged on how accurately they could reproduce the axioms, definitions, and theorems the instructor had given them to memorize. Sometimes the students were given problems to solve. They were asked to manipulate formulas that the instructor had previously chalked onto the blackboard for them to copy into their notebooks.

The days when students worked in the laboratory were hardly any better. Students strived as best they could to duplicate experiments from a workbook. Inasmuch as the results had to match those in the workbook, students could scarcely hope to find any surprises. There was little possibility that they would be astonished or given occasion to wonder at anything.

A NEW APPROACH FOR PHYSICS

A difficult and demanding subject and a way of teaching it that made it seem tedious and boring—it could almost be thought that the traditional high school physics class was intentionally designed to put students off physics for the remainder of their lives. It practically guaranteed that most students would come to loathe the subject and try to forget everything they had been forced to learn about it.

Yet in spite of all this some actually found physics fascinating. Two of our new explorers, Jim Hicks and Chris Chiaverina, happily number among these fortunate few. After high school they went on to study physics at college and graduate level. The more they learned, the more they came to appreciate and love the wonders of this branch of science.

To these men it seemed only natural that the world should share their passion. So they returned to the place where it all began, to the high school physics classroom.

HIGH SCHOOL PHYSICS CLASSES designed by the authors include an annual excursion to the local swimming pool, to investigate the dynamics and behavior of waves in a liquid.

99

Chris Chiaverina

HOW TO WEIGH A CAR WITH A *stopwatch. Because mass, force and acceleration are interrelated, any one of these components can be evaluated by measuring the others. Stopwatch in hand, a physics student calls out regular time intervals as her assistant drops a marker to indicate progress so far, while other students provide the muscle. The steadily increasing distance between the markers will yield the acceleration, from which the car's mass can be easily calculated.*

They realized that they had chosen an un-usual place to express passion. But they had ideas for a revolutionary approach for teaching the wonders of physics.

Their first change was to strengthen the role of the student. No longer would young scholars sit at a desk and take notes. Instead Hicks and Chiaverina wanted students to take a more active part in class. The way to do this, they proposed, was to get students to ask ques-tions about the physical world. Moreover, they did not want students to ask just any questions. They wanted students to ask questions that the students themselves cared about.

Chris Chiaverina

Chris Chiaverina

A SESSION ON THE DODGEM CARS *offers an ideal first-hand demon-stration of the validity of Newton's first law of motion. When dodgems collide, they stop abruptly but their passengers momentarily continue.*

side-to-side movement

direction of pulse

A SLINKY TRANSVERSE WAVE. *In a transverse wave the particles of the medium move perpendicular to the direction of travel.*

Chris Chiaverina

They also changed the instructor's role. No longer was he or she there to provide answers. Instead, it was the instructor's responsibility to launch students in the search for answers. In-structors were there to help students see how physics can provide some very powerful, service-able tools to aid them in their investigations. But the students themselves were to be responsible for the actual answers.

Jim Hicks and Chris Chiaverina believe that physics is within the reach of anyone who is willing to take the time to explore it. For their new program all that was needed was a way to engage students in the learning process. And the best way to do this, they believe, is to encourage students to learn for themselves.

A PHYSICS LABORATORY, 1990s *style. The physical behavior of fluids is very different from that of solids, and wave pools, swimming pools, and waterslides offer many opportunities to explore these differences.*

THE FILM OF WATER BETWEEN *the chute and the boy's body allows a free interplay between the centripetal and centrifugal forces that swing him high on the turns, low on the straight stretches.*

These teachers want to stimulate curiosity in their students, to nurture a desire to know. They hope to show students that the effort of searching for answers can be every bit as rewarding as the answers themselves. In the words of Richard Feynman, one of the great physics teachers of this century, they want students to experience "the pleasure of finding things out."

AN ENTHUSIASTIC INVESTIGATOR *demonstrates that, though the wave moves, the water itself does not.*

CLASS STRUCTURE

Physics classes always have been divided into units of study, such as time and motion, optics, waves, mechanics, and so forth.

Jim Hicks and Chris Chiaverina begin each unit with hands-on demonstrations. Banished from introductory sessions are all definitions, axioms, laws, and anything else abstract. Hicks and Chiaverina merely ask students to watch demonstrations and to manipulate laboratory equipment. Moreover, students are encouraged to experiment with equipment in any way they can think of. It is important only that students

Banked Curve

To reduce chances of skids, highway curves are often banked so the roadbed tilts inward. The road then will provide an inward force on the car.

TO KEEP AN OBJECT MOVING IN a circle, an inward (centripetal) force must act on the object. If this force is removed the object will fly off in a straight line at a tangent to the circle.

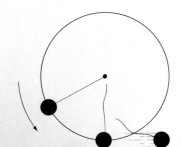

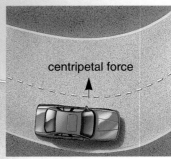

centripetal force

USUALLY THE FRICTION between a car's tires and the road is enough to provide a car with the centripetal force it needs to make a turn. If the friction between the tires and the road is reduced by slippery conditions, the car will skid off on a tangent to the curve as in the diagram above.

Chris Chiaverina

THE STUDENTS ARE CHECKING whether the speed limit on the sign is appropiate for the curve.

observe and ask questions about what they observe. There are no wrong or right questions.

Later phases of the introductory sessions are used for discussion. Hicks and Chiaverina encourage students to share ideas about the demonstrations they had witnessed earlier. Also, this is an occasion for students to reflect and speculate on the unit to come.

While talking about earlier experiments and demonstrations, students frequently come across key vocabulary words and sometimes even begin

to view the demonstrations as road maps to many of the important ideas in the unit. The main thing, however, is that through hands-on experiences and discussion everyone gets a feel for the subject matter and begins to generate some questions about it.

If the introductory concrete sessions have been successful, by the end of them students will feel an overriding curiosity about what they have seen and discussed. Such curiosity leads naturally to the next phase of study, the abstract stage. This stage begins with demonstrations that illustrate key mathematical relationships in the unit of study. Not only are many important ideas in the unit developed here, but students find that they also have some very powerful tools that can help them answer many of the questions they have raised.

In this stage Hicks and Chiaverina have all but discarded the workbook approach for laboratory assignments. To engage students in the learning process and to get them to think for themselves, they give them the sketchiest of goals for experiments and only the most essential suggestions for how to go about devising these.

Hicks and Chiaverina use the last series of class discussions to summarize the entire unit of study. It is here that students and instructor try to tie together the various strands of course material. Together they draft a document stating the basic principles and pertinent equations they have studied, and they discuss the practical applications of these in the real world.

REAL WORLD PHYSICS

A point Jim Hicks and Chris Chiaverina love to make is that physics may be one of the easiest disciplines to teach because it is everywhere. All that is needed is the imagination to see it. The real world outside the classroom provides the best physics laboratory available.

One of the most unusual and creative aspects of their revolutionary approach to teaching physics is the way they make use of this giant laboratory. No program anywhere takes fuller advantage of the physics in students' lives.

Classrooms, gymnasiums, hallways, playgrounds, school auditoriums, and roads all

become components of their students' experiments. Swimming pools, for example, allow students to experience action-reaction forces on a large scale. Hallway walls become part of experiments that demonstrate the motion of particles. Large-scale auditorium demonstrations are used to illustrate interference in and the properties of sound waves.

But probably the most ingenious idea that these new explorers have come up with is "The ultimate physics laboratory: the amusement park." Any physicist, they say, will tell you that such places offer an unparalleled opportunity for everyone, from the most elementary physics student to the most sophisticated graduate, to study at first hand the laws of motion. These giant playgrounds are a paradise for illustrating Newton's laws of motion, energy transformations, momentum conservation, and rotational motion of every kind.

For years Jim Hicks and Chris Chiaverina have been taking their students on all-day excursions to amusement parks. In fact in 1975 they wrote their own amusement park laboratory manual. The excursions have become

Chris Chiaverina

THE SPEED AT WHICH A SKID IS *likely to occur is directly related to the degree of banking. Here a class measures the slope of the roadway with a spirit level and ruler.*

RIDERS ON THE EDGE AT THE *famous motorcycle racetrack at Donnington, England, are precariously balanced by opposing centripetal and centrifugal forces.*

R. Parker/Horizon

so popular that Six Flags Great America near Chicago now has an annual "Physics Day." In May 1992 "Physics Day" attracted over 5,000 physics students from four states.

But probably the most unusual field trip they take with their students is a five-day excursion to Orlando in Florida, to Epcot and the Magic Kingdom. While there they challenge students to answer questions about the physics behind many of the exhibits. Working in small groups, students must apply and summarize what they learned throughout the year.

A three-page laboratory assignment is devoted just to the airplane ride. While using a homemade accelerometer during take-off, students plot acceleration vs time and estimate the take-off speed. Later, students derive the lift force for a banked curve flight in terms of the mass of the airplane, speed of the airplane, and the acceleration of gravity. Force diagrams play a crucial role when computing such things as the time of skidding and angular impulse to each wheel during touchdown.

Epcot itself provides a field day for the physics adventurer. As well as completing a ten-page physics laboratory packet, each student is required to keep a journal containing their reflections and experiences during their stay in Orlando. One student wrote, "Epcot used to be boring and senseless as did MGM Studios. Now that I have studied everything, I have absolutely enjoyed myself. I feel like a little kid again."✪

Chris Chiaverina

George Patterson Advertising

Gabe Palmer/Stock Photos

AN OBJECT EXPERIENCES *momentary weightlessness as its energy state shifts from potential to kinetic, a phenomenon experienced by every rollercoaster rider at the stomach-lifting instant at the summit (left), before the terrifying high-speed descent (below left).*

MODERN MEANS OF TRANSPORT *of all kinds are designed according to advanced analysis of simple physical relationships.*

PHYSICS STUDENTS ARE ASKED TO *observe that, regardless of the weight of the riders, all chairs on this ride (even the empty ones) maintain the same angle relative to the spinning central wheel. They are then invited to explain why, by using the elementary laws of angular momentum.*

Luis Castaneda/The Image Bank

◁ A STUDY IN APPLIED VECTOR *analysis. At every point on the ride, the track is engineered in such a manner as to oppose the momentum of the moving car it carries, so preventing it from coming off the track.*

THE FASTEST OF THE WORLD'S
land animals, the cheetah was once
prized by royalty as a hunting
companion. Today it is endangered
in much of its remaining habitat.

AMAZING CREATURES

A BALD EAGLE ON THE CHILKAT
*River, Alaska. Bald eagles in
Canada and Alaska have always
sustained a healthy population,
but the population inhabiting the
southern United States steadily
collapsed under the multiple threats
of human persecution, habitat
destruction, and pesticide poisoning,
until a census in 1963 could locate
only 417 nesting pairs, down from
possibly 20,000 last century. A
captive rearing program spearheaded
by the George Miksch Sutton Avian
Research Center in Oklahoma has
enjoyed encouraging success in
attempts to restore the numbers
of this magnificent bird.*

➢ ON JUNE 20, 1782, THE BALD
*eagle (then known as the "American
eagle") was adopted as the national
emblem of the United States
of America.*

Flight for Survival

JAMES W. GRIER

Thirty years ago when James Grier first climbed 70 feet (22 meters) into the upper branches of a tree to look at an eagle's nest, he did so only to satisfy his curiosity about bald eagles. Never in his wildest dreams did he suppose that one day this eagle's very survival would depend on what he and others would learn from their work in the field. Yet this is exactly what happened. Today Dr. Grier teaches in the Zoology Department at North Dakota State University. He is considered one of the world's foremost authorities on the bald eagle.

ENTHRONED IN A TREE COVERED *by a flowering flame vine, two bald eagles ready their nest in Florida, home state of about 90 percent of the total southern population.*

As the bald eagle soars overhead with its brown body, white head, and white tail standing out against a blue sky, or as it perches majestically, high in a tree, its strength and beauty are obvious. In spite of its natural grandeur, however, until recently little has been known about the bald eagle, and people have viewed it with mixed emotions. In fact, it nearly became extinct. But during recent years people have learned much about the species and gained a whole new appreciation of it. The result is that the bald eagle is now making a comeback. This is the story of the bald eagle's decline and recovery, and of the new explorers who helped make that recovery happen.

The bald eagle has a power and mystique that make it a potent symbol. Perhaps this is one of the reasons the United States adopted the bald eagle as its official emblem in 1782. Even then, however, not everyone held the bald eagle in

NUMBERS OF BALD EAGLE *nesting pairs in the lower 48 states have gradually increased, showing the species' recovery from near-extinction in the 1960s.*

TOTAL NUMBER OF NESTING PAIRS

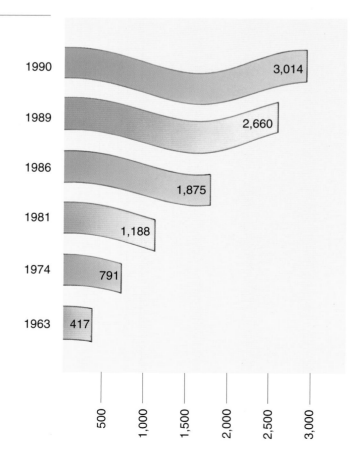

Year	Nesting pairs
1990	3,014
1989	2,660
1986	1,875
1981	1,188
1974	791
1963	417

500   1,000   1,500   2,000   2,500   3,000

high regard. Many people feared or simply disliked this large bird. Others felt that the bald eagle threatened their fish, game, and livestock. For many years the bald eagle was shot and trapped, and in some areas, such as Alaska, a reward was offered for killing bald eagles .

The bald eagle was also an innocent victim of many other human activities, including land development and pollution of its natural habitat. Many bald eagles could not tolerate the presence of people and buildings nearby, and so they were driven from their habitats. Several toxic chemical contaminants in the environment began causing problems for the bald eagle. One of the worst proved to be DDT.

EARLY RESEARCH

Because so little was known about the bald eagle, it took some time for researchers to understand the impact of human activity. Up until the 1920s the only information about the species came from scattered and mostly incidental reports from ornithologists, amateur

Leonard Lee Rue/Bruce Coleman Limited

RENDERED UNIQUE BY A *combination of white head and tail plumage, the bald eagle,* **Haliaeetus leucocephalus,** *is one of a group of large sea eagles spanning the northern hemisphere, Africa, and Australasia. Its European counterpart, the white-tailed sea eagle, has had a roughly parallel history of collapse followed by a gradual restoration.*

birdwatchers, and egg collectors. Then, from 1921 to 1933, a lone pioneer in the study of the bald eagle, Francis Herrick at Western Reserve University, studied the home life of the bald eagle in Ohio. His work was followed by a few other studies of the bird, including a long-term study of nesting eagles in Florida and a large banding project in Florida carried out by Charles Broley, an energetic retiree. He started his studies of eagles in 1939 at the age of 59, climbing into hundreds of nests at the tops of tall trees and banding over 1,100 nestling bald eagles!

During the twenty years that Charles Broley worked with bald eagles in Florida, he noticed a decline in the number of young eagles being produced. He was the first to alert the world to this problem. The species had been officially protected in the US by an Act of Congress in 1940 but many people did not take the law seriously; and eagles were still being shot for bounty in Alaska. During the late 1940s, 1950s, and early 1960s the bald eagle was going into a slow decline that could have led it to extinction.

BALD EAGLES OCCASIONALLY *nest on the ground, but most pairs prefer to build high in the largest available tree, with a commanding view over the surrounding country-side. Nests are reused annually for decades, enlarged, and refurbished before each breeding attempt.*

111

America's National Emblem

Bald eagles are found only in North America, and they tend to congregate where the food supply is abundant. As their favorite food is fish, they are mostly found along seacoasts, rivers, reservoirs, and larger lakes. They breed in Alaska, Canada, and the United States in the Rocky Mountains, the Great Lakes area, and along the Pacific and Atlantic coasts as far south as Florida and California. They winter mostly along rivers south of the Canadian border.

Not all eagles migrate. The migratory patterns of the ones that do appear to depend on the food supply. In the late fall, as food becomes scarce in their own habitats, northern eagles migrate south.

THE EAGLE'S NEST

Bald eagles generally make their nests in old pine or cypress trees. For protection from the sun they build below the canopy of the tree. But for better visibility and flight approaches, and for protection against insects, eagles prefer to build as high as possible. So their nests typically are 60 to 100 feet (18 to 30 meters) off the ground.

For building supplies, sticks sometimes as long as 6 feet (1.8 meters) plus grass, moss, and other soft materials for lining are the favored materials.

The largest eagle's nest on record measured 12 feet (3.6 meters) from top to bottom and was estimated to weigh 4,000 pounds (1,800 kilograms). This nest also had the longest history of use: it was occupied for 35 years.

An eagle family will use the same nest for years, sometimes even for several generations. In the spring, when eagles return to their breeding territories, they then add new sticks and grass to the nest. For some eagles this seems to be purely a routine performance. The nests of these eagles remain substantially the same size year after year. Other eagle families, however, are more industrious. Each year they add new material on to their nests until they become massive structures such as the one already mentioned.

Another interesting variation among eagle families is the way they maintain their nests. Some are meticulous "housekeepers," who promptly remove uneaten food and generally keep their nest very clean. Others let food accumulate and constantly bring fresh lining materials to the nest to hide the old uneaten food. And still others are truly messy and allow large amounts of rotting meat to pile up underneath them.

THE BALD EAGLE'S ARSENAL OF ATTACK *equipment includes long broad wings for effortless soaring, moderately long tail for maneuvrability, incomparably keen eyesight, long sharp talons for a vice-like killing grip, and a powerful, sharp-toothed beak for tearing prey apart.*

ANATOMY

The bald eagle is larger than almost all other species of birds. Generally, males are somewhat smaller than females. An adult eagle's length varies from about 2 feet 6 inches (75 centimeters) to over 3 feet (1 meter). Its wingspan ranges from 6 to 8 feet (1.8 to 2.4 meters). Its weight ranges from 7 to 14 pounds (3 to 6 kilograms).

Compared to other animals, such as mammals, an eagle's weight may seem light, but this is necessary for

primaries

secondaries

tail

THE TERM "EAGLE-EYED" HAS BECOME
a byword for exceptionally keen vision.

Adult plumage is fully acquired in the fourth or fifth year. Bald eagles also have large yellow bills, yellow feet, and yellow eyes. Their talons are black. Younger birds lack the white heads and tails, and have dark eyes and beaks.

THE EAGLE'S EYESIGHT

In myth and legend eagles are famous for their eyesight. In colloquial English, for example, the phrase "eagle-eyed" is used to describe someone with exceptionally keen vision. While it was formerly thought that eagles could see about eight times better than humans, more recent studies have shown their sight to be only a little over two to three times that of a human.

Scientists do not have a complete understanding of why eagles are able to see so well. They know that the eagle's eye is large relative to its skull, and so it has a relatively large light-sensitive retina. A factor scientists puzzle over is a structure called the pecten, which extends into the eye from the retinal area. The eye of the eagle, like that of many other birds, differs from other vertebrates in having two retinal foveae in each eye. The sensory cells in the fovea are unusually dense.

Scientists theorize that this density of sensory cells increases the resolution of any image projected onto the retinal surface. Also, the nerve connections behind the sensory cells are exceptionally dense and promote complex neural processing of the image.

flight to be possible. To keep the eagle strong while reducing its weight to size ratio, nature has made numerous adaptations to its structure, such as feathers and hollow bones. The result is a creature with large, powerful wings which is a strong, maneuverable flier. Eagles have been known to prey on animals larger than themselves and to reach flight speeds of 35 to 45 miles (60 to 70 kilometers) per hour in level flight, and well over 100 miles (160 miles) per hour during a dive.

As for the bald eagle's coloring, perhaps it can be best understood in terms of its scientific name, *Haliaeetus leucocephalus*. *Haliaeetus* is the Greek word for "sea eagle," and signifies those eagles that live along the shorelines of rivers and ocean coasts and hunt fish. *Leucocephalus* means "whiteheaded." The bald eagle was given its name because its head and neck are covered with white feathers. Strictly speaking the bald eagle is not actually bald in the contemporary sense of the word.

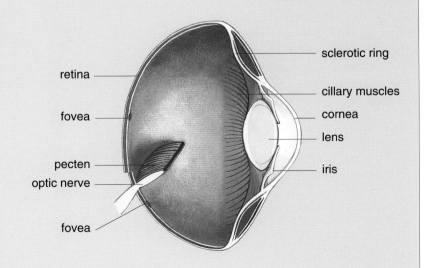

retina

fovea

pecten

optic nerve

fovea

sclerotic ring

cillary muscles

cornea

lens

iris

WITH A HIGHER CONCENTRATION OF SENSORY CELLS THAN IN ANY
other vertebrate, an eagle's eye is more than twice as efficient as a human's eye.

NEARLY READY FOR RELEASE, *an adolescent bald eagle is tagged for subsequent identification. A numbered aluminum band allows its place of origin to be traced should it ever be found dead.*

Then, in 1962, Rachel Carson brought the problem to the attention of the general public with a book titled *Silent Spring*, in which she described a spring with no birds calling. Conservationists concerned about the bald eagle and other species, such as the peregrine falcon, the osprey, the brown pelican, and the whooping crane, started to get together to share notes and discuss what could be done, both to better understand the problems and to correct them.

INFORMATION ACCUMULATES

Several events during the 1960s helped to provide information about the bald eagle and to focus attention in the proper direction. Two major bird conferences were held (in Madison, Wisconsin, in 1964, and in Ithaca, New York, in 1969) to discuss the plight of the peregrine falcon and other birds of prey. Following the 1964 conference, a new organization of concerned scientists and other interested people, the Raptor Research Foundation, was formed. Then Derek Ratcliffe in England discovered a correlation between the thicknesses of falcon egg shells in museums and the use of DDT in the environment. Later studies undertaken in North America by Joe Hickey and one of his students, Dan Anderson, yielded similar results.

1

HERE BALD EAGLES CONGREGATE *at a major wintering area on the Chilkat River in Alaska, where about 3,000 to 4,000 have been counted along a 10 mile (16 kilometer) stretch. Northern bald eagles are markedly less territorial than their southern relatives, a factor that may have had some bearing on their comparative success, in that they exhibit a consequently greater ability to reoccupy vacant territories in new areas.*

BREEDING DISPLAYS

2   3   4

There were also several developments in the study of bald eagles specifically. The National Audubon Society, led by its research director Alexander Sprunt IV, began coordinating meetings of researchers. In the central part of North America large-scale bald eagle nesting surveys and banding projects began. Jim Grier's work in northwestern Ontario was one of these. He eventually discovered and visited over 800 bald eagle nests, banded over 1,100 nestlings, and conducted several different research projects involving these birds over more than thirty years. He worked in close association with the Ontario provincial and Canadian federal governments plus several conservation organizations. Elton Fawks initiated a long-term survey of numbers and age ratios of wintering bald eagles along the Mississippi River in Iowa and Illinois.

Most of these studies are continuing, and there have been significant new developments. A large number of studies of nesting, migrating, and wintering bald eagles have been initiated from coast to coast throughout the US and Canada. These involve many researchers and agencies. Present studies include investigations

of the impacts of human disturbance on bald eagles; their blood chemistry and genetics; radio telemetry to follow eagle movements; analyses of eagle vocalizations; computer modeling of their populations; and a number of studies of other aspects of their biology and management.

OTHER TYPES OF ACTION

While better scientific information on the species was accumulating, several people and groups were taking other kinds of action. DDT, after long and acrimonious debate, was finally banned in the US in late 1972. The use of DDT was actually already declining in the US, partly because of concerns over its effects and partly because many insects were becoming resistant to it and so it was losing its effectiveness.

The laws protecting bald eagles were strengthened, and the birds received additional legal protection under revised international treaties and the new Endangered Species Act. The bald eagle was declared an endangered species in 1978 and recovery teams were established to make recommendations about research and management.

LIKE MOST RAPTORS, BALD eagles mate for life and maintain their pair bonds with elaborate and spectacular aerial displays before breeding each year. One dramatic display involves a mock attack from above, in which (1) the birds are flying at different levels, then (2) the "attacker" swoops down. (3) The "victim" (usually the female) rolls on her back and the eagles fleetingly lock talons. (4) Both birds regain their original flight pattern.

Kurtis Productions

JIM GRIER CLIMBS TO A BALD eagle nest to remove an egg for transfer to a rearing facility.

The Hacking Program

Most vital component of the entire process, the prime function of the hacking tower is to gradually accustom the eaglet to life in the wild. The part of the tower used by the birds is essentially two adjoining squares on stilts. One square is walled on three sides, and contains a nest, perch logs, and grass or hay so the birds can lie down. Its back wall is equipped with one-way glass and screens, so that observers can watch the young eagles from a third compartment without being seen. The observers leave and enter the tower only during hours of darkness. Food is supplied through a chute from this back wall. The other square is a feeding platform for the birds, designed to closely mimic the high, open, exposed environment of a genuine eagle nest. A group of 5 to 12 eaglets is transferred to the hacking tower when about 11 weeks old and, unaided, each learns to fly, handle prey, and orient itself to the surrounding countryside. Each eagle develops at its own pace. Food is constantly provided so the birds can return on occasion for up to a year after they depart.

M.Alan Jenkins/Avian Research Center, Inc.

M.Alan Jenkins/Avian Research Center, Inc.

M.Alan Jenkins/Avian Research Center, Inc.

CRADLED IN FOAM AND SECURED BY cord netting, a precious cargo of two eggs lies packed in a portable field incubator. The eggs must be protected from vibration, and maintained at a constant temperature.

AS WELL AS ARTIFICIAL INCUBATORS, broody hens are sometimes used as surrogate parents to hatch the eggs. Eggs may have been obtained from captive breeding or from healthy populations in the wild.

HATCHING TAKES ABOUT A DAY, A grueling process beginning when the baby uses a tiny tooth atop its bill to chip an air hole in the shell and ending when it has struggled free of the last broken fragments.

DINNERTIME AT A BALD EAGLE residence. In bald eagles, both parents feed the young, but in many other birds of prey, the father only fetches food. The mother tears it apart and feeds it to her chicks.

AN ARCTIC BALD EAGLE BRINGS a rock ptarmigan for its chicks. Found only in North America, bald eagles may begin to breed in their fifth or sixth year, and sometimes live for 30 years or more. Broods typically consist of two young.

REMAINING DISCREETLY IN THE background, a technician uses a puppet to feed a new-hatched chick. Remote stance and momma model are part of the tactics used to prevent the chick from imprinting on humans instead of eagles.

Bounties in Alaska were dropped, and the table on bounties was actually reversed! The new regulations, with supplementary rewards from the National Wildlife Federation, provided rewards for information leading to the arrest and conviction of anyone who killed eagles.

Bald eagles that were injured or sick were looked after at the new Raptor Rehabilitation Center at the University of Minnesota, under the guidance of Dr. Pat Redig and Dr. Gary Duke. Numerous smaller rehabilitation projects started elsewhere. These projects developed new techniques for treating injured and sick eagles, including advanced surgery for repairing broken bones and removing objects from eyes. Many of the patients were successfully returned to the wild once they recovered, or they were saved for public display or captive breeding.

BOOSTING EAGLE POPULATIONS

There were also several attempts to boost the populations of bald eagles in the wild by reintroducing birds into areas which had mostly or entirely lost their native bald eagle populations. The pioneering work was done in New York

under the direction of Peter Nye. Projects in other states and provinces, including Tennessee, Ontario, and Oklahoma, such as at the Sutton Research Center, followed.

These reintroductions were accomplished with eggs or chicks from captive breeding or from populations in areas such as the Great Lakes states, central Canada, and Alaska. Captive breeding was accomplished primarily at the US Patuxent Wildlife Research Center in Maryland and at a few zoos and other breeding projects.

For captive-bred bald eagles to be released back to the wild, they first have to be reared to a stage where they can feed themselves but are not quite old enough to fly. If the birds are obtained as eggs from the wild, they usually require a period of time of artificial incubation, either in mechanical incubators or under surrogate parents such as broody hens, until hatching. Then the chicks require a period of hand raising. The young birds are then released through techniques based on a centuries-old method known as hacking.

They are taken to "hacking towers" where they live and from which they can eventually fly.

Jeff Foott/Auscape International

This has led to the third major factor in the bald eagle's recovery. In an environment of more positive human relationships and greatly reduced persecution, a new generation of eagles has grown up which better accepts the presence of humans. More and more young eagles in the wild are growing up with human activity, vehicles, and buildings nearby, so that they become accustomed to people. Eagles that are artificially returned to the wild by hacking programs have been used to seeing people in the distance from an early age. As all of these young eagles mature and begin nesting, they are less likely to be bothered by humans, who become just another part of their environment.

THE FUTURE

The bottom line is that the rate of bald eagle survival has soared and, with it, eagle populations. There are still some residual problems: for example, pollution in the Great Lakes affects bald eagles in that immediate area. Another problem is the continuing human population growth and associated developments that may squeeze out the last remaining habitat for bald eagles in the Chesapeake Bay area on the east coast of the US and parts of the southeastern and southwestern states. But aside from these mostly regional problems the future for bald eagles looks fairly bright and secure.✪

NO LONGER REGARDED AS A pest, the bald eagle is increasingly valued for its grace and beauty.

Here humans supervise, and assist by providing food, but the people stay hidden behind barriers. The birds must not have too much contact with people or they will become too tame, or be "imprinted" on humans. Hacking continues to be a successful way of reintroducing captive-bred bald eagles to the wild.

A SUCCESSFUL PROGRAM

The results of all of these efforts and projects have led to success in restoring the species. Basically, three major things have happened. First, the ban on DDT reversed the reproductive decline. Second, people generally have a more informed and positive attitude to bald eagles. The number of bald eagles being shot has been greatly reduced, thanks to stricter laws and regulations, better enforcement, and rewards for information on violations. Publicity through the mass media and from conservation groups such as the Audubon Society and the National Wildlife Federation has greatly enhanced the bald eagle's image. Most of the bad feelings about eagles have gone and, instead, Americans have started loving and protecting "their" bald eagle.

Don Klumpp/The Image Bank

BADGE OF MATURITY, THE BALD eagle's white head is not achieved until four to six years of age, until which time a dull brownish immature plumage probably serves to suppress aggression from territorial adults. Referring to snowy whiteness rather than hairlessness, the name "bald" reflects an earlier and now obsolete meaning of the word.

SIBERIAN CRANES FLY THOU-
sands of miles over wetland corridors
to reach their summer habitat in
northern Siberia. Totally dependent
on the fast-disappearing wetlands
along the migration routes, this rare
and majestic bird has the longest,
most dangerous migration of all
crane species.

➤ NEWLY HATCHED SIBERIAN
crane chicks bear little resemblance to
the sleek adults they will become.

Jean Paul Ferrero/Auscape International

Journey to Save a Crane

GEORGE ARCHIBALD

With body feathers as white as new fallen snow, wings edged in black, and a face showing splashes of brilliant red, the Siberian crane has long been thought a thing of rare beauty and elegance. Scientists will tell you that the crane is among the oldest surviving species on the planet. Yet cranes today have diminished in such numbers that it is now a species threatened with extinction. Dr. George Archibald, one of the world's acknowledged authorities on cranes, is the Director of the International Crane Foundation. He has devoted his life to the study of cranes and to keeping these creatures alive and free in their natural state.

THEIR MIGRATION PATHS TAKE Siberian cranes over the freezing wastelands, arid deserts, and inhospitable mountains of seven nations. During their long migration these soaring birds with their 7 foot (2 meter) wingspread, red faces, and long pink legs are easy targets for hunters.

LIKE MOST CRANES THE ELEGANT Siberian crane is "cold-hardy." Its winter migration is caused by lack of food, not winter temperatures.

Peter Jackson/Bruce Coleman Ltd

George Archibald

Think Siberia and most likely your mind will conjure up a place where life is hard. In your mind's eye you will see barren plains and snow and distant mountains. Probably, if there are any humans in your picture, they're men dressed in rags huddled together in the cold. Usually such men are standing in the long shadows of other men who themselves are dressed in coarse overcoats and who cradle weapons in their arms.

Now, for a larger perspective, pull back from this picture. Probably you will see a scattering of little settlements, usually constructed of crude materials, each settlement isolated and distant from the others. Maybe here you will think to yourself, as others have, "Siberia—an archipelago of prison fortresses and human torment!"

Yet what to us in our imaginations is sheer torment is paradise to one of the rarest and most elegant creatures that share our planet—the Siberian crane. Since times untold the wetlands of northern Siberia have been home to these enormous white birds with red faces. It is there in the skies overhead that the lingering echoes of their cries have reverberated for millennia. And

THE MATING DANCE OF THE SIBERIAN CRANE

male female

1

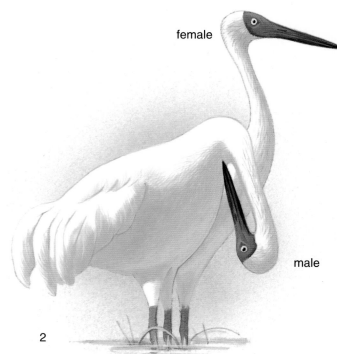

female

male

2

it is there that they have pleased each other with their dances, and found mates, and nested, and raised generations of young.

Were you to visit Siberia, and were you fortunate enough to gaze upon one of these magnificent cranes in its natural habitat you would look, in the words of Gretchen Schoff, "backward to the beginnings of geologic time and forward to the future we are building for our grandchildren." For while Siberian cranes are among the oldest surviving species on the planet, they are also among the most endangered.

HABITAT LOSS

Cranes have been hunted for their feathers probably since people began to adorn themselves with ornaments. So, certainly, hunters must share some responsibility for their dwindling numbers. Yet by far the greatest threat to their survival can be traced to the destruction of their wintering grounds in southern Asia.

In the early fall, as the days grow shorter and arctic winds begin to sweep across the wetland plains of Siberia, the cranes lift themselves in a sudden flutter and start their long, dangerous migration across Siberia, southward to the gentler wetlands of India and Iran. For centuries cranes have been traveling these same migration corridors and making their winter home in these same wetlands.

The problem is that with the staggering increases in human population that have occurred in this century, and with the ambitious development programs in countries like Iran and India, the wetlands that the cranes rely on are fast disappearing. They are being drained, then converted into farms, and later into towns and cities. As the wetlands vanish, much of the animal life that found a home there vanishes with them. So the key to the survival of the Siberian crane is to protect the wetlands along their migration corridors.

But this is easier said than done—the corridors extend some 5,000 miles (8,000 kilometers) and cross many national boundaries. Protecting the wetlands along them would involve the cooperation of several countries. Scientists and others interested in saving these cranes quickly saw that nothing less than an international conservation effort was required.

THE INTERNATIONAL CRANE FOUNDATION

Twenty years ago, when the plight of the Siberian crane was first recognized, there were major political barriers to any international effort. Communication among conservationists in the Asian nations that share Siberian cranes was almost nonexistent. And so a tiny organization headquartered in the north-central United States was founded—the International Crane Foundation (ICF).

The goal of the ICF was to bring about the required international collaboration to save the Siberian crane. But what could a tiny organization so far removed from the cranes' traditional migration corridors do?

Steven E. Landfried

HUNTERS IN THE AFGHANISTAN *and Pakistan countryside often capture cranes alive. The cranes are tamed, then trained as "watch dogs" to guard the hunters' property.*

(1 AND 2) THE MALE SIBERIAN *crane initiates the mating dance by using rapid bowing movements. (3) After bowing, he stretches his wings and utters a lengthy cry. The female responds with a call of high-pitched double notes. (4) The male then imitates the female's call in a lower pitch. During the dance, both birds shake their heads vertically.*

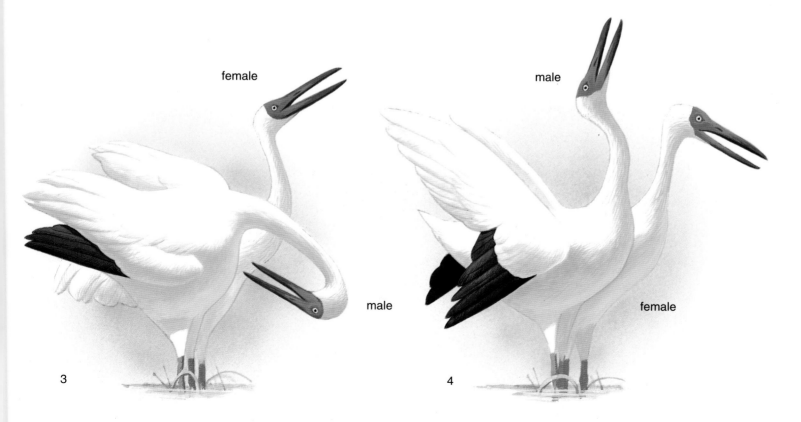

female

male

3

male

4

female

Steven E. Landfried

BILL KURTIS VISITS GEORGE
Archibald at the 160 acre (65 hectare) grounds of the International Crane Foundation. Here, new explorers are developing strategies to preserve the wetlands used by Siberian cranes and halt the species' slide to extinction.

The first step towards saving the crane was simple. The ICF had to find out how many cranes had survived and where these cranes were living. What scientists knew was that in winter and on migration the Siberian cranes are absolutely dependent on the wetlands' wide expanses of shallow water, where they probe in the mud for tubers and roots of aquatic plants. Unlike more successful crane species that forage in winter on gleanings in agricultural fields, Siberian cranes are "tied" to these wetlands.

So, with encouragement from the ICF, scientists from many countries met, banded together in small groups, and began to collect a record of the whereabouts and movements of cranes. Later they contributed their separate records to a common fund of knowledge. This fund, or data base, today contains all we know about Siberian cranes.

THREE WILD FLOCKS

Siberian cranes have three distinct populations: the Western Flock, the Central Flock, and the Eastern Flock. Of the three, the Central Flock, which winters in the Keoladeo National Park in India, is the most studied. Although strictly protected in India, the cranes of this flock are still sometimes slaughtered by the hunters who traverse the mountains of Pakistan and Afghanistan. In the mid-1960s the best estimate was that about 125 cranes belonged to the Central Flock. By the winter of 1991–92 researchers could find only six surviving cranes.

Numbers of the Western Flock, which winters in Iran, have remained steady at around ten or eleven birds for the past ten years. This is the least known and the least studied of the three flocks. Although its breeding area has yet to be discovered, we do know that one or two juveniles accompany the adults to Iran each winter. The population of this flock, however, is not increasing. So, at present, the most urgent question researchers face with respect to the Western Flock is why its population remains stagnant. Continued research is also needed to find its migration route and breeding area.

Only one breeding area is known in western Siberia. Although population figures suggest that it is used by the Central Flock, it may be that this area is used by the Western Flock as well, or instead.

The Eastern Flock, which winters in China, contains the majority of the world's Siberian cranes. During the 1970s Russian ornithologists estimated that there were between 200 and 300 in eastern Siberia on the tundra where they breed. But the location of their wintering grounds remained a mystery. Finally, after a two-year search, the Chinese located about 400 Siberian cranes wintering at Poyang Lake in southern China. Local people, however, were still hunting these cranes for their feathers, which were greatly prized in the manufacture of fans. With encouragement from the ICF the Chinese government protected the northwest corner of Poyang Lake as a nature reserve.

A RARE AND WONDROUS SIGHT,
the Eastern Flock is returning to its winter habitat in the mud flats along Poyang Lake in southern China.

Sture Traneving

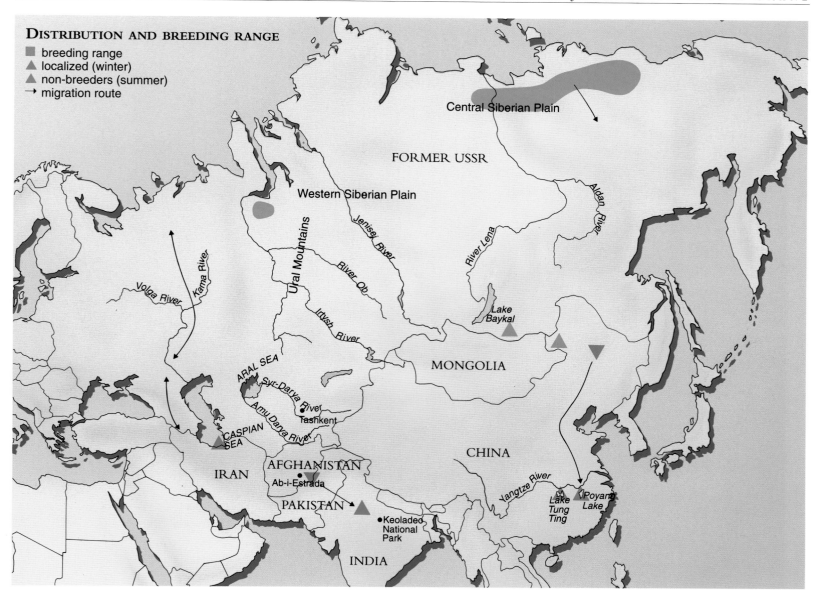

DISTRIBUTION AND BREEDING RANGE

- ■ breeding range
- ▲ localized (winter)
- ▲ non-breeders (summer)
- → migration route

Central Siberian Plain

FORMER USSR

Western Siberian Plain

Ural Mountains

Volga River
Kama River

Jenisei River

River Ob

River Lena

Aldan River

Irtush River

ARAL SEA

Syr-Darya River
Amu Darya River
Tashkent

CASPIAN SEA

Lake Baykal

MONGOLIA

IRAN

AFGHANISTAN
Ab-i-Estrada

PAKISTAN

CHINA

Yangtze River

Lake Tung Ting

Poyang Lake

Keoladeo National Park

INDIA

Because of these measures the winter count of the Eastern Flock has increased dramatically to as many as 2,626 birds.

But the ecological balance of Poyang Lake is threatened by a new dam proposed for the Yangtze River at Three Gorges. To save Siberian cranes, we must conserve their breeding habitats, wintering grounds, and a chain of critical wetlands between these destinations. Strained international relations have restricted cooperative international programs to help the cranes. Nevertheless, most of the nations that share the Siberian crane seem committed to conservation.

BREEDING IN CAPTIVITY

One of the goals of the ICF has been to establish a "species bank" of captive Siberian cranes in Baraboo, Wisconsin, at the ICF headquarters. These cranes breed in the far north in May and June when there is continual daylight. Hoping that long days might trigger breeding, ICF staff equipped the birds' pens with floodlights,

THE SURVIVAL OF THE SIBERIAN *crane population depends on the conservation of their breeding habitats and wintering grounds, and a chain of critical wetlands between these destinations.*

THE SIBERIAN CRANE IS ONE OF *the oldest surviving species on our planet, as well as one of the most endangered.*

Cranes in Myth and History

Christie's London/The Bridgeman Art Library

According to legend, it is the custom of cranes each evening to flock together in a wheel round their king. From this nightly conclave a select few cranes are chosen to watch over the others while they rest. To a crane there is no greater honor than to be among those chosen for this responsibility, for between dusk and dawn the fate of all their brothers and sisters depends upon the vigilance of these few awake cranes.

And that is why from time to time you will spy a crane standing on one foot. These are the guardians who are watching over the flock. They stand on one leg because in their other foot, which they keep raised and close to their breast, they grasp a stone. It is their intention, should they grow drowsy and relax their grip, that this stone will fall on the foot that supports them. By this means guardian cranes remind themselves of the responsibility with which they have been entrusted.

This myth of the guardian crane belongs to the tradition of story-telling that comes to us from medieval Christian Europe. It is only one of the many crane stories and legends that have appeared throughout most of human history, in all corners of the globe.

That cranes fly for thousands of miles at great heights inspired poets to call them the messengers to the gods. In Chinese story-telling the ancient sage either traveled to heaven riding on the back of a crane or entered heaven after being transformed into a crane. For the Hopi Indians in the American Southwest cranes are the guardians who carry the souls of the dead to the afterworld. In India the crane is protected as sacred.

CRANES ARE A SYMBOL OF LUCK, HAPPINESS, AND PEACE IN JAPAN *and they were a popular subject in Japanese art. This six-leaf painted screen dates from the eighteenth century.*

Russian folklore says that when a soldier dies, a crane appears. Even today Australian Aborigines mimic the moves of cranes in their ritual dances, while at the other end of the world reindeer hunters in Siberia also copy in dances these same crane movements before their winter hunts.

Because cranes mate for life and are long-lived—some have been known to enjoy a life span of eighty years or so—they symbolize monogamy, fidelity, longevity, and good luck. In the old African tale, "Arap Sang and the Cranes," cranes are celebrated for the extraordinary kindnesses they show a weary old man who turns out to be a king. In Imperial China only court officials of the highest order were permitted to wear robes embroidered with a white crane, which to these officials was a symbol of nobility. In Tibet the crane is a symbol of auspicious fortune.

But nowhere more than in Japan is the crane a symbol of luck, happiness, and peace. The Japanese decorate their palace walls with pictures of cranes, and likenesses of cranes are often found on their wedding altars and bridal kimonos. One of the most popular ways in Japan of using the crane is in origami, the art of paper folding. Japanese children have strung up chains of a thousand origami cranes as a way to make their wishes come true and as a prayer for peace.

simulating the long daylight hours of the far north. To the delight of ICF staff, the females came into breeding condition and laid. Because the females stop laying once they have eggs to incubate, the new-laid eggs were taken away, to be incubated by other means.

At first staff tried placing Siberian crane eggs in incubators under conditions proven for other species of cranes. All the embryos, however, died. Then, in 1981, the staff decided to use another species of cranes as surrogate parents to incubate fertile Siberian eggs. The embryos survived that spring and two eggs hatched. For the first time, Siberian cranes had been hatched from captive-produced eggs.

Within a decade approximately fifty Siberian cranes had been established at three centers: the ICF in Baraboo, the Vogelpark Walsrode in Germany, and the Oka State Reserve in Russia. With these "species banks" captive birds were being reproduced fast enough to provide chicks for release into the wild.

Being able to reproduce captive birds on a regular schedule was a step in the right direction. Now, ensured of a supply of Siberian crane chicks, ICF staff were ready to take on the next crucial problem—that of "imprinting."

During the eight months that juvenile cranes spend with their parents, they learn many things. For example, immediately after crane chicks hatch they look up to see enormous white birds standing above them. Soon the

chicks are responding to these adults. Everything the adults do—the food they bring their chicks, their behavior, their flights as they leave the nest—is impressed on the young cranes. ICF staff were afraid that if female juvenile cranes learned to associate with humans rather than cranes, they might misidentify themselves as humans. If this happened, the young cranes would not be equipped to survive on their own in the wild.

An example of this kind of misidentification, or erroneous "imprinting," are Ramsar and Tanya, two hand-reared female Siberian cranes living at ICF. After trying unsuccessfully to pair these confused females with male cranes,

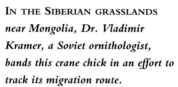

IN THE SIBERIAN GRASSLANDS *near Mongolia, Dr. Vladimir Kramer, a Soviet ornithologist, bands this crane chick in an effort to track its migration route.*

RESEARCHERS AT THE *International Crane Foundation artificially inseminate "Hirakawa," a young female crane, as part of the effort to reestablish the species.*

TWO DAYS OLD, THESE HATCH- *ery chicks have mirrors and crane feathers nearby to reduce the risk of them "imprinting" with humans.*

THIS VERY WET PEN AT THE *International Crane Foundation simulates the Siberian crane's natural wetlands habitat.*

127

Steven E. Landfried

AT THE PATUXENT WILDLIFE *Center in Maryland researchers attach a satellite tracking device by fitting a harness to the crane and stitching the harness ribbons together.*

WEARING A WHITE CRANE *costume and holding a hand puppet resembling a Siberian crane's head and neck, a researcher at the International Crane Foundation helps rear captive chicks which later will be released into the wild.*

ICF staff finally resorted to providing them with a human mate. Tanya, a dainty and extremely feminine crane, danced a lot but never laid an egg. Ramsar, a robust and aggressive female, danced with intensity, came into breeding condition and laid three eggs, all of which were fertilized by artificial insemination, using semen from a neighboring male. All three eggs hatched and two of the chicks were released in 1991 with the wild cranes in western Siberia.

SATELLITE TELEMETRY

In recent years new field techniques have been developed that may help save the Western and Central flocks. Satellite telemetry, for example, works by attaching tiny radios in small back-packs to the cranes. These radios establish a communication link-up between the cranes and a satellite. For the first time, by using such sophisticated technology, we can accurately track the migrations of Siberian cranes across Asia.

Once the migration routes for these cranes have been determined, ground studies can be made to document the biology of Siberian cranes throughout the wide range of their migration corridors. ICF staff hope that such information will provide a basis for improved management of crane populations in the wild. They also hope to incorporate what they learn into programs aimed at educating hunters.

ISOLATION-REARING

Another technique for increasing the number of cranes in wild flocks is to hatch and rear young chicks in their natural habitat in strict visual and vocal isolation from humans. This technique reduces the risk of erroneously imprinting the young cranes with human behavior, and is especially important to ICF staff because they have found that crane chicks reared in captivity show more than a little reluctance to return to their natural habitat.

Sture Traneving

George Reszeter/Oxford Scientific Films

A SYMBOL OF BEAUTY AND *grace, this elegant Siberian crane is wintering at Keoladeo National Park in India.*

George Archibald

INTERNATIONAL CRANE FOUND- *ation staffers frequently use other crane species such as this sandhill crane to incubate Siberian crane eggs. Both males and females share incubation duty.*

In 1991, efforts were made to have two Russian-reared Ramsar chicks become part of a wild Siberian crane family in western Siberia. Unfortunately, the wild family of cranes then migrated before a stong bond was formed with the captive-reared juveniles and they were left behind. They were held all winter at the Oka Nature Reserve. With two captive-reared 1992 chicks (one from Ramsar and one from a female at the Oka Reserve), the two 1991 birds were again released with the wild family of cranes. However, the two 1991 birds would not leave the release camp and were returned to Oka Reserve. One of the 1992 chicks was killed by a golden eagle. The remaining chick may now be joining the wild cranes: ICF anxiously awaits news from Russia. Efforts may be made to release the two 1991 birds with the wild cranes on their wintering grounds in India.

In August 1992 satellite radios provided by NASA and researcher Dr. David Ellis of the US Fish and Wildlife Service were placed on one Siberian crane chick of the wild cranes nesting in western Siberia, and two radios were placed on juveniles of the Eastern Flock in Yakutia. ICF staff await the historic results.

In addition, more eggs will be taken from captive flocks to the wilderness for isolation-rearing and release with the wild cranes. To avoid the problem of wild cranes migrating too early, the ICF plans to raise chicks from eggs laid earlier in the season. Satellite radios attached to the isolation-reared chicks may map the migration route. By combining the techniques of isolation-rearing and satellite telemetry, scientists may be able to help save the Central Flock.

THE FUTURE

Sustained international cooperation for decades to come is vital if the Siberian cranes are to survive the challenges that threaten their survival. Under the auspices of the Bonn Convention on Migratory Animals, an "Agreement on the Conservation of the Siberian Crane" is being drafted. It is hoped that through this agreement, the eleven nations that support the Siberian cranes will meet every two years to continue to discuss cooperative efforts to help conserve the cranes. Researchers, conservationists, and educators must combine forces for years to come, to keep this "lily of birds" in Asian skies.✪

DOLPHINS ARE FAMOUS FOR
*their spectacular aerial leaps. Known
as breaching, such playful leaping
also serves a practical purpose. It
helps dolphins communicate with one
another, herd food, and even defend
themselves from predators.*

➢ THIS INSIDE VIEW OF A
*Cretan drinking cup from the sixth
century* B.C. *shows an image of the
Greek god, Dionysus, in a boat. The
dolphins patrolling around the boat
are preserving Dionysus from harm
and guiding him to a safe harbor.*

Why Is This Dolphin Smiling?

RANDALL L. BRILL

History is filled with reports of dolphins who have guided exhausted swimmers to shore. Now new explorers are studying this remarkable animal to unravel the secrets of the most sophisticated sonar system known to humans. Dr. Randy Brill, a specialist in sensory psychology, is dedicated to learning how the dolphin uses echolocation. Dr. Brill was Supervisor of Marine Mammal Training at the Brookfield Zoo, Chicago, Illinois. He is now a staff scientist with the Naval Ocean Systems Center Laboratory in Hawaii where dolphins are being trained in search and report missions.

HISTORY IS FILLED WITH STORIES *of dolphins who have befriended children. Here a young girl plays with a bottlenose dolphin.*

Many legends exist about the dolphin. Tales of its affinity with humans were an accepted part of Greek mythology. The ancient Greeks told stories of children who played and rode in the waves with dolphins, and about a musician who when rudely cast into the sea was borne to safety on a dolphin's back.

Cretan sailors believed that the god Apollo changed himself into one of these mysterious creatures and swam ahead of their ships to guide them into safe harbors. The Greek temple at Delphi was named after dolphins. And to Delphi they went to have the future revealed to them and to ask for guidance about what they should do to avoid catastrophe.

In part, our fascination with dolphins can be explained by the fact that dolphins are mammals. Moreover, by virtue of common branches on the family tree of evolution, dolphins share a close kinship to human beings. They breathe air, have warm blood, bear live young, and nurse those young with milk. Yet they look like fish.

But perhaps what is most fascinating about the dolphin is that its home is in the ocean, underneath the waves—in an environment that is unknown and alien to humans. So it is especially ironic that this creature, that humankind has revered as a friend for over 2,500 years, now finds us its worst enemy. Tuna fisheries and drift-net fisheries, pollution, and our collectively thoughtless treatment of the environment are seriously threatening its very survival.

Aristotle, in Athens in the fourth century B.C., was the first to attempt a methodical description and classification of the dolphin. Today, the work that Aristotle began continues among scientists in universities, oceanariums, and research establishments. It is here, in these institutions, that we increase our understanding of dolphins and learn what it will take to ensure their continued survival on this planet.

The Dolphin's Place on the Evolutionary Tree

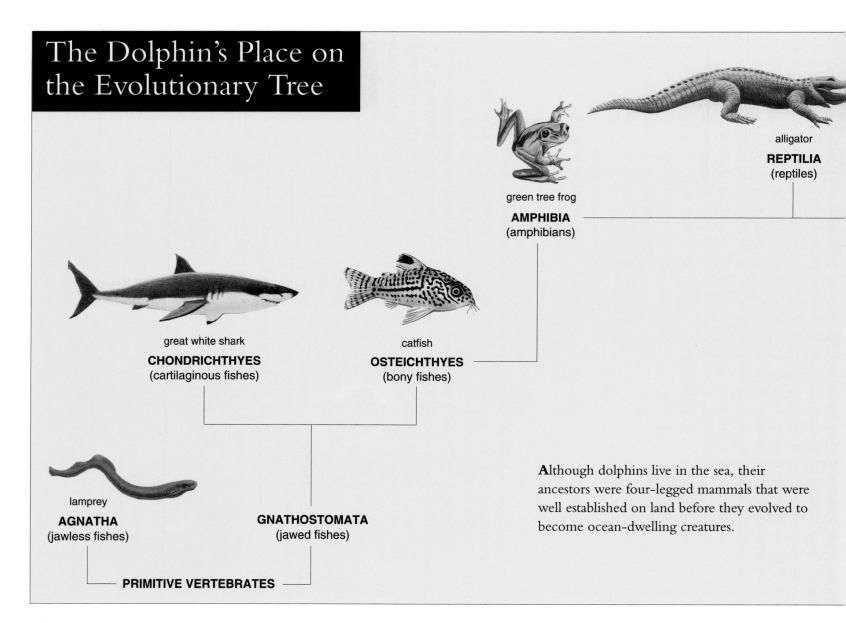

green tree frog
AMPHIBIA
(amphibians)

alligator
REPTILIA
(reptiles)

great white shark
CHONDRICHTHYES
(cartilaginous fishes)

catfish
OSTEICHTHYES
(bony fishes)

lamprey
AGNATHA
(jawless fishes)

GNATHOSTOMATA
(jawed fishes)

PRIMITIVE VERTEBRATES

Although dolphins live in the sea, their ancestors were four-legged mammals that were well established on land before they evolved to become ocean-dwelling creatures.

C. M. Dixon

TWO DOLPHINS PAINTED IN A fresco from Knossos, Crete, which dates from 1700 to 1400 B.C. Archaeologists think that this fresco probably came from a queen's apartment in the Minoan royal palace. The ancient Greeks endowed dolphins with human virtues such as generosity and selflessness.

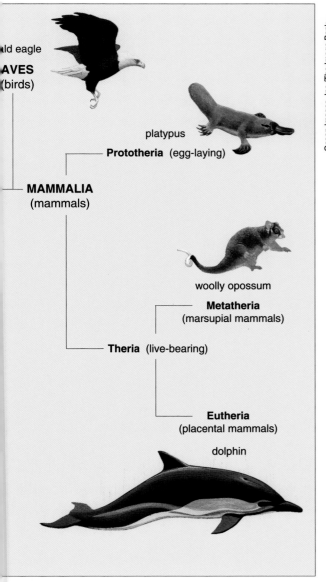

Ocean Images, Inc./The Image Bank

DOLPHINS' STREAMLINED SHAPE makes them one of nature's more formidable swimmers.

THE DOLPHIN'S EVOLUTION

A remarkable product of evolution, some species of dolphins as we know them have existed for 60 million years.

The commonly accepted model for the evolutionary process is life beginning in the sea as simple organisms, which over hundreds of millions of years evolve into higher order organisms, change shape, and ever so gradually emerge from the sea onto land. The dolphin's evolution is a reversal of this model. The dolphin's ancestors were four-legged mammals that were well established on land before they evolved back into the sea.

Fur, external ears, and hind limbs disappeared giving way to a streamlined shape. Forelimbs became flippers or pectoral fins. The tail flattened and large horizontal flukes developed to provide propulsion. The nostrils migrated to the top of the head to allow the dolphin to breathe effortlessly while moving swiftly through the water.

133

The Friendly Marine Mammal

Dolphins belong to an order of mammals called Cetacea, which is the Latin word for whale. One of two suborders of Cetacea is toothed whales, or Odontoceti. Biologists, ever intent on more accurate classification, identify the 30 to 36 species (the number varies in different classification schemes) of dolphins as belonging to this suborder. Thus to a biologist a dolphin is actually a small toothed whale.

common dolphin (Delphinus delphis)

Over millions of years dolphins have become one of nature's most formidable swimmers. Some species of these amazing creatures are able to reach speeds in excess of 25 knots per hour. For power and speed, its tail evolved and flattened, growing large horizontal fins known as flukes. It acquired a smooth, hairless, streamlined shape, eliminating frictional drag and turbulence. The complex mathematics of its surface contours make the dolphin a near perfect form for propelling through water.

Like other mammals, dolphins need air to live. They breathe through an opening at the top of their heads called a blowhole, which is a hinged flap of skin. When a dolphin dives this flap becomes a watertight valve that seals off and protects the dolphin's nostrils. Dolphins have evolved into such proficient breathers that they can empty and refill their lungs in less than a second. This allows for effortless breathing as they lunge across the ocean's surface.

But dolphins are not merely formidable swimmers, they are also excellent divers. Under ideal conditions, some dolphins have been known to dive to depths of 1,550 feet (475 meters).

HABITAT

Like many of their mammalian cousins, dolphins tend to be very adaptable. Different species of dolphin are found in a huge variety of different habitats, including all the world's oceans, tropical waters and cold polar seas, and many of its rivers and harbors. Most species, like the Atlantic bottlenose dolphin, have very definite home ranges, and tend to spend most of their time within them.

spinner dolphin (Stenella longirostris)

Little is known about the ranging patterns of the species that do travel. Their movements appear to be related to the seasonal movement of the schools of fish that make up their diet. Some scientists theorize that variations in ocean temperature also play a role in their movements.

Although these extremely social animals have been known to travel in family-sized groups, usually they travel in larger groups. Occasionally small groups will break off from the larger group, only to return a few days later. Scientists believe that dolphins in large groups are better

Henry Ausloos/NHPA

DOLPHINS ARE FOUND IN ALL OF THE WORLD'S OCEANS. THESE *bottlenose dolphins are pictured in the Red Sea.*

able to protect themselves from shark attacks. This may explain why dolphin species of the open ocean are found in very large groups of hundreds of animals.

Their safety at sea depends on their ability to communicate with one another by whistle signals. Members of the group contact each other when danger threatens. They also signal each other when foraging together for fish.

SOCIAL INTERACTION

Although they can be very aggressive at times, dolphins are mostly non-aggressive and cooperative. They nurture their young and have particularly strong mother-infant ties. Dolphins will take turns caring for a sick or injured dolphin. Scientists have watched dolphins lifting sick schoolmates to the surface so that the sick could breathe.

Commerson's dolphin (Cephalorhynchus commersonii)

pantropical spotted dolphin
(Stenella attenuata)

And dolphins have been known to try to assist stranded animals, even when such assistance places them at risk.

Dolphins do not appear to form permanent pairs. Because most species bear a single calf only once every four or five years, when a female is fertile the competition between males can be fierce. Although playful, willing alliances between a male and female occur, scientists are finding evidence from one dolphin population that male dolphins in their mating strategies often form intricate and changing social alliances in order to gain advantage over females and sometimes other males. Teams of males in this one group have been observed recruiting teams of other males in something akin to a battle plan. The goal usually is to steal fertile females from other dolphin bands.

Ganges River dolphin
(Platanista gangetica)

Dolphin young are born after a gestation period of 9 to 14 months, varying with the species. For the Atlantic bottlenose, for example, gestation takes 12 months. Births can occur year-round but can peak in particular seasons, such as spring and summer, in some species. Usually at least one other female dolphin is present during the birthing process to help the mother. A dolphin calf is born underwater. Because dolphins are mammals and must breathe air, the calf usually enters the world tail first, although there are successful head-first births in several species.

A newborn calf is roughly one-third the length of an adult. The bottlenose dolphin calves are from 35 to 51 inches (90 to 130 centimeters) at birth, and most species are about this size, although some are smaller and some are larger. A newborn dolphin's mother or one of the assisting dolphins often will accompany the calf to the surface for its first breath. The tie between calf and mother, or its mother's female associates, appears to be strong. It often continues into adulthood.

blowhole

mouth

to lungs
to stomach

BEFORE DIVING, DOLPHINS BREATHE RAPIDLY AT THE SURFACE THROUGH *the blowhole, which is a hinged flap of skin on the top of the head. When they dive, the flap becomes a watertight seal. Returning to the surface, the dolphin breathes out explosively as the blowhole plug opens by a muscular effort.*

The Photo Library, Sydney

LEAPING HIGH INTO THE AIR, A DOLPHIN PERFORMS *at a water show. Dolphins are capable of learning through observation. They also have good memories.*

ECHOLOCATION

In contrast to land-bound mammals, the most remarkable evolutionary adaptations dolphins have made are in their senses, and nowhere more so than in the dolphin's extraordinary sense of hearing.

To paraphrase Patrick W. B. Moore, merely to say that a dolphin can hear is comparable to passing off Michelangelo as a simple craftsman who could paint church ceilings. The dolphin is a mammal whose hearing system accommodates several basic factors. First is the frequent and rapid change in water pressure that dolphins experience while diving. Second is the physical phenomenon that sound travels five or six times faster in water than in air. Third is the ambient noise of the aquatic environment. Fourth, and certainly the most intriguing, is that dolphins possess a natural sonar system so sophisticated that human beings have yet to understand it fully or to duplicate it.

Indeed, dolphins are among the most talented acoustic creatures known to us. Their echolocation skills and hearing are so acute that many scientists theorize that they have contributed to their evolutionary survival. Supporting this theory is the dolphin's brain size. While it rivals a human's in weight and volume, the major portion of the dolphin's brain is composed of auditory cortex. In other words, most of this mammal's brain is dedicated to dealing with sounds. A dolphin's brain deals with sounds ten times higher in frequency than anything a human being can hear and can process these sounds at remarkable speed.

The dolphin's extraordinary acoustic ability is enhanced by a process called echolocation.

135

AT CHICAGO'S BROOKFIELD
Zoo's dolphinarium a member of Dr. Brill's team slips a soft rubber hood over Nemo's head and snout.

HIS EYES COVERED AND WEARING
the neoprene chin guard designed by Dr. Brill, Nemo inserts his head into an underwater hoop in readiness to be tested.

➢ **NEMO AND RANDY BRILL**
enjoy a brief respite from the rigors of scientific research. For the experiment to succeed, it was vital for Dr. Brill to win Nemo's trust and confidence.

Echolocation works on the same principle as a bat's sonar system. The dolphin projects sound waves and when these waves strike an object, they are echoed back to the animal. The animal then hears the echoes and extrapolates information about the object from them.

Over the last three decades we have learned a great deal about what the dolphin can do with echolocation. For example, a dolphin can detect a 3 inch (8 centimeter) metal sphere at 300 feet (90 meters) and can recognize minute differences in size that are visually impossible for any human being to detect. The dolphin's echolocation abilities are so robust and reliable that the United States Navy employs dolphins in search and recovery missions.

Even so, scientists have only begun to learn how the dolphin's echolocation system works. Most mammals listen to sounds that are transmitted through air. Compared to the way sound behaves in air, water plays havoc with sounds. The question researchers are asking is: how does a dolphin, a mammal, produce and listen to sounds in an aquatic environment?

FOREHEAD-JAW THEORY
A quarter of a century ago, Professor Ken Norris hypothesized that the series of high-frequency clicks, which are the sounds dolphins make when they echolocate an object, are produced somewhere in the dolphin's forehead behind a body of fat called the melon. According to Norris the melon functions as a kind of acoustic lens, focusing sound into a well-defined beam which echoes off any objects in its path. The returning echoes are best received at the sides of the dolphin's lower jaw. There they travel along pathways of specialized fat to the inner ear.

This theory was considered innovative and radical for two reasons. First, land-bound mammals produce sounds in the larynx of their throats. And second, the sounds we hear come to us not through pathways of specialized fat, but through an anatomical structure we call the auditory canal.

But Norris's theory was based on sound anatomical observations. The dolphin's lower jaw is hollow and filled with an oily fat that runs from the jaw to the auditory bulla, which houses the middle and inner ears. The fat in the jaw is like that of the melon and unlike fat anywhere else in the dolphin's body. Both bodies of fat possess molecular structures that

make it possible for sound to pass between tissue and water without losing much energy.

Thus, among the scientists who study dolphins a great controversy arose. On one side were those who supported Ken Norris's "forehead-jaw" theory. On the other side were those who supported the more conventional "larynx-auditory canal" theory. The controversy took the form of learned discussion that was carried on in scientific journals and professional meetings. The hope, among everyone engaged in this discussion, was that all the debate might lead to a better understanding of the dolphin's ability to echolocate objects under water.

If Dr. Randy Brill and his team could learn how dolphins receive echolocation signals, such learning might shed light on their extraordinary accomplishment of surviving 60 million years. Researchers hoped that new knowledge would add to our understanding of the process of evolution—how and why some species become extinct, while others evolve, and while still others remain largely the same.

CONFIRMING THE FOREHEAD-JAW THEORY
In the years since Ken Norris first proposed the forehead-jaw theory a great deal of evidence has accumulated in support of it. Researcher Ted Cranford has identified a sound-producing mechanism beneath the dolphin's blowhole and just behind the melon. Dr. Whitlow Au has shown dolphins indeed emit sounds as well-defined beams. And there is now a plentiful supply of anatomical, electrophysiological, and biochemical evidence to support sound conduction through fat in the lower jaw.

When Dr. Brill and his team commenced their work, the only evidence that was missing was confirmation from an actively echolocating dolphin. If the forehead-jaw theory was to be proven, the researchers had to find some method of blocking the echolocation process earlier described by Ken Norris.

Mike Greer/Chicago Zoological Society

To Dr. Brill the solution was naively simple. Train a dolphin to perform an echolocation task. Then ask the dolphin to perform the same task under conditions that would make it impossible for returning echoes to reach the lower jaw.

But how do you soundproof a dolphin's lower jaw? This was the first problem Dr. Brill and his team had to solve. From the laws of physics they knew that under water an air bubble is an effective acoustic reflector. They also knew that closed-cell neoprene, the material that diving wet suits are made of, is actually a bundle of small air bubbles. So the solution seemed obvious: fit a piece of closed-cell neoprene over a dolphin's jaw.

But how do you make a piece of neoprene rubber stick to the smooth, rubbery surface of a dolphin's skin? If the neoprene could not be kept in place, the researchers would be unable to argue that sound had been blocked from reaching the dolphin's lower jaw. After months of searching for a solution, the answer came to Dr. Brill one morning as he sleepily looked into the mirror over the vanity unit: small suction cups, the kind that are used in bathrooms everywhere to hold soap dishes and other appliances to slippery bathroom walls! Dr. Brill cut a piece of neoprene rubber to fit over the lower portion of a dolphin's jaw, and to this neoprene hood he attached the small suction cups.

The team was ready. The researchers selected a dolphin named Nemo from Chicago's Brookfield Zoo's dolphinarium. With the aid of the small suction cups and straps that went over the back of Nemo's head and his snout, the hood stayed in place.

Now another problem arose. If Nemo could see the target, the researchers could not be certain that he was depending exclusively on echolocation to detect it. Thus, Nemo would have to wear a blindfold. The researchers, however, were lucky with this problem. Soft rubber suction cups placed over the eyes are standard equipment in the world of dolphin echolocation research. So Nemo already had years of experience wearing eyecups while demonstrating his echolocation skills in the zoo's dolphin shows.

The problem was in persuading Nemo to wear the new soundproof hood at the same time as he wore the blindfold. For the experiment to be effective, Nemo would have to allow the researchers to deprive him, if only for a few brief moments, of his two major senses: vision and hearing.

Needless to say, the researchers' initial attempts to persuade Nemo to wear the hood were met with clear signs of disapproval on Nemo's part. He would calmly rest his head on the side of the pool and allow the hood to be fitted in place. Then he would slip back into the water and shake his head vigorously until he threw off the hood. Finally, displaying his still cooperative nature, Nemo calmly would retrieve

Mike Greer/Chicago Zoological Society

ALWAYS EAGER TO PLAY, NEMO *at first would shake his head vigorously until he threw off the neoprene hood, then calmly retrieve the piece of rubber on his snout, whip his head around, and throw the offending object at his trainer.*

137

Francois Gohier/Photo Researchers, Inc.

BOTTLENOSE DOLPHINS ARE *capable of bursts of speed up to 17 miles (27 kilometers) per hour. They are able to achieve such high speeds by leaping from the water in a series of curves.*

Gerard Lacz/NHPA

DOLPHINS LOVE TACTILE *contact. Often they can be seen stroking one another with the penis or with flippers, swimming belly to belly, or touching flippers.*

the hood on his snout, whip his head around and throw the offending object at his trainer. Months of careful but frustrating training were devoted to Nemo getting used to the hood and eyecups. Above all, Nemo had to be comfortable wearing this equipment while performing the assigned echolocation task.

To perform the task Nemo had to position his head in an underwater hoop. Then, using only his echolocation ability, Nemo would be asked to determine whether a steel cylinder or a sand-filled ring had been lowered into the water some distance away. The task would be conducted under three conditions: without a hood, with a hood that allowed echoes to pass through it, and finally with a hood that blocked out echoes completely.

In the end it was the trusting relationship between dolphin and trainers that made the difference. Nemo had always been taught that nothing a trainer asked him to do would ever bring him harm. Over time and through patience he learned that what the researchers were trying to do now was no exception. After almost two years of planning, designing the experiment, building equipment, and trial and error, the day finally arrived when Nemo calmly wore the hood over his lower jaw, swam comfortably underwater to position his head in a hoop, allowed his eyes to be covered, and then echolocated on targets.

After an additional eighteen months of collecting both behavioral and acoustic data, this team of new explorers had made history. They had proven that Nemo could not successfully echolocate while wearing the soundproof hood. This was the best evidence yet in support of the theory that dolphins depend on their lower jaws when listening for echoes to the sound waves they project ahead of themselves.

TWO HEARING SYSTEMS

Scientists have described complex social behavior for several species of dolphins. Sound is as important in social communication as it is in echolocation. Dolphins, in attempting to identify objects by means of echolocation, produce and listen for sounds at frequencies far in excess of anything a human can hear. In communicating with other dolphins, however, the dolphin relies on whistle-like sounds that are well within the human hearing range. Scientists also know that dolphins are fully capable of producing whistle signals at the same time as they produce echolocation signals. This suggests that they are able to listen to both types of signals at the same time.

The "jaw-hearing" research and a number of other studies point to the possibility that high-frequency sounds are received best by the fat in the lower jaw while low-frequency signals, like whistling, may be received best along the tissues of the auditory canal. Could it be that dolphins have a two-channel, frequency-dependent peripheral hearing system? This is a question that researchers need to answer.

INTELLIGENCE AND COMMUNICATION

In the early 1960s John Lily and several colleagues pursued and popularized the idea that dolphins could "talk" and that we humans might be able to converse with them by means of some common language. Computers were used to attempt to translate human speech into sounds that dolphins could easily hear and mimic. While Lily's efforts provided food for thought, his methods steadily moved away from accepted scientific practices. Today, many scientists would agree that while dolphins obviously communicate with each other, we have no reason to suspect that they use what we would recognize as "language" to do so.

More importantly, research has shown us that dolphins have cognitive abilities to learn and understand symbolic languages. Dolphins are capable of memorizing impressive vocabularies of acoustic and visual symbols and the rules of syntax that govern their use. Dolphins can even recognize changes in meaning conveyed by rearranging combinations of these symbols.

But scientists have learned that dolphins are not the only non-primates capable of performing such tasks. One African gray parrot and some sea lions have demonstrated abilities with symbolic languages that rival their dolphin counterparts. Should we be surprised? Dr. Brill believes not. Virtually every living creature, in-

cluding the amoeba, has some means of communicating with others of its kind. We should be as impressed by the chirping sparrow or the stridulating cicada because while they may not be as attractive or endearing as dolphins, they are communicating as effectively. What is important is that scientists are developing amazing tools and techniques to probe the cognitive abilities of animals around us and that they hope to unlock some of nature's most amazing secrets.

We humans possess an insatiable desire to believe in something that exceeds our limited physical and mental capabilities, something that embodies our highest hopes and dreams. Thus, we are fascinated with the possibilities of UFOs, lost cities beneath the sea, entities from other planes of existence channeling through our frail human shells, and talking dolphins. These things are intriguing, but scientists such as Dr. Brill have learned to empirically question such dreams. We must realize that every phenomenon and every creature that inhabits the earth is a mystery—not because they somehow may be better than us, but because their existence, alone, regardless of any romantic attraction, makes them precious and warrants their study. It should not be necessary to find that a creature is as physically attractive or as intelligent as us humans before we assign intrinsic value to its place in our world. ❂

THE INCREDIBLE SPEED, *maneuverability, and sonar capabilities of dolphins have made them an object of military research. From 1960 to 1989 the US Navy is known to have trained and worked with 240 dolphins, which were taught to detect enemy mines, to locate lost military equipment, and to guard military bases.*

RELATIONSHIPS BETWEEN *dolphins of different species are not always amicable. Nevertheless, there are many well-documented cases of cooperative behavior between dolphins of the same species. In some populations dolphins develop stable associations with each other that last for years.*

Echolocation in Dolphins

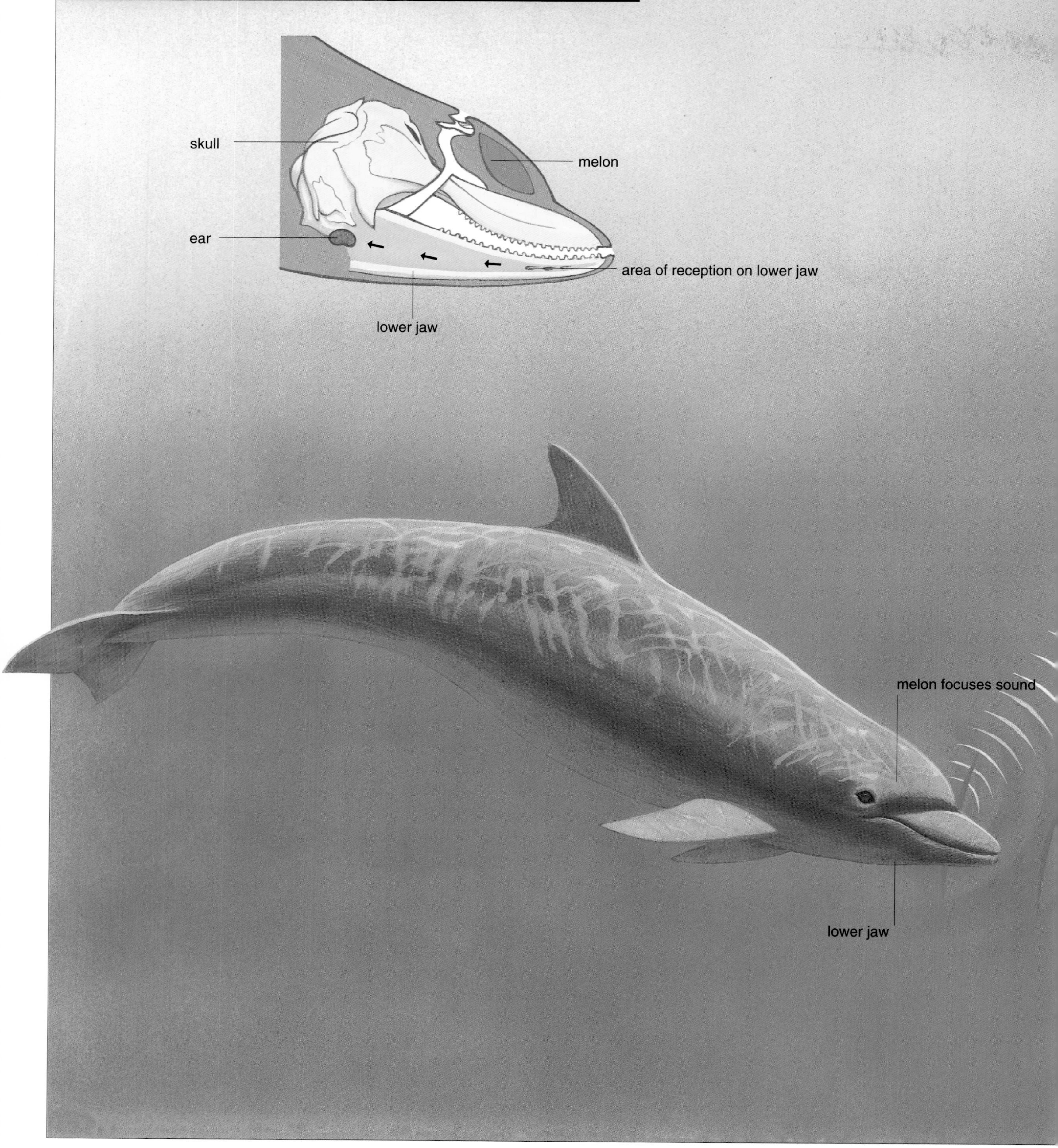

skull

melon

ear

area of reception on lower jaw

lower jaw

melon focuses sound

lower jaw

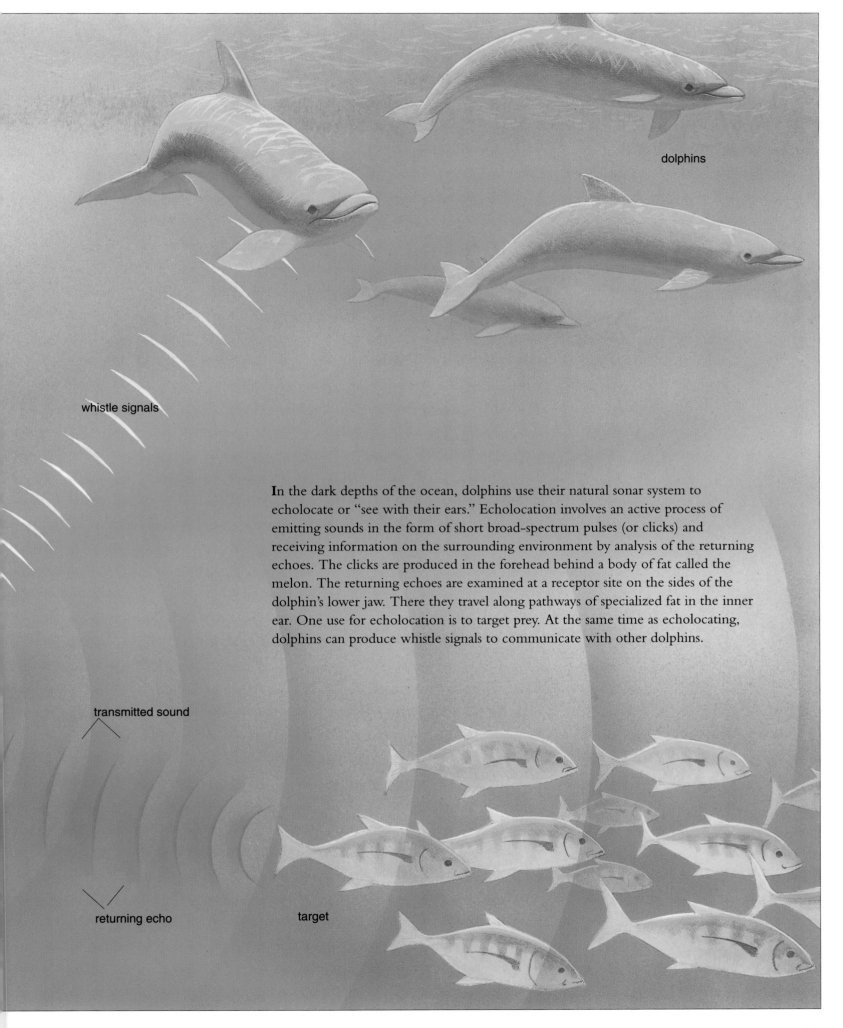

dolphins

whistle signals

In the dark depths of the ocean, dolphins use their natural sonar system to echolocate or "see with their ears." Echolocation involves an active process of emitting sounds in the form of short broad-spectrum pulses (or clicks) and receiving information on the surrounding environment by analysis of the returning echoes. The clicks are produced in the forehead behind a body of fat called the melon. The returning echoes are examined at a receptor site on the sides of the dolphin's lower jaw. There they travel along pathways of specialized fat in the inner ear. One use for echolocation is to target prey. At the same time as echolocating, dolphins can produce whistle signals to communicate with other dolphins.

transmitted sound

returning echo   target

SHROUDED IN MIST AND FOG,
with every bough and limb moss-
draped, virgin cloud forest still
survives on Cerro de Pantiacolla.
Isolated from the main ranges of the
Peruvian Andes by some 50 miles
(80 kilometers) of flat lowlands, this
mountain ridge serves as refuge for
many bird species rare or vanishing
elsewhere. Researchers exploring this
pristine wonderland found evidence
to suggest that these isolated and
unexplored forests may also act as
the point of origin for the gradual
evolution of entirely new bird species.

➢ THE BUFF-THROATED TODY-
tyrant is one of the rarest and least
known of rainforest birds elsewhere
in South America but the research
team found it unexpectedly abundant
on their study plots in the cloud
forests of Cerro de Pantiacolla.

Loren McIntyre

Islands in the Jungle

JOHN W. FITZPATRICK
AND DAVID E. WILLARD

The mountain Cerro de Pantiacolla is a beautiful isolated ridge rising about 4,000 feet (1,220 meters) above the flat lowlands, about 50 miles (80 kilometers) out from the main slopes of the Peruvian Andes. For years John Fitzpatrick and David Willard had dreamed of being the first scientists to explore its highest ridgetops. Eventually they achieved their dream, in a six-year-long series of expeditions for the Field Museum of Natural History in Chicago. These expeditions established the evolutionary importance of these isolated ridges which act as "islands in the jungle."

ONE OF THE MOST GORGEOUS *and spectacular birds of South America, the pavonine quetzal,* **Pharomachrus pavoninus.** *This fruit-eating canopy-dweller is found in highland forests from Colombia to Bolivia.*

Barbara L. Clauson

AN ANDEAN COCK-OF-THE-*rock,* **Rupicola peruviana.** *The richness and diversity of South American birdlife is unrivaled anywhere. A third of the world's approximately 9,500 bird species occur on that continent.*

Barbara L. Clauson

A MAP SHOWING THE LOCATION *of Manu National Park and the authors' study area. For sheer range and species diversity in a biologically critical region, Manu is one of the world's most important national parks.*

Throughout its hundred-year history, Chicago's Field Museum has continued the tradition of the great natural history museums of the world, which have always conducted expeditions to unknown places. Great expeditions to the Galapagos, South America, Africa, Southeast Asia, and the Pacific have brought back to Chicago nearly 20 million specimens and artifacts for study and display.

Throughout their history, museums have accumulated hundreds of millions of specimens from almost all corners of the world. Some are as huge as an elephant skull or a whale's backbone, while most are as tiny as a mite or a flea. Each has careful documentation about its origins, its natural setting, and its physical condition when collected. Properly protected and compared, these myriad museum specimens have led to some of humankind's greatest historical and scientific discoveries.

Only a tiny fraction of museum specimens ever emerges for people to admire. Most are stored and carefully protected for study in the back rooms and top floors of the museums. These huge collection areas in many ways form the real museums, protecting vast libraries of an ever-changing world so that humans might see and better understand their world hundreds of years later. For example, the bird collection of

John W. Fitzpatrick

the Field Museum contains almost 400,000 specimens, some of which date back to the original explorations of the interior of Brazil in the early 1800s.

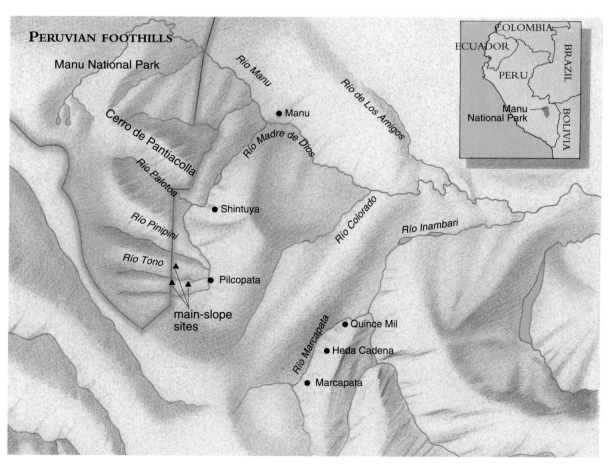

John W. Fitzpatrick

CERRO DE PANTIACOLLA, SEEN *from the Río Palotoa. Unremarkable at a casual glance, such forested foothills along the length of the Andes are often isolated from the main range, harboring a host of unique plant and animal species. Few such areas have been systematically explored by biologists.*

CALLED "VALLEY OF SMOKE" BY *its natives, the forested slopes of the Cosnipata Valley stretch away to the lofty peaks of the Andes 50 miles (80 kilometers) or so to the west.*

"Islands" and Evolution

KOEPCKE'S HERMIT, SHOWN IN THIS *painting by J. P. O'Neill, is a new species, first described in the 1970s.*

John W. Fitzpatrick

Can mountains act as islands, even though they are not surrounded by water? Early musings over this question began in the 1960s and 1970s with the discovery of many new, undescribed species of birds on outlying mountain ridges in eastern Peru.

Biologists have long known about the importance of islands in evolution. Islands frequently give rise to new species, because populations that become isolated on them may begin to change their physical and genetic structure. Sometimes this happens by accident, simply because island populations tend to drift genetically toward some new look. Other times, island habitats may be different enough from the mainland to cause selection for new characteristics that are better adapted to the island's environment.

In addition, islands may retain populations of species whose ancestors have long vanished from the mainland.

Such "relict" species persist on islands among plant and animal communities that contain fewer species than the mainland, so that there is less competition.

Island populations the world over are known for their strange and different forms of life. Indeed, assemblages of strange forms on the Galapagos Islands helped Darwin deduce how evolution proceeds via natural selection.

Loren McIntyre

CLOUD FOREST. ALMOST CONSTANT RAIN AND FOG MAKES THIS A *difficult environment for birds, and its inhabitants are often highly specialized.*

145

Andean Slopes

alpine grassland
(puna)

10,500 feet (3,200 meters)

elfin forest

8,200 feet (2,500 meters)

cloud forest

3,300 feet (1,000 meters)

upper tropical forest

lowland tropical forest

1,300 feet (400 meters)

At the base of the main slopes is lowland and upper tropical forest. Gradually this gives way to cloud forest. The higher the altitude, the more stunted the trees become, giving way to mossy elfin forest with very stunted trees. This

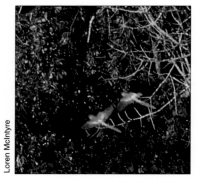

Loren McIntyre

MACAWS ARE AMONG THE *largest and gaudiest of all parrots. Here, seen from a low-flying aircraft, parrots patrol the rainforest canopy. A world apart from the shade below, and difficult to reach from the ground, rainforest canopies constitute a new frontier of zoological research in the tropics.*

THE VALLEY OF SMOKE

Where the Peruvian Andes come together with the Amazonian forests below, they break into isolated ridges, or foothills, forming some of the wettest places on earth. Indians call one such place Cosnipata (the "Valley of Smoke"). The "smoke" is actually condensing water vapor, swirling almost constantly between the steamy Amazonian lowlands and the cool upper slopes. Huge afternoon thunder clouds can drop rain on these slopes virtually every day of the year. The forests cloaking the steep ridges and rocky gorges of these mountain foothills are some of the richest and least disturbed montane forests to be found anywhere in the Americas. They are home to 1,000 species of birds—more than 10 percent of the species known in the entire world! The diversity of mammals, insects,

flowering plants, and almost every other form of tropical life is equally staggering.

John Fitzpatrick and David Willard's interest in the region, and particularly the Cerro de Pantiacolla, began in the 1970s with their many trips into the great Manu National Park, probably the most biologically diverse park in the world. Their interest stemmed partly from the very richness of the area, and partly from its unique archipelago of foothills. This complex of ridges extends into the Amazonian lowlands, in some areas for nearly 60 miles (100 kilometers).

They began to suspect the evolutionary importance of the foothills after their own expeditions in 1975 and 1976 had turned up no fewer than four undescribed bird species on one isolated mountain in extreme northern Peru. They wondered whether these ridges were

then gives way to alpine grassland (puna) at the very top. On the isolated ridges (such as the pesk below) the strata are similar but they usually occur at lower elevations and are compressed. The top zone is frequently missing.

elfin forest

cloud forest

acting as ecological "islands," allowing certain species to survive and evolve in isolation, while their ancestors became extinct on the main mountain slopes. If this were the case, then countless ridges of the eastern Andean foothills might be places where new species evolved through time. This would not only help to explain the unparalleled species diversity in the western Amazon and Andes, but it also would suggest an important conservation message: the Andean foothills need to be protected from over exploitation, because they are both preserving life forms from the past, and generating many of the new species for the future.

IN THE PERUVIAN CLOUD FOREST

The especially wet vegetation that grows on the summits of the cloud-drenched slopes is known

as "cloud forest." Cloud forests are fairylands of stunted, gnarled trees covered with ferns, orchids, bromeliads, and lichens as well as huge skirts of moss and liverworts. Animals and plants of the cloud forest are adapted to life in the windblown mist. Species found in these forests rarely if ever descend to the steamy lowland forests only a few hundred yards below.

Because the cloudy ridgetops are separate from the cloud forest on the main slopes, the ridges support distinct, isolated patches of upper montane habitat. These remote ridgetops are ecological "islands" supporting life forms cut off from the rest of their kind just as if the intervening lowlands were nothing but ocean.

Fitzpatrick and Willard's suspicions about the importance of isolated mountains were just ideas, theories that could be tested against reality only with a huge amount of back-breaking work. A six-year-long series of expeditions to the region to gather specimens and data for testing these theories followed.

Their brief but unforgettable first ascent up the Pantiacolla in 1980 established that the small land area of this ridgetop cloud forest supported a much reduced bird community compared to the equivalent forests of the main Andean slopes. This is characteristic of islands which typically have fewer species than nearby mainlands.

More surprising still, many of the birds that inhabited the ridgetops were extremely rare. Fitzpatrick and Willard identified two particularly abundant birds (the graytailed piha, *Lipaugus subalaris*, and the buff-throated tody-tyrant, *Hemitriccus rufigularis*) as two of the rarest birds in all the Andes. Here, they were abundant! Moreover, of two very numerous hummingbirds in the forest understory, one, Koepcke's hermit, *Phaethornis koepckeae*, had been described only a few years before, when it was found on a

THE GRAY-TAILED PIHA, ONE OF *the most common small birds in the cloud forests of Cerro de Pantiacolla.*

ABOUT 30 SPECIES OF MONKEYS *range the forests of Central and South America. Most widespread are howler monkeys, successful mainly because of their ability to subsist on leaves in addition to the more nutritious standard monkey diet of fruit and insects. This is a youngster.*

HIGHLAND RAINFOREST. UNLIKE *temperate woodlands elsewhere in the world which are normally made up of very large numbers of very few tree species, tropical forests like this are made up of small numbers of very many species.*

distantly isolated mountain ridge several hundred miles north; the other, the rufous-webbed brilliant, *Heliodoxa branickii*, was so poorly known that no female specimen had ever been collected! This forest was full of scarcely known birds. On later trips, two species entirely new to science were found, plus a host of others previously known from only a few early collectors.

THEORY CONFIRMED

The beginning of Fitzpatrick and Willard's final expedition in 1985, the culmination of five years' research, was an adventure in itself. First the dugout canoe carrying the supplies had to be dragged up the rocky rapids of the Río Palotoa, then a machete trail was hacked out of one of the mountain's few easily climbed ridges.

The 1985 expedition had two major goals. The first was to complete a thorough inventory of the bird life of the upper slopes and summit of Cerro de Pantiacolla. The second, even more crucial, goal was to finish making an inventory of the bird life at various elevations on the main Andean slopes, a task begun in 1981 after the two scientists first suspected the island-like role of the Pantiacolla. This tedious process was necessary in order to prove conclusively that the

John W. Fitzpatrick

birds suspected to be "ridge-specialists" did not in fact occur on the main Andean slopes.

These new explorers spent nearly three months in the unspoiled splendor of the Pantiacolla ridgetops, one of the most pristine and little-explored corners of the Peruvian rainforest, achieving the first goal. But their final main-slope campsite was a heartbreaking place. The Río Tono tumbled its last mile or so down the mountain through forest that only a few years before had been as virgin as the Pantiacolla's. Now, however, muddy roads and chainsaws had penetrated deep into the interior. Loggers and settlers were now threatening the unprotected border of the Manu National Park. Although every effort was made to get as far

LADEN WITH SUPPLIES AND *equipment, the expedition's boat is pushed upstream.*

◄ **TROPICAL FORESTS SHELTER** *a biological diversity found nowhere else. A plot like this may be home to hundreds of plant and bird species, and thousands of species of insects and other small life.*

BIRDS ARE MOST EFFICIENTLY *captured for study in mist nets. Woven of fine dark nylon, these nets are about 33 to 100 feet (10 to 30 meters) long. Unable to see the fine mesh, flying birds strike the net and lie entangled until the researcher arrives. Sometimes the specimen is collected, but more often the bird is thoroughly examined, weighed, and measured, marked with a uniquely numbered tag, and released unharmed. Disentangling the bird without injury is a delicate task.*

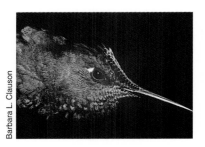

A VIOLET-FRONTED BRILLIANT, *glittering jewel of the cloud forest. Hummingbirds are the smallest of all birds.*

away from them as possible, it was hard to find the necessary expanses of untouched forest in which to set up the mist nets. Mist nets are made of dark nylon mesh and are so fine that they cannot be seen against the background by birds flying through the forest understory. They are used to catch the birds, which remain alive and unharmed until their release after the investigator identifies and marks them. Despite the efforts made to avoid them, the final six weeks were spent with a distant hum of chainsaws, and sickening crashes and thumps of huge trees being felled. With the disappearance of these ancient forests, hundreds of species of birds would be another step closer to extinction.

After six weeks the inventory work was almost completed. Netting and collecting at

elevations between 2,300 and 3,300 feet (700 to 1,000 meters) on the main slope yielded no trace of any of the specialty birds so common at the same elevations on the Pantiacolla. Also, as predicted from observations made on the first expedition, the number of bird species here far exceeded those on the outlying ridge.

On the last day of fieldwork Fitzpatrick and Willard made a discovery that confirmed one of their most important predictions. At Cerro de Pantiacolla the two closely related hummingbird species, the violet-fronted brilliant, *Heliodoxa leadbeateri*, and the rufous-webbed brilliant, *Heliodoxa branickii*, do not have overlapping ranges on the mountain. This kind of "ecological segregation" is typical of closely related species on tropical mountain slopes. If

New Age Expeditions

CAREFULLY LABELED AND PREPARED FOR *later study back at the museum, a tray of bird specimens is laid out to dry.*

Modern expeditions have much in common with the expeditions of earlier days: rugged, exhausting work in remote and beautiful places; long hours worked day after day with little time for relaxation; and the careful preparation, documentation, and transport of specimens. Following these techniques, Darwin collected and used specimens to deduce the process of evolution by natural selection. Modern scientists are still interpreting and expanding that theory, and carefully documented specimens are still a most important means of studying evolution.

Today's scientists also recognize and respect the need to be careful conservationists as well as collectors, even though collections of specimens from remote, little-studied regions are still essential to further the understanding of each species across its range. Such collections allow scientists to piece together the origins of species, and the interactions among hundreds of species. Today, scientists never collect truly rare or endangered species, and take only a few specimens of each species. Their most important principle in collecting is never to leave any lasting effect on the population level of any species at any locality.

On today's expeditions each animal sacrificed receives "individual attention" unmatched in the history of expeditions. For example, for birds, besides the traditional preservation of feathers, skin, and a few bones, scientists

preserve whole skeletons and often the whole bird—inside and out—in formalin and ethyl alcohol. Each specimen's mites and lice are preserved, and the stomach and gut of most specimens are analyzed for information about their feeding habits. Writing the complete specimen label can take as long as preparing the specimen! In this way, every individual is made as valuable as possible for future generations of scientists, and so ultimately for the species itself.

In recent times representative portions of internal tissues have been preserved by freezing them in the field in a tank of liquid nitrogen. These tissue samples allow detailed comparative analyses of DNA structure. These samples provide a whole new way to study the ancient origins and evolutionary histories of living things.

THE EXPEDITION MEMBERS SPENT SEVERAL WEEKS IN THE CLOUD FOREST, *using camps like this as their base, gathering both information and specimens.*

COMMON FROM LOWLANDS TO *altitudes of about 1,600 feet (500 meters), the russet-backed oropendola is a colonial rainforest bird that builds long, pendent nests.*

QUITE APART FROM THEIR *enormous species diversity, the tropical rainforests of the world act as global air-conditioners, adjusting atmospheric levels of oxygen, carbon dioxide, and water vapor.*

one species is present at a particular level its close relative is absent. On the Pantiacolla the violet-fronted brilliant was restricted to above 4,270 feet (1,300 meters) while the rufous-webbed brilliant was very common below that level. Fitzpatrick and Willard already knew that the rufous-webbed brilliant was not known on the main slopes, so they predicted that the violet-fronted brilliant would extend its range down-slope in the absence of its counterpart. Minutes before they struck the mist nets and began the long trip home, they found a male violet-fronted brilliant captured in the mist nets at 2,460 feet (750 meters). So, on the main slope on the last day, they had found an explicit confirmation of their hypothesis: in the absence of the rufous-webbed brilliant its competitor occurred further down the slope almost to the mountain's base.

COMING TO CONCLUSIONS

The last day of the trip had proved as exciting and rewarding as the first. What Fitzpatrick and Willard had proven, after five separate expeditions spanning six years, was that the mountain ridges of eastern Peru form a mosaic of distinct bird communities, each ridge some-what different from every other one. As true ecological islands, the outermost of these ridges have an extremely important evolutionary role: they give refuge to species that become extinct on the intensely competitive, main mountain slopes. These relict populations can continue evolving and become distinct species.

These new explorers had discovered why the tropical and montane forests of western South America have the richest bird diversity in the world. Possibly for millions of years, the tropical isolated mountains of the eastern Andes have been "islands in the jungle," continually serving as species refuges and species generators. Today, their history may be almost over. The great forests of the Andean foothills are being cut down and converted to plantations of hill rice, coffee, cocoa, and tea.

As each precious mountain ridge is logged, a unique chapter in the evolutionary history of South America is wiped out forever. As Fitzpatrick and Willard's expeditions suggest, also disappearing with the forests are the newly evolving species of tomorrow.

The long-term solution lies in setting aside some of these vast mountain areas, including their flanking ridges, to preserve both the species remaining from the past and those yet to come in the future. In this respect, Peru has become a leader in South America, committed to protecting a major fraction of its forested land. Today, people live in harmony alongside the splendid Manu National Park.

Hopefully, the work of Fitzpatrick and Willard in the Valley of Smoke and their specimens preserved in Chicago's Field Museum and Lima's Museo de Historia Naturale "Javier Prado" will continue to inspire the protection of these and the other timeless treasures of tropical South America.✪

THESE CHILDREN AT THE *entrance to their forest shack live close to the beauty of the Manu National Park.*

151

LORD OF THE MOUNTAINS, AND
*much the strongest animal in North
America, the grizzly bear once
ranged across the western part of the
continent, including the prairies. But
bears and humans make poor neighbors, and with the opening up of
western rangelands during the nineteenth century, grizzly numbers
collapsed from an estimated 100,000
to its current precarious level of about
1,000 individuals in the whole of
the lower 48 states.*

➤ IN SUMMER MANY GRIZZLY
*bears eats thousands of army cut-
worm moths a day. The protein and
fat from these moths help grizzlies
build up reserves for winter sleep.*

The Legendary Grizzly

MARILYNN GIBBS-FRENCH
AND STEVEN P. FRENCH

Respected, feared, and held sacred, the grizzly bear has been the subject of legends since it was first seen by humans. However now people are looking beyond the myths and discovering new things about the grizzly. Since 1983 Dr. Steven French and Marilynn Gibbs-French have been following the bear's tracks, hiking deep into the Yellowstone ecosystem. Their discoveries may help save Yellowstone's endangered population of about 300 grizzlies. As other researchers and scientists begin to study the bear's unique metabolism for cures for human diseases, the Frenches work through their Yellowstone Grizzly Foundation to save this endangered creature.

FOR OVER HALF A CENTURY, THE opportunity to feed wild grizzly bears attracted many tourists to Yellowstone National Park, as shown in these photographs taken in 1925 (upper) and 1963 (lower).

For thousands of years the grizzly bear roamed freely over most of western North America, living comfortably off the abundant wildlife and plants. It lived in harmony with native Americans who respected the bear's power and who cherished its similarity to humans. Native Americans learned from the bear by watching it forage for edible plants, and the bear became an important symbol in their spiritual ceremonies and legends.

When European settlers moved further west, humans' peaceful relationship with the grizzly began to change. By the turn of the nineteenth century the pioneers' rapid expansion in search of new beginnings brought with them a combination of forces that heavily reduced the grizzly population. As the pioneer population expanded, the grizzly's habitat was overtaken by farms and grazing livestock. The grizzly itself came to be regarded as a ferocious brute that needed to be exterminated. Its size and stamina led to frontier legends of its strength and near invulnerability. Its description by frontiersmen became the basis for the scientific name it was given in 1815: *Ursus horribilis.*

When modern weapons, such as the repeating rifle, were introduced, it was the beginning of the end for the vast majority of grizzly bears. For many hunters, the killing of one of these mighty bears was a matter of prestige, though it was also killed to sell its hide and meat. Sometimes a grizzly was captured alive for public spectacles such as bear and bull fights.

For two hundred years the western wilderness had drawn more and more settlers.

The beleaguered grizzly was forced to take refuge in remote wilderness hills and mountains. But even these isolated grizzlies were not safe from human encroachment. By the end of the nineteenth century, the population of approximately 100,000 grizzlies in the lower 48 states was reduced to less than 1,000. And less than 1 percent of its original habitat remained.

THE YELLOWSTONE REFUGE

In 1872, when Congress acted to create Yellowstone, the nation's first national park, the grizzlies finally had a refuge that was protected against human settlement and habitat destruction. As the park began to draw tourists, the food they left behind began to attract both black and grizzly bears. Tourists and park administrators left discarded food in open-pit dumps in and around the park. For the grizzly, the strong urge to feed on the high-energy garbage overcame its normally shy and reclusive nature. Grizzlies began congregating in large numbers at the abundant garbage dumps and as they became bolder, feeding during daylight, they also became a tourist attraction.

At first the park service saw no harm in these food habits. The bears were helping them with their garbage problem, and the growing tourist population could view the bears in predictable areas. But the food available from the garbage dumps reduced the need for the grizzly's traditional foraging habits and had a significant influence on its natural behavior.

To gauge the grizzly's needs and to better manage it within the ever more popular park,

"NATIVE CALIFORNIANS Lassooing a Bear". During the nineteenth century, frontiersmen almost universally regarded grizzly bears as ferocious brutes to be exterminated by any means available. Recently it has been appreciated that these formidable animals have an important role to play in healthy wilderness ecosystems.

◄ *A MAJESTIC GRIZZLY AT HOME, a sight to send a shiver up any backpacker's spine. The grizzly differs from the more amiable black bear that shares its environment by its multicolored fur, smaller ears, characteristically dished face, and the marked hump over its forequarters.*

155

Yellowstone National Park

A GRIZZLY RAIDS A GARBAGE *dump. Closure of Yellowstone's garbage dumps was controversial because some researchers felt that the grizzly would not survive without this source of easily available food.*

Erwin and Peggy Bauer/Bruce Coleman Limited

GRIZZLIES ARE INQUISITIVE AND *extraordinarily persistent foragers, and will thoroughly investigate campsites for overlooked food scraps and anything else that might be edible, including such items as soap and toothpaste.*

GIBBS-FRENCH AND FRENCH USE *a naturalist's approach to studying their grizzlies, relying on spotting scopes and telephoto lenses to observe the bears undetected from a distance. They operate throughout the summer from this high-country base camp.*

information was needed on the grizzly's feeding habits, its social organization, and its ecosystem.

A major study of Yellowstone's grizzly bears was begun in 1959 by Dr. John Craighead and Dr. Frank Craighead. Until then the grizzly had been the subject of legends and there was very little scientific fact. Its shyness, its nocturnal habits, and the sheer danger of getting too close had limited the gathering of reliable information. The Craighead study lasted until 1971. For 12 years the Craighead team gathered information primarily about the bears that gathered at the garbage dumps, developing and refining techniques for trapping, anesthesia, marking, and radiotracking.

During the 1960s, while the study was still underway, the park policy changed. The new policy was intended to return the park to a more primitive state. And for the grizzly that meant no more human garbage. Other new policies also affected the grizzly, although this was not immediately obvious. Strict fishing regulations were introduced, the annual elk herds were no longer reduced, and a natural fire policy was developed. But none of these had the same immediate impact on the grizzlies as the closures of the open-pit garbage dumps. And the new policy was controversial, because many feared that the grizzly would not be able to survive. After nearly a hundred years of dependence on human garbage, the Yellowstone grizzly suddenly had to survive on its own.

Unfortunately many grizzly bears couldn't adjust to foraging for food as their ancestors had: During the two years after the dumps were closed, grizzlies were killed in record numbers as they trespassed into human developments in search of the food they had grown accustomed to. Many bears wandered into the surrounding national forests, in search of food, and were killed during the legal sport hunting seasons.

Because of this increased level of human-caused mortality, concern was mounting about the status and future of the Yellowstone grizzly population. As a result, the Interagency Grizzly Bear Study Team (IGBST) was created in 1973 to monitor the population trends and to collect and analyze a variety of demographic data on the Yellowstone grizzly population following the closures of the garbage dumps.

By 1975 the grizzly bear population in the Yellowstone region was threatened with extinction. In that same year they were listed as a threatened species under the Endangered Species Act. It was estimated that less than 200 bears were left in Yellowstone National Park and the surrounding area.

To protect this small population, changes were begun. Among the first was the ending of the sport hunting of grizzly bears in the three states surrounding Yellowstone. Another change, which was perhaps the most important, was the government's interagency cooperation, allowing the bear's recovery in its natural ecosystem.

Marilynn Gibbs-French/The Yellowstone Grizzly Foundation

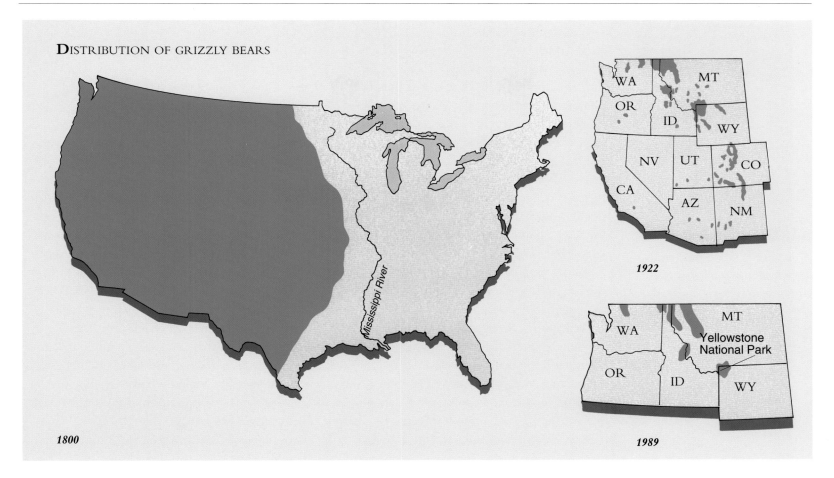

DISTRIBUTION OF GRIZZLY BEARS

Mississippi River

1800

1922

Yellowstone National Park

1989

DOCUMENTING BEAR BEHAVIOR

By the early 1980s what was left of the Yellowstone grizzly population had become the subject of scientific debate and further study. In fact, of all the animal populations in North America, none had been more studied for their demographics than Yellowstone's grizzlies. (Both the Craighead study of 1959 to 1971 and the IGBST study from 1973 to the present are extremely detailed.) Yet very little research had ever been conducted on grizzly behavior within its ecosystem, that is, in the wild.

Could the grizzly relearn its ancestral foraging behavior and could it do so before the population died out? Could the shrinking wilderness provide for its needs? Could the small, threatened population ever be vital again?

To find some answers to these questions, Steve French and Marilynn Gibbs-French began an independent study in 1983. They studied the grizzly using the traditional naturalist's approach: intensive observation in the field. They wanted to document the bear's behavior in its environment without disturbing the animals or allowing the animals to become aware of their presence. Because of this approach, along with safety concerns, the Frenches never attempted to develop a relationship with any of their subjects. Instead, after hiking behind the bears, following

the tracks, they use spotting scopes and telephoto lenses to observe the bears from distant vantage points, generally from 1,300 to 2,000 feet (400 to 600 meters) away.

Observing a wild animal in the field presented plenty of logistic difficulties. Since the bears no longer congregated at the open-pit garbage dumps, they were difficult to find. A single bear's home range could extend from 300 to 700 square miles (about 775 to 1,800 square kilometers). And as grizzlies searched for natural foods in the ecosystem, they moved into remote and rugged areas. But when the Frenches did locate and observe them (and they made thousands of such observations), they were able to collect a library of information. Their detailed field notes and film records have filled the gap in knowledge of the grizzly's natural behavior.

During their long-term study they have succeeded in filming behavior few people have ever seen. They have watched bears during mating season bonding for a month at a time. They have observed the patience a mother shows for an injured cub. They begin their fieldwork in the spring when the grizzlies emerge from their dens to look for the first foods of the season. And they continue their watch throughout the summer and fall as the grizzlies bulk up on the calories they need for the winter hibernation.

BEFORE EUROPEAN SETTLEMENT *the grizzly roamed unhindered west of the Mississippi River. Over a century later, the expansion of settlers westward had severely reduced the grizzly population. Today the American grizzly is only found in a handful of northwestern states near the Canadian border.*

Stan Osolinski/Oxford Scientific Films

A GRIZZLY TRAVERSES A *meadow. Grizzlies are more likely to be abroad by day, while black bears forage mainly after dark.*

A GRIZZLY CLAWS A TREE APART.
Though grizzlies feed largely on berries, tubers, fish and carrion, they also tear logs and tree trunks to get at grubs and wild honey.

FORAGING IN THE WILD

Another very important finding of the Frenches' study was that bears were exploring and developing the hunting skills they had all but abandoned when garbage was available. Increasing numbers of grizzlies were stalking and killing the now abundant elk calves. Some individual bears became deliberate predators of the calves, chasing down and killing one or more each day. Overall, the new and important finding was that the elk calves had become a valuable natural food for a significant portion of the Yellowstone grizzly population.

Other bears concentrated on fishing. The now healthy populations of cutthroat trout lay their eggs in the tributaries of Yellowstone Lake and Yellowstone River. When the trout are spawning in these shallow, narrow streams they are easy and abundant prey for the grizzly bears. For individual bears the trout came to be a very important food. One bear fished 11 spawning streams over a 10 day period. It seemed to reach a fishing frenzy as it caught and ate 24 fish in

28 minutes on one stream. During that 10 day period it caught at least 100 fish each day. Other grizzlies also fished on these streams. The cutthroat trout also appears to have become a valuable food source for many grizzlies.

The Yellowstone grizzlies were also discovering "new" natural foods. Since 1988 the Frenches have been studying the importance of the alpine habitat to grizzly bears. They have found that at least 100 different grizzly bears spend most of the summer on alpine talus slopes feeding extensively on moths. Although historical data is limited, these alpine aggregations of army cutworm moths once may have been part of the grizzly's diet. But sport hunting had been prevalent in the same area, which may have suppressed this feeding behavior by generally reducing the grizzly population, and in particular selectively removing moth-feeding bears who were vulnerable while they were feeding on the exposed talus slopes. Until hunting was banned and garbage was less available, the grizzlies may have suppressed their appetite for moths.

GRIZZLIES CAN BE FORMIDABLE
predators, bringing down with ease animals as large as deer and elk. This sow and her first year cubs are feeding on an elk carcass.

THIS SNARLING CLOSEUP
shows the grizzly's small eyes and ears, compared with the snout, reflecting its dependence on smell rather than sight and sound to investigate the surroundings.

➤ THE DIET OF A GRIZZLY
varies according to the season and availability of prey. Grizzlies are skillful hunters and foragers, using several methods to obtain their food.

Diet of a Grizzly Bear

SPRING

elk calf

spring beauty

carrion

LATE SPRING

cutthroat trout

Mary Evans Picture Library

**LATE SPRING
EARLY SUMMER**

Evert's thistle

SUMMER

army cutworm moth

FALL

red squirrel and whitebark pine tree nuts

bull elk

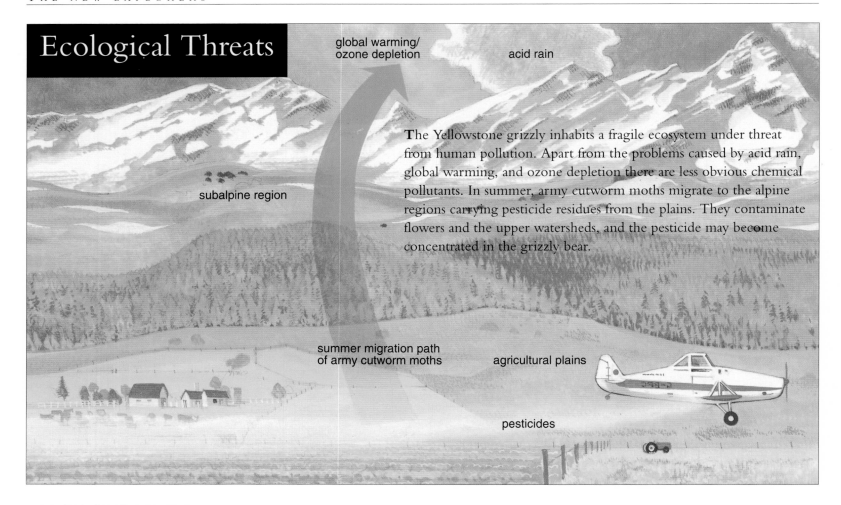

Ecological Threats

global warming/
ozone depletion

acid rain

subalpine region

The Yellowstone grizzly inhabits a fragile ecosystem under threat from human pollution. Apart from the problems caused by acid rain, global warming, and ozone depletion there are less obvious chemical pollutants. In summer, army cutworm moths migrate to the alpine regions carrying pesticide residues from the plains. They contaminate flowers and the upper watersheds, and the pesticide may become concentrated in the grizzly bear.

summer migration path
of army cutworm moths

agricultural plains

pesticides

A GRIZZLY SOW AND HER CUBS *dig for roots. The cubs learn their mother's foraging techniques when still very young.*

The moths play a large role in the grizzly diet. They provide a significant amount of nutrition, primarily fat, to a large portion of the grizzly population each summer and early fall, when bears are storing layers of fat needed for hibernation. Many bears feed on moths for as many as six hours each day, with some bears eating hundreds of thousands of moths a year.

Based upon the field work of Steve French and Marilynn Gibbs-French, we now know that the Yellowstone grizzly bear population has overcome its dependence on human garbage and has successfully relearned its natural foraging skills. The ongoing demographic research by the IGBST and their own work have shown the Frenches that the grizzly is healthier today than it has been in the past hundred years, and more as it was before the European explorers arrived.

AN INSECURE FUTURE

Unfortunately, the future of the Yellowstone grizzly population continues to be in doubt despite their successful adaptation to natural forage and despite the cooperation of agencies towards their ecosystem management. The grizzly population in the Yellowstone ecosystem is relatively small (estimated to be 200 to 300), and is vulnerable to high levels of human-caused

mortality because of its low reproductive rate—one of the lowest of all land mammals. A female breeds, on average, only once every three years, and 50 percent of bear cubs die.

The loss of genetic diversity is also a major concern. Yellowstone's bear population is not only small, it is also geographically isolated. The future gene pool will be limited to those individuals currently present.

The grizzly's new feeding behavior also has an alarming component. The army cutworm moth that supplies so much nutrition is hatched in agricultural communities, and during its larval stage it is sprayed with chemical pesticides. When the adult moths reach the alpine areas they shelter in loose rock fragments and feed on the nectar of the alpine flowers. The pesticide residues may contaminate not only the alpine flower communities and watersheds, but may also concentrate within the bears.

The grizzly's current habitat in Yellowstone holds yet another concern. Within what is known as the Grizzly Recovery Zone there are more than 24 jurisdictional zones. Each has its own management agenda and each is under pressure to turn the land over to development.

Observations in the field indicate that the grizzlies are still finding new and important natural foods. Knowledge of the habitats and the foods they need is incomplete. Before this fragile land and isolated population is further tampered with, much more needs to be learned.

Habitat insecurity is not limited to lands managed by government agencies. The private lands within and adjacent to their ecosystem are used by grizzlies either as travel corridors or as a source of natural foods. These lands represent only about 1 percent of the ecosystem, but as many as two-thirds of all conflicts in the ecosystem between grizzly bears and humans occur on private lands. Private lands are not yet oriented towards grizzly conservation, yet it is vital to the bears' future to find security within them. Conserving the grizzly population in the Yellowstone ecosystem may require sacrifices. Some useful measures might include compensation for the ranchers if bears attack their livestock, direct purchase of private land, easements for conservation, and cooperation from private citizens.

SAVING A SPECIES

There are many reasons for humans to conserve a wild species. One of the most important is knowledge. With the demise of a species, the opportunity to learn its hidden secrets is lost. Understanding the grizzly bear's unique metabolic pathways during the mysterious process of hibernation may have applications for a wide variety of human ailments.

The species' place in the ecosystem is another point of conservation. As our global environment becomes more threatened, the grizzly remains at the head of a complex ecological web that holds together the flora and fauna of a delicate ecosystem. By preserving this magnificent animal, we will preserve other plants and animals that otherwise would attract little or no attention or protection. And in doing so, our efforts will set an example for other conservationists to follow.

Last, but not least, we must not forget the species' symbolic power. The grizzly bear is a symbol of the wilderness of the Yellowstone ecosystem. It is also a symbol of the energy and power of the once vast American western wilderness. Two hundred years ago the grizzly symbolized the danger of the frontier. Now it may be a symbol of our willingness to enter another frontier and conserve the few wild places that remain on our planet.✪

Paul McCormick/The Image Bank

A GRIZZLY CUB. *Grizzly populations grow only slowly: females do not become sexually active until their fifth or sixth year, then mate only every second or third year. On average, half of all cubs die before reaching independence.*

CHARACTERIZED BY THEIR *shaggy fur and flat-footed gait, bears are the largest and most powerful of all land carnivores, grizzly males often weighing well over 400 pounds (180 kilograms).*

Hibernation

THE HIBERNATING GRIZZLY

The winter slumber of the grizzly bear is still one of nature's mysteries. For up to six months of each year Yellowstone's grizzlies avoid the food shortages and severe weather conditions that exist outside their comfy dens. During this extended period, the bears do not eat, drink, urinate, or defecate. Yet without nutrition and without disposal of their wastes, they manage to emerge from their dens with essentially no loss in lean body mass.

THE GRIZZLY'S WINTER HOME

The hibernation den is typically located in remote, rugged areas in order to avoid disturbance during hibernation. This is especially important to pregnant females who give birth while in the den. Bears seem to choose a topography that with the prevailing winds creates a substantial snow cover over the den entrance. The typical den has an entrance tunnel 2 to 4 feet (0.6 to 1.2 meters) long (although it can be much longer) and a sleeping chamber 3 to 4 feet (0.9 to 1.2 meters) in diameter. Bears may use leaves and other material from the forest floor to build a bed in the chamber.

Most dens are dug at the base of supporting structures such as the roots of a tree, but occasionally grizzlies use an existing structure such as a rocky cavern or hollow tree. Although dens are seldom reused, individual bears show fidelity to a general denning area.

THIS DEN HAD A FALLEN *log supporting the roof of the entrance tunnel. A grown man easily fits through the entrance, although it may be a little tighter for a 600 pound (270 kilogram) grizzly.*

Marilynn Gibbs-French/The Yellowstone Grizzly Foundation

A TYPICAL GRIZZLY HIBERNATION DEN DUG INTO THE ROOT SYSTEM *of a substantial tree. The roots are used to form the den ceiling.*

Grizzlies generally stay in the den in the hibernating state unless disturbed by other animals or humans. They may come out briefly during warm periods in mid-winter. Unlike other animals, bears can rise quickly from their sleep if disturbed and also birth and nurse their young during hibernation.

THE SCIENTIFICALLY AMAZING GRIZZLY

In preparation for hibernation a grizzly will eat up to 20,000 calories (about 84,000 kilojoules) per day during the late summer. It builds up a store of body fat equal to what it will need to survive. During hibernation it burns up to 4,000 calories (16,700 kilojoules) a day. All the bear's energy and water requirements are derived from the combustion of its stored body fat.

As it rests, the bear's body temperature reduces only a few degrees. Its metabolism, however, markedly decreases and the heart rate and respiration rate drop by half.

Despite being inactive and non-weight-bearing, the bear is able to preserve muscle and bone mass during

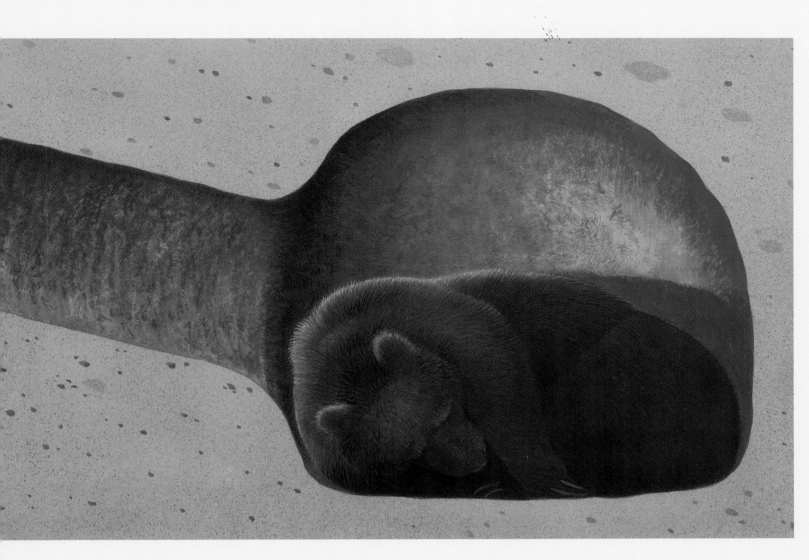

hibernation. The bones of other mammals, including humans, thin after months of inactivity. Yet scientists have found that bears are able to recycle the calcium their bones leak as they sleep, redepositing it to form new bone.

And while bears do not excrete for months, their bodies do not accumulate urea, the toxic byproduct of mammal metabolism. In humans such an accumulation would destroy the kidney and eventually, if not eliminated, poison the body. In bears, the urea appears to be reabsorbed through the bladder and then recycled into components that help form protein.

HUMAN APPLICATIONS

Scientists are looking to the hibernating bear with increasing interest, hoping its unique metabolism and bone growth pattern will have applications for human ailments. They are searching for a chemical in the bear's blood that may promote bone growth. Such a chemical could treat osteoporosis, a disease in which bones waste away. It could also help bedridden patients who quickly

lose bone mass. And it could allow astronauts, who lose bone mass when they are weightless, to go on extended space expeditions. The bear's blood also may contain chemicals that prevent kidney disease and may provide clues to heart disease and eating disorders.

Jim Brandenburg/Planet Earth Pictures

GRIZZLIES OFTEN EMERGE EARLY IN SPRING FROM THEIR WINTER DENS, *before the snow has gone, perhaps to take advantage of winter-weakened prey.*

IF THE HISTORY OF LIFE ON *earth could be compressed into a single year, and all times reduced in corresponding proportion, then the dinosaurs arose in early August and ruled until late November, when they abruptly vanished for reasons that are still unclear. On this scale, humans arose a few minutes before midnight on 31 December. In this reconstruction, a* Minmi, *a heavily armored plant-eater, munches quietly in the foreground while an* Allosaurus, *a giant carnivore, hunts behind.*

➤ THE SKULL OF
Protoceratops, *a plant-eating dinosaur of the late Cretaceous period in Mongolia and China. (The Cretaceous period was from 145 to 65 million years ago).*

Where the Dinosaurs Came From

PAUL C. SERENO

More than any other fossil group, dinosaurs stir popular imagination. But can extinct creatures be the subject of serious scientific inquiry? The answer is not just yes, but rather that the study of dinosaurs and their close relatives also presents a great opportunity for the exploration of evolution. Paleontologist Dr. Paul Sereno, a professor of evolutionary biology at the University of Chicago, is one of the world's leading researchers of dinosaur evolution. He travels to distant lands searching for and studying fossil bones that will help to reconstruct the dinosaur family tree, and shed light on the way dinosaurs evolved.

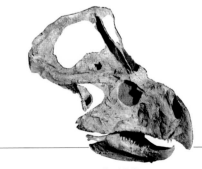

Paul C. Sereno

BREAK-UP OF PANGAEA DURING *the age of dinosaurs: (1) shows the early Triassic, 245 million years ago; (2) early Jurassic, 190 million years ago; (3) end Jurassic, 150 million years ago; (4) late Cretaceous, 95 million years ago; (5) end Cretaceous, 65 million years ago.*

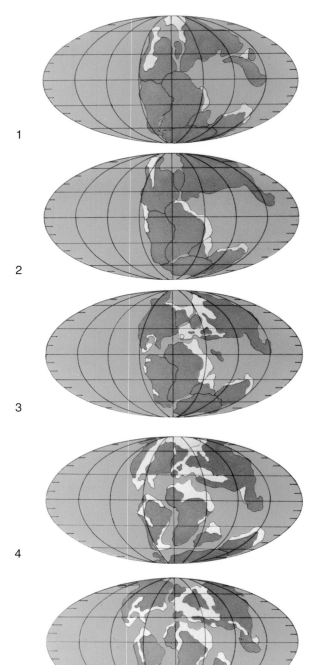

1

2

3

4

5

Paul C. Sereno

THE LEFT HAND OF **Herrerasaurus,** *the earliest known dinosaur. Its strong talons and various other features indicate that it was an agile, active predator.*

Dinosaurs first appeared about 225 million years ago as relatively inconspicuous predators of moderate body size. At that time the earth's major land masses were united in a single supercontinent, Pangaea. As Pangaea fragmented and drifted apart into continent-sized islands, dinosaurs evolved into a spectacular array of forms that included the world's largest land animals and the most adept vertebrate fliers. Then, for reasons that are still unknown, they all died out and suddenly the Age of Dinosaurs was over.

What can these once dominant creatures tell us about how evolution works? What patterns can we see in the way they evolved? To answer these questions, Dr. Sereno and his team of students are preparing a family tree that will detail the dinosaur dynasty and its evolution from the very beginning. They are visiting fossil collections all over the world to study every variety of dinosaur, looking for the missing evidence to answer questions about the branching evolutionary history of dinosaurs. Using computers, they log every feature shared by dinosaurs and look for group patterns. As they explore the fossil evidence, they start with a few basic questions that have gone unanswered until recently. Just what is a dinosaur? And what did the earliest dinosaurs look like?

TRACKING THE FIRST DINOSAUR

In 1988 Dr. Sereno led an expedition to the barren lands at the foot of the Andes Mountains in Argentina to look for skeletons of the earliest dinosaurs. Limb fragments of the earliest dinosaur, *Herrerasaurus*, were found here 30 years ago. The expedition's objective was to find a complete skeleton of this dinosaur, to record the

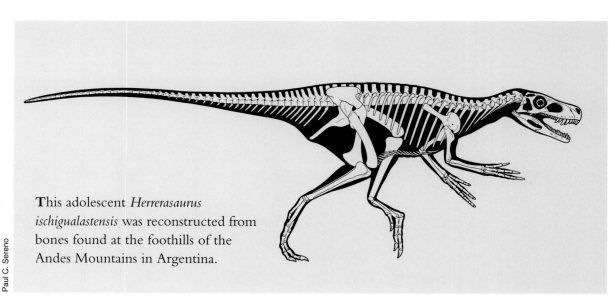

This adolescent *Herrerasaurus ischigualastensis* was reconstructed from bones found at the foothills of the Andes Mountains in Argentina.

Paul C. Sereno

American Museum of Natural History

Paul C. Sereno

SINCE ONLY BONES SURVIVE, WE *must rely on the interpretive skills of artists for impressions of how dinosaurs might have looked in life. The American artist Charles Knight was the earliest and one of the most famous of these illustrators. This 1897 painting portrays two* **Dryptosaurus** *in combat.*

FOSSILS OF OTHER ANIMALS HAVE *been found in the same deposits that yielded* **Herrerasaurus.** *Here, one of Dr Sereno's students examines the skull of one of these, a crocodile-like creature called* **Proterochampsa.**

Paul C. Sereno

HERRERASAURUS WAS FOUND *here in the badlands of the Ischigualasto Valley, north-western Argentina, in the 1950s.*

habitat in which it lived, and to determine the age of *Herrerasaurus* by analyzing volcanic ash found near the bones.

Three weeks of the expedition had passed and still only fragments of *Herrerasaurus* had been found. One day, while investigating a remote ravine, Dr. Sereno spotted some fossil bone on a sandstone ledge. He soon realized that what lay before him was an almost-complete skeleton of *Herrerasaurus*. The slender neck and narrow skull were partially exposed on the surface of the rock. The expedition team decided to remove the heavy blocks of sandstone in which the skull and skeleton were buried and transported them back to the laboratory for cleaning. After specialist technicians spent months carefully removing the surrounding rock, a well-preserved skull and entire skeleton of *Herrerasaurus* emerged.

This new discovery from Argentina provided the first complete picture of an early dinosaur. This particular animal, in human terms, was a teenager, judging from the moderate size of its bones as compared to larger bones of the same species. Its skeleton is approximately 8 to 9 feet (2.4 to 2.7 meters) long. The skull, 1 foot (30 centimeters) in length, clearly indicates that *Herrerasaurus* was an active predator. The lower jaw has an unusual sliding joint midway along its length for flexing around struggling prey, much like the jaws of a

snake. The hind limbs indicate it was powerfully built and clearly supported all of the weight of the animal. The forelimbs, by comparison, are relatively short except for the hands. The very elongated, clawed hands were designed for grasping and capturing prey. By studying the remains of *Herrerasaurus* and positioning it on the family tree with its early relatives, Dr. Sereno began to reconstruct the branching pattern of dinosaur descent.

The evolutionary adaptation of *Herrerasaurus* required a close look at the other early dinosaurs and dinosaurian precursors. These earlier reptiles provided more clues to piecing together the origin and early evolution of dinosaurs.

THIS ARTISTIC RECONSTRUCTION *shows giant pterosaurs congregating to feed at a dead* **Triceratops** *about 135 million years ago. With a wingspan extending to about 40 feet (12 meters), some pterosaur species were the largest of all flying animals.*

Jane Burton/Bruce Coleman Limited

American Museum of Natural History

KNOWN FROM EUROPE AND *possibly South America,* **Plateosaurus** *of the late Triassic was a plant eater (the Triassic period was from 245 to 200 million years ago). Details of its anatomy and body proportions suggest that it may have reared up on its hind quarters to browse on tree foliage.*

RULING REPTILES

Dinosaurs and their living descendants, birds, are part of a larger group of reptiles called archosaurs ("ruling reptiles"), which also includes living crocodiles. Both the dinosaur-bird lineage and the crocodile lineage are easily traced back to about 240 million years ago, when they lived side-by-side with a variety of carnivorous, superficially crocodile-like xarchosaurs and bat-like pterosaurs

The crocodilian branch of the archosaur family tree included the largest predators of the day. The hallmark of their anatomy was an unusual ankle joint that can be seen today in the hind feet of living crocodiles.

The dinosaur-bird branch of the family tree included the winged pterosaurs and several small dinosaur precursors. These early dinosaur precursors were the first land vertebrates to evolve a bipedal (upright) posture, in which only the hind limbs were used for locomotion. This two-legged stance, similar to human posture, appears to have promoted the evolution of wings among pterosaurs and the evolution of grasping hands among the first dinosaurs.

The first dinosaurs (for example *Herrerasaurus*) appeared 10 to 15 million years later and are characterized by a series of modifications in the bones of the hand, hip, and ankle. These modifications arose in the common ancestor of all dinosaurs at the base of the family tree and constitute the scientific definition of a dinosaur. The first dinosaur's traits included increased muscle in the forearm, reduced length of the outer fingers of the hand, and a strengthened pelvic girdle. The key to understanding dinosaur origins lies in identifying the subtle anatomical modifications that go with the branches of the family tree.

DINOSAURS ARE DIVIDED INTO *two major lineages based on the structure of their pelvis. The "bird-hipped" ornithischians (above) are not related to birds although, like birds, they had backward-pointing hip bones and tended to carry their bodies parallel to the ground. The "lizard-hipped" saurischians (right) had front-projected pelvises similar to those of lizards or crocodilians.*

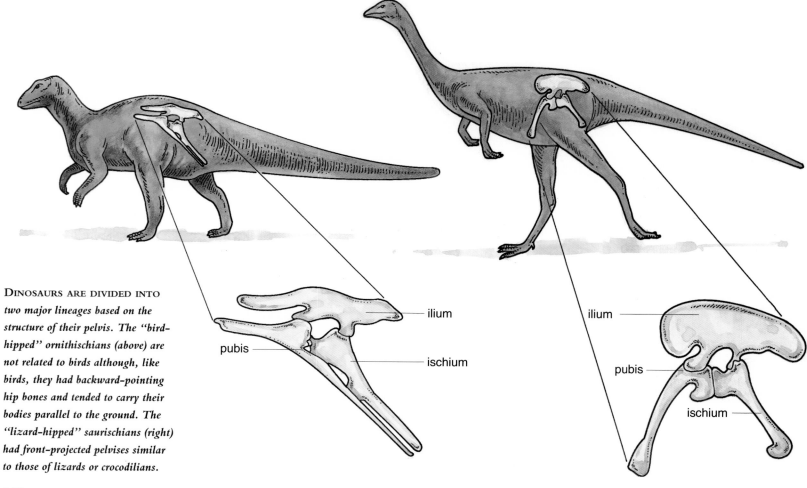

ilium

pubis

ischium

ilium

pubis

ischium

Retracing the Family Tree

Pseudhesperosuchus jachaleri

Saurosuchus galilei

Stagonolepis robertsoni

Eudimorphodon ranzii

Riojasuchus tenuiceps

Rutiodon sp.

Herrerasaurus ischigualastensis

Lagosuchus talampayensis

ORNITHODIRA

CRUROTARSI

ARCHOSAURIA

Euparkeria capensis

Vjushkovia triplicostata

Proterosuchus vanhoepeni

ARCHOSAURIFORMES

Paul C. Sereno

To understand more about the origins of dinosaurs paleontologists have constructed a family tree to show the earliest dinosaur, *Herrerasaurus ischigualastensis* (top right), with its more primitive dinosaur relatives.

Paul C. Sereno

A RECONSTRUCTED SKELETON OF *the North American dinosaur* Stegosaurus, *which is a member of the ornithischian lineage.* Stegosaurus *lived from the mid-Jurassic to the late Cretaceous period (about 170 to 65 million years ago).*

STEGOSAURUS WAS EQUIPPED *with long bony spikes on its shoulders and tail, and the large, sail-like plates along its spine may have functioned as cooling fins.*

CHARTING DINOSAUR DESCENT

During the 150 years since the first discoveries of dinosaur fragments, more than 500 dinosaur species have been described. However, most of what we know about dinosaurs is based upon the remains of about 200 species. These species, each of which lived only a few million years, evolved during the Mesozoic era or "Age of Dinosaurs," a period that spanned 160 million years, from the end of the Triassic period (200 million years ago) through the Jurassic period (150 million years ago) to the end of the Cretaceous period (65 million years ago).

By the time dinosaurs first appeared in the fossil record they had already diverged into two major branches, the ornithischians ("bird-hipped") and the saurischians ("lizard-hipped"). The ornithischians evolved plant-eating habits, evidenced by their triangular, leaf-cutting teeth. All subsequent ornithischian dinosaurs maintained this leaf-eating habit, diversifying into spiky-plated stegosaurs, armored ankylosaurs, thick-headed pachycephalosaurs, duck-billed hadrosaurs, and horned ceratopsians.

K. Perkins/J. Beckett/American Museum of Natural History

"CROSSING THE FLATS", A *reconstruction of* Mamenchisaurus hochuanensis. *This enormous vegetarian, stretching nearly 88 feet (27 meters) from snout to tail-tip, lived in China during the late Jurassic period (about 150 million years ago). It is notable for its extra-ordinary neck, which has 19 vertebrae and extends some 50 feet (15 meters).*

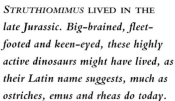

STRUTHIOMIMUS LIVED IN THE *late Jurassic. Big-brained, fleet-footed and keen-eyed, these highly active dinosaurs might have lived, as their Latin name suggests, much as ostriches, emus and rheas do today.*

ONE OF THE MOST FORMIDABLE *predators of all time, an* Allosaurus *is shown straddling its* Apatosaurus *kill. Researchers have very little to go on in reconstructing dinosaur colors and patterns, but modern animals with similar lifestyles are streaked, spotted and marked for very good reasons, and it seems probable that the same influences controlled color patterns in dinosaurs as well.*

The saurischians split into two great branches, the long-necked, vegetarian sauropodomorphs and the flesh-eating theropods. The sauropodomorphs evolved into the largest terrestrial animals that ever existed, most of which were specialized for browsing in the succulent canopy of Mesozoic era forests. *Brachiosaurus,* for example, evolved to add several vertebrae to its neck so that when extended vertically, it reached a height of nearly 40 feet (12 meters).

The flesh-eating theropods were a diverse group of two-legged predators and scavengers that, midway in the course of their evolution, gave rise to birds. The earliest theropods inherited the flexible lower jaw of *Herrarasaurus* that could bend around struggling prey preventing escape, and hands with only three strong claw-tipped fingers that were designed for grasping. At several points in their evolution, theropods evolved large skulls and very reduced forelimbs, such as *Tyrannosaurus.*

Other theropods evolved slender limbs and fleet-footed habits similar to living ostriches. These evolved a beak and either reduced or lost all of their teeth. Some theropods, like

Dilophosaurus, were ornamented with cranial crests and may have hunted in small groups.

The flesh-eaters were always less numerous than the larger herbivorous dinosaurs, but nevertheless they persisted as the principal terrestrial predators and scavengers until the end of the dinosaur era some 65 million years ago.

DINOSAURS AND LAND BRIDGES

Dr. Sereno and his team have also investigated the dinosaurs of western North America and Asia and placed them on the family tree.

They have determined that the lines of descent cross from North America to Asia and back to North America again, indicating that some dinosaurs were able to cross the Bering Land Bridge which at that time connected these two land masses when the sea level was low. These small groups of colonizers soon evolved into new species as they adapted to conditions in their new habitats.

TRACHODON WAS A MEMBER OF *the* **Hadrosaurus** *group, which are known as the duck-billed dinosaurs from the distinctive structure of their jaws. Up to 50 feet (15 meters) in length, these plant eaters inhabited Europe, Asia, and America during the late Cretaceous period (about 70 million years ago).*

Formation and Discovery of a Fossil

Most plants and animals leave no trace of their existence. When they die, their bodies rot and the soft tissues, such as skin, rapidly decompose. Within months these tissues are fully integrated with the soils. Harder tissues, like bones, may remain for several years, depending on prevailing conditions. In almost all cases, however, bones, too, are dissolved by acidic soils or broken down and scattered by predators, scavengers, or geologic forces.

In rare instances, the carcasses of dead animals and the remains of plants are buried quickly before total decomposition has occurred. These remains become buried in loose sediment, usually mud or sand, that keeps out oxygen and thus the bacteria that causes decay. These sediments compact as the weight of the ever-thickening overlying material exerts pressure, squeezing out all moisture and air from between the sediment particles. Eventually these sediments will form a rock layer.

Over a period of thousands of years, groundwater percolates through these sediments, altering the chemical composition of the buried animal and plant matter, saturating the pores of the remains, replacing the original bone minerals and woody plant tissues with rock minerals that had been dissolved in the groundwater. It is these minerals that form the fossil casts or fossil bones that survive. Even soft tissues such as skin and the fronds of plants may be preserved, although usually they remain only as impressions or as carbonized replacements.

Only a very small fraction of the few individual animals and plants that become fossils are discovered by paleontologists. Many of the fossils are destroyed by erosion or are buried far beneath the surface by younger rock layers. Only those fossils that are exposed near the surface in areas that are not covered by soils are candidates for discovery. Paleontologists must take advantage of that small window in time, perhaps only a few months or years, when erosion has exposed, but not yet destroyed, a fossil.

SOMETIMES FOSSIL SKELETONS ARE FOUND ALMOST ENTIRELY *undamaged, like this* **Mesosaurus** *in a Permian deposit in Brazil.*

Telling Time

RELATIVE DATING

The most common method for estimating the age of fossils or the rock layers that contain them is called relative dating. Generally, each rock layer preserves fossils of animals and plants that lived when the sediment was formed. Researchers have studied the fossil record from different regions and established a general succession of stages of development for animals and plants that documents major transitions in animal and plant life, such as the evolution and extinction of dinosaurs. Fossils discovered at a new site can be compared to this established succession to reliably determine the general age of the site. If one finds a dinosaur skeleton, for example, the site would be considered Mesozoic in age (the Mesozoic era occurred 245 to 65 million years ago) and older than other sites that are dominated by fossil mammals.

RADIOMETRIC DATING

This relative age, however, does not specify the age of the site in terms of exact numbers of years, but rather only its age relative to other sites. For a numerical value, or absolute date, paleontologists must study the radioactive minerals contained in the rock layers at a site. Radio-active minerals change their composition at a constant clock-like rate which can be measured precisely. To establish an absolute date, researchers must obtain a sample of rock that contains radioactive minerals, such as some forms of potas-sium, that crystallized at the same time that the sediments or fossils were buried.

Rocks come in three varieties: igneous (formed from molten rock), metamorphic (formed from existing rocks metamorphosed by heat and/or pressure), and sedimentary (formed from eroded

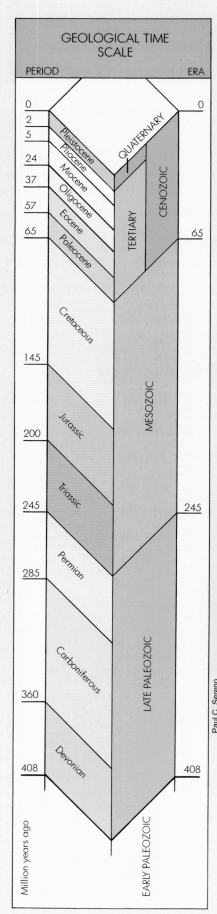

GEOLOGICAL TIME SCALE

PERIOD		ERA
0		0
2	Pleistocene	QUATERNARY
5	Pliocene	
24	Miocene	
37	Oligocene	CENOZOIC
57	Eocene	TERTIARY
65	Paleocene	65
145	Cretaceous	
200	Jurassic	MESOZOIC
245	Triassic	245
285	Permian	
360	Carboniferous	LATE PALEOZOIC
408	Devonian	408
		EARLY PALEOZOIC

Million years ago

particles of existing rock). Fossils are found almost exclusively in sedimentary rocks.

The most common source of radio-active minerals for dating fossil sites is volcanic ash. Fortunately, evidence of volcanic activity is relatively common in sedimentary rocks. Since potassium is a constituent of most minerals in volcanic or igneous rocks, a potassium-argon dating system is commonly used. The potassium crystals in the volcanic ash will then be measured to give a fossil a birthdate, give or take a million years.

When volcanic lava cools, potassium atoms are locked or frozen into a crystal structure. As soon as some of the radio-active potassium isotopes are locked into this crystal structure, they begin to decay and their "clock" starts. Measurements of the ratio of this original radioactive mineral and its decay products provide an estimate of the age of the deposit and the fossils it contains.

Paul C. Sereno

DR. SERENO CAREFULLY EXCAVATES A SAUROPOD *leg bone from the ground in which it has lain for more than 130 million years.*

THE HISTORY OF LIFE ON EARTH CAN BE DIVIDED *into eras and then subdivided into periods. The boundaries of these divisions are marked by significant events such as the mysterious extinction that wiped out 96 percent of marine species about 250 million years ago.*

Paul C. Sereno

ABOUT 135 MILLION YEARS AGO *this slab was part of the sediment on the bed of an ancient Chinese lake. It bears a fossilized skeleton of the sparrow-sized* **Sinornis santensis,** *one of the oldest known birds.*

ANCIENT BIRDS AND THE ORIGIN OF FLIGHT

The placement of birds on the dinosaur family tree has always been somewhat troublesome because the fossil record of birds is practically barren for a 50 million year interval following the appearance of the oldest bird, *Archaeopteryx*, 150 million years ago. On the one hand, *Archaeopteryx* is considered a bird because it had the feathers which were unique to birds. On the other hand, its skeletal anatomy closely resembled the carnivorous dinosaurs from which it evolved. Yet, after *Archaeopteryx*, there is a wide evolutionary gap until the appearance of *Ichthyornis* 80 million years ago. *Ichthyornis* is a toothed bird with the same avian skeleton that allows modern flight performance and perching.

This mystery in bird evolution has been solved with the recent discovery of sparrow-sized bird skeletons in China. The new fossil bird, dubbed *Sinornis* or "Chinese bird," appears to be only 10 to 15 million years younger than *Archaeopteryx*. Some primitive skull and skeletal features of *Sinornis* are also found in *Archaeopteryx* dinosaurs but are absent in all other birds, indicating that *Sinornis* represents an early avian offshoot, an important link in the dinosaur family tree.

Other skeletal features suggest that *Sinornis* marks a key point in bird evolution, when advanced features related to powered flight first appeared. *Sinornis* lost the long balancing tail of *Archaeopteryx* and theropod dinosaurs, replacing it with a blunt, fused tail bone. In living birds this bone supports a fan-like array of tail feathers which enhance aerial maneuverability and function as a brake during landing. The shortened tail also shifts the center of mass from above the hind limbs towards the forelimbs, as in modern powered fliers.

The feet in *Sinornis* were capable of grasping, with the first toe being swung around to oppose the other toes.

Thus in *Sinornis*, as in dinosaur evolution in general, we see that profound changes in the skeleton can occur rapidly, over a few million years, and result in adaptations to a new lifestyle. These large scale changes most often first appear in small animals which later give rise to larger species. There are many examples of this pattern of size increase in dinosaur evolution, with *Tyrannosaurus*, as one example, representing the last and largest of the big-headed carnivores.✪

ARCHAEOPTERYX
Fossil evidence shows that although **Archaeopteryx lithographica** *could fly, it apparently could not fold its forelimbs during flight or at rest as a modern bird can.*

A SPECTACULAR SPRINTER, THE *cheetah is the fastest of the world's land animals. The cheetah's hunting style requires large open areas for stalking and then running down its prey. In a chase that lasts less than a minute, this most streamlined of felines can reach speeds of 68 miles (110 kilometers) per hour.*

➤VEHICLES SUCH AS THIS ONE *are well suited to carrying tourists on wildlife-viewing safaris. Cheetahs, now an endangered species, can still be seen in parts of Africa.*

How Long Will the Cheetah Run?

LAURIE MARKER-KRAUS
AND DANIEL KRAUS

Prized for its speed and grace, the cheetah was once the favored pet and hunting companion of royalty. Its domain extended from Africa to India. Today the magnificent cheetah is extinct in India and endangered in Africa. Where it survives in the wild, it lives in small, isolated, and dwindling populations, and seldom breeds in captivity. Its fate lies with the conservation efforts of people like cheetah experts Laurie Marker-Kraus and Daniel Kraus. The Krauses are co-founders and co-directors of the Cheetah Conservation Fund, a program based in Namibia, Africa, that aims to save the world's last cheetahs.

A. & M. Shah/Planet Earth Pictures

HUNTING WITH CHEETAHS *became a royal passion for mogul emperors from the thirteenth to the sixteenth centuries. Trained within a few weeks of being caught, cheetahs were carried on horseback to a hunt with their eyes hooded. The hood was removed only when the prey was within range.* Cheetah and Stag with Two Indians, *by George Stubbs, 1724–1806.*

Manchester City Art Gallery/Bridgeman Art Library

D. Parer & E. Parer-Cook/Auscape International

AFTER OVERTAKING PREY, SUCH *as this impala calf in Kenya's Masai Mara Game Reserve, the cheetah administers the coup de grâce. The cheetah bites down on the neck, squeezing the throat and causing death by strangulation.*

From the time of the pharaohs to the early years of the twentieth century, from the palaces of Asia to the royal hunting lodges of Europe, princes and emperors have supplied themselves with cheetahs. They are the fastest of all animals on land. They have been prized for their speed and grace, for which they received the name of the "hunting leopard."

Only the dog was more popular than the cheetah as a hunting companion. Cheetahs were particularly well suited to the royal sport of coursing, that is, hunting game by sight rather than by scent. Crusaders brought back to Europe stories of cheetahs used to hunt gazelles in Syria and Palestine. Marco Polo wrote that Kublai Khan kept hundreds of cheetahs for deer hunting. Akbar the Great, an Indian mogul in the sixteenth century, was reputed to have owned 9,000 cheetahs during his lifetime, keeping up to 1,000 in his stables at any one time. Practically every Italian Renaissance court maintained cheetahs.

But the great numbers of cheetahs captured for hunting began to drain the wild populations. Because cheetahs did not breed in captivity, stocks of hunting cheetahs had to be continually replenished from free-ranging populations in the wild. By the beginning of the twentieth century the stock of cheetahs in Asia was so depleted by the demands of hunters that Indian moguls had to import their cheetahs from Africa.

A DIFFERENT KIND OF CAT

The cheetah is a unique and highly specialized member of the cat family. Classified as *Acinonyx jubatus*, it is the only species in its genus. In both anatomy and behavior it is markedly different from the other 36 species of the family Felidae. Nature has designed the cheetah for speed. Larger in chest, leaner and lighter in body, with longer legs than other big cats, adult cheetahs weigh from 70 to 140 pounds (32 to 64 kilograms). For a big cat this is considered lightweight. Excluding the tail, the head and body are only about 4 feet (1.2 meters) long.

The word cheetah comes from the Hindu word *chita* meaning "spotted one." Its distinguishing marks are the long teardrop-shaped lines on each side of the nose, from the corner of its eyes to its mouth. The cheetah's coat is tawny, with small black spots in between larger spots measuring about 1 inch (2.5 centimeters) across. On the tail, the spots merge to form four to six dark rings. The tail usually ends in a bushy white tuft.

Unlike other cats, which are nocturnal, cheetahs rest and sleep at night. They leave their hunting until early morning and early evening. They are found in a variety of habitats, from open grasslands to semi-deserts and thick bush. Cheetahs prefer flat, open habitats where their view of the surrounding area is unobstructed. This allows them to see both prey and predators.

John Downer/Planet Earth Pictures

THIS SOLITARY CHEETAH SURVEYS *one of the few areas where cheetahs enjoy large expanses of open territory: Kenya's Masai Mara Game Reserve.*

IN 1900, CHEETAHS ROAMED *over at least two-thirds of the African continent. By 1975, hunters, poachers, ranchers, predators, and habitat destruction as well as a loss of genetic variation had reduced cheetahs' numbers significantly. By 1992 population groups were scattered. Once a common animal found on five continents, the cheetah is now an endangered species.*

1900

1975

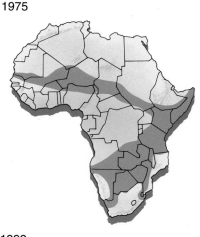

1992

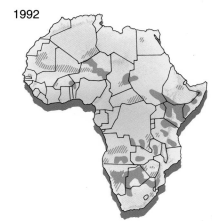

Research undertaken in Namibia can benefit not only the local wild population, but also wild and captive populations in other countries. Of the approximately 1,000 cheetahs in captivity in 160 of the world's zoos in 36 countries, virtually all have come from Namibia or are descended from Namibian founding stock. Yet very little is known about the behavior and biology of Namibia's cheetahs.

The Namibian conservation program began with a comprehensive survey of all the districts in Namibia where cheetahs still exist. This survey included distribution patterns, availability of prey, attitudes of farmers toward the cheetah, and current livestock and wildlife management practices and their impact on the cheetah.

CONFLICT WITH THE FARMERS

Surveys showed that in Namibia, 70 percent of wildlife lives on farmlands ranging from 10,000 to 40,000 acres (4,050 to 16,200 hectares). Ninety-five percent of the cheetah population lives on these private lands, where prey is available and other large predators are generally absent. But private ownership of wildlife has caused unique problems for conservation. Each farmer has particular opinions about how to deal with "his" or "her" wildlife, even though the chee-tahs move from farm to farm; female cheetahs

will cover over 450 square miles (1,200 square kilometers) and males over 300 square miles (800 square kilometers). Sometimes as many as 10 to 20 cheetahs have been seen together near farm dams or on roads. This large gathering together is an unusual characteristic of the Namibian cheetah.

Historically, the cheetah has been viewed as a pest and a threat to the livelihood of livestock farmers. Since it is legal in Namibia to shoot an animal that interferes with one's property and livelihood, three generations of farmers have done their best to eliminate the species. Yet, by the late 1970s, a population of 5,000 to 6,000 animals remained.

In the 1980s, because of a variety of circumstances which included severe drought, a 50 percent decline in the wildlife populations due to the drought, and the continued over-stocking of livestock on rangelands, cheetah populations came into even greater conflict with farmers. And, during this period, 80 percent of one of the cheetah's main prey, the kudu, died due to an outbreak of rabies. As a result of these combined events, the cheetah resorted to prey-ing on domestic livestock, causing an all-out war against the species. By the latter part of the 1980s, the cheetah population had been reduced by more than half.

181

The conflict continues. Indiscriminate trapping remains a pressing problem. The live traps are set at "playtrees." These have not been reported in any other area of Africa but they are a focal point for cheetahs in their large home ranges in Namibia. Playtrees have sloping trunks and large horizontal limbs that the cheetahs can easily climb. They visit the playtrees regularly and scent mark them with scat (droppings) and urine. Farmers whose properties include playtrees can trap all the cheetahs that visit the trees. Most of the trapped cheetahs are then shot and killed.

PRACTICAL CONSERVATION

The cheetah's survival requires that conservationists develop a clear understanding of the farmers' problems with cheetahs and strive to reach a compromise. Since almost all huntable wildlife belongs to the landowners and has an economic value through live sale, meat production, and trophy hunting, wildlife conservation strategies are developed along with livestock and pasture management practices.

Conservationists are also introducing farmers to farm management practices used

THE TRAP SET BY A FARMER *at this "playtree" is surrounded by thorn bushes that allow the cheetah only one entry way—through a box trap. Such live traps are legal in Namibia. Cheetahs in Namibia use playtrees as social centers.*

Laurie Marker-Kraus

Nature's Greatest Sprinter

The cheetah is unmatched in the animal or automotive world for its acceleration from 0 to 40 miles (64 kilometers) per hour. It can reach a full speed of 68 miles (110 kilometers) per hour in a matter of seconds. In comparison, a championship racehorse runs up to 40 miles (65 kilometers) per hour.

As the cheetah runs, only one foot touches the ground at a time. In a sprint each stride covers 20 to 25 feet (6 to 7.5 meters). There are two points in each stride when there are no feet touching the ground—as the cheetah is fully extended, and then when it is totally doubled up. Nearing full speed, the cheetah runs at about 3½ strides per second.

The cheetah's anatomy is uniquely specialized for its high-speed sprints. For its explosive use of energy, the cheetah is endowed with a powerful heart, an oversized liver, and large, strong arteries. For aerodynamics, it has a small head, a flat face, a reduced length of muzzle which also allows the large eyes to be positioned for maximum binocular vision, enlarged nostrils, and extensive sinuses.

Its body is narrow and lightweight, deep-chested and narrow-waisted. It has long, slender feet and legs, and specialized muscles which act simultaneously for high acceleration and greater swing to the limbs. Its hip and shoulder girdles swivel on a flexible spine that curves up and down as the limbs are alternately bunched up and then extended when running, giving greater reach to the legs. Its long, muscular tail acts as a stabilizer or rudder to balance it when accelerating in fast turns.

The cheetah is the only cat with short, blunt claws that are exposed even when retracted. They help grip the ground like cleats for traction when running. Their paws are less rounded than those of other cats, and their pads are like tire treads, to help them in fast, sharp turns.

Yet this gifted sprinter runs on average for only 20 seconds at a time. During its high-speed chases, the cheetah's respiratory rate climbs from 60 to 150 breaths per minute. The increased rate means the cheetah can only run 1,200 to 1,800 feet (about 365 to 550 meters) before it is exhausted and must stop to recover.

Karl Ammann/ACE Photo Agency

AROUND THIS EUPHORBIA *tree cheetah littermates are practicing the play behavior that helps refine their hunting techniques. Littermates usually remain together for several months after their mother separates from them. Male littermates may stay together for life, hunting in groups called coalitions.*

locally and internationally to protect livestock from predators. Some of these include reducing calf losses by keeping cows closer to the homestead during calving time; placing donkeys with calving herds, as donkeys are aggressive toward intruders and chase away cheetahs; and promoting more aggressive breeds of cattle, such as *Bos indicus* and indigenous breeds. Solutions for protecting small stock like sheep and goats include employing herders and large breeds of guard dogs; placing bells on several individuals in a herd, which seems to confuse and scare cheetahs; and raising baboons with the herds, since baboons then become very protective.

The cheetah can survive only if its habitat is preserved and if it is able to support populations of healthy wild prey. Since the cheetah generally prefers wild game, the maintenance of wild prey reduces conflict with livestock farmers. One of the main objectives of long-term conservation is to educate an often skeptical public to the importance of predators and prey in a healthy ecosystem. For example, as a selective hunter, the cheetah plays a major role in the health of prey populations. By seeking the oldest and weakest animals in a herd, it helps the strongest to survive and helps strengthen the species as a whole. Also, by leaving remains of their kills, cheetahs help to feed other animals which are

important in the ecological cycle including jackals, porcupines, badgers, civet and genet cats, vultures, and insects.

Most importantly, a local outreach center for conservation fieldwork, such as that of the Cheetah Conservation Fund, provides researchers and farmers alike with information and help. The farmers' participation in conservation strategies is actively encouraged. They are invited to collect data about cheetah sightings and tracks on their farms, so that patterns of movement between farms can be developed. Meanwhile, samples of blood and tissue are being collected from cheetahs trapped on farms to assess the overall health and genetic makeup of the free-ranging population. Since some cheetahs continue to be killed each year, these condemned cats will at least supply information about the species that, in the end, will help to provide solutions to the complex issues of their conservation.

Conservationists at the Cheetah Conservation Fund are also working with government ministries of wildlife, tourism, and agriculture, with veterinarians, and with all individuals concerned for the cheetah's future. Every effort toward conservation and education allows this unique and magnificent species a little more time for its run.✪

Cheetah Preservation Fund

LOCAL VETERINARIAN, DR. *Reimer Hassel, assists the Krauses with a tranquilized cheetah trapped on a farm in Namibia. They are collecting blood and tissue samples for genetic and disease analysis.*

BYPRODUCTS OF A GROWING
population and modern industry
together pose a major threat to the
environment. Pollution of many
kinds is threatening our planet.

184

THE FRAGILE EARTH

ONE OF THE MOST DRAMATIC
*sights in nature, a stream of molten
lava spills from the central crater in
this view of Kilauea in eruption.
Kilauea has been under constant
scientific scrutiny since Hawaii's
Volcano Research Institute was
founded in 1912 and is one of the
most carefully studied volcanoes on
earth. The research institute is
located in the same area where the
high priests of ancient Hawaii
watched over this abode of the gods,
long before the coming of Europeans.*

➢ LAVA BREAKS DOWN INTO
*rich volcanic soil which quickly
regenerates plant life.*

Rivers of Fire

R O B E R T N . Y O N O V E R

Between the years 91 and 89 B.C. the ancient city of Pompeii withstood a long siege by the famous Roman general Sulla. Yet in A.D. 79 this same city was overpowered in a few days when Mount Vesuvius erupted with a force so explosive that it buried the city. Until recently volcanoes were thought of as one of those mysterious eccentricities of nature. Today science has pushed far beyond this. Thanks to the work of Dr. Robert Yonover, Dr. Frank Trusdell, and other scientists and scholars who study activity deep inside the earth, we are learning more every day about volcanoes and about the fragile composition of our planet.

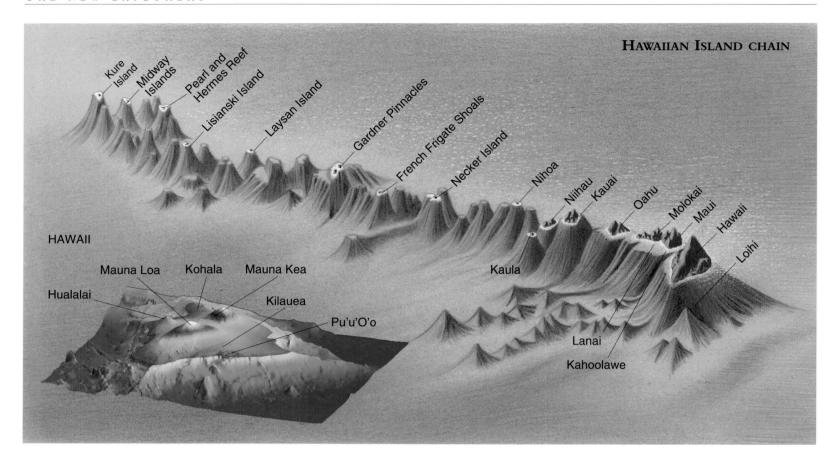

HAWAIIAN ISLAND CHAIN

Kure Island · Midway Islands · Pearl and Hermes Reef · Lisianski Island · Laysan Island · Gardner Pinnacles · French Frigate Shoals · Necker Island · Nihoa · Niihau · Kauai · Oahu · Molokai · Maui · Hawaii · Loihi · Kaula · Lanai · Kahoolawe

HAWAII · Hualalai · Mauna Loa · Kohala · Mauna Kea · Kilauea · Pu'u'O'o

BRAVING HEAT AND FUMES,
Bill Kurtis goes about the dangerous and uncomfortable task of sampling a lava flow. Seething at temperatures well over 2,200°F (1,200°C), the material comes directly from the earth's interior, sometimes tens of miles beneath the surface.

On July 18, 1986, a team of scientists, including Dr. Robert Yonover and Dr. Frank Trusdell, were camped on a terrace 500 feet (150 meters) above Pu'u'O'o, Hawaii.

Pu'u'O'o is a large cinder and spatter cone some 850 feet (260 meters) high. It is located on the slopes of the Kilauea Volcano on the island of Hawaii. The scientists were there because all indications suggested that the time was right for Pu'u'O'o's next eruption, and they wanted to observe lava rising to the earth's surface. The immediate goal was to learn everything they could about the triggering mechanisms for volcanic eruptions.

CYCLE OF ERUPTIONS

For almost three years Pu'u'O'o had been erupting regularly. The team had collected enough data on these eruptions to enable them to guess at both the force and time of Pu'u'O'o's next eruption. Although cautious about the risks inherent in their work, no one on the team was particularly troubled by questions of safety.

The last thirty or so eruptions had followed a regular pattern. On average, before an eruption, Pu'u'O'o would accumulate molten material for approximately 25 days. The eruption itself would last roughly 18 hours, after which the vent would shut off and Pu'u'O'o would resume accumulating magma. After an

eruption the conduit to the eruption site from the summit magma chamber remained open. It was this chamber and the material in it that interested the scientists.

The cyclic pattern observed in past eruptions, however, was not the only guide the scientists used for predicting the volcano's next eruption. At their disposal they had even more powerful tools.

For example, they had used a laser ranging device to measure the expansion of the volcano's crater, or caldera. A volcano's crater functions as a kind of reservoir for magma, or molten material, which accumulates inside it just before an eruption. Tilt meters measure the angle of the summit crater. A sudden swelling from the accumulating magma causes tilt to increase. After an eruption, when the magma has been released from its prison, the crater deflates and the angle of its summit tilt decreases.

But the most sensitive tool that the team used was a seismometer, a machine that registers and locates earthquakes and earth tremors. As a volcano gets ready to erupt, summit seismic activity increases to a daily count of 450 to 500 earthquakes. Because the seismic activity around Pu'u'O'o was increasing, the team concluded that a small eruption was imminent.

That night Dr. Yonover and Dr. Trusdell's team was there to collect molten lava samples, to take temperatures of the lava, and to record any out-gassing events that could signify a change in the volcano's state.

It was important to measure the temperature of the magma because magma stored in the Pu'u'O'o vent, or vertical conduit, for a period of time would be cooler than molten material that had just recently moved up into the vent. A rise in temperature would signal the arrival of more juvenile or fresh magma from inside the earth and hence the onset of a volcanic eruption.

A CLASSIC FIRE FOUNTAIN

The eruptive style of Pu'u'O'o is a classic fire fountain in which magma is ejected forcibly several hundreds to a thousand feet into the air. This type of eruption occurs when the magma is charged with gas. When the pressure of the magma accumulating inside the volcano becomes too great, the volcano erupts. The pressure release causes the gas to rush to the surface, carrying molten rock hundreds of feet into the air. The effect is to create a standing fountain or column of "red hot" rock.

The team already knew that a column of old, hardened lava was "plugging" Pu'u'O'o's vent. This lava, they hypothesized, functioned much the way a cork functions in a champagne bottle. It would keep Pu'u'O'o's gases bottled up until the pressure inside became so strong that it could not retain them any longer. Then the plug would blow and the fire fountain would start.

The question team members asked was how could molten rock act as a "cork"? Their working hypothesis was that the lava in Pu'u'O'o's vent had degassed and cooled since the volcano's last eruption. Lava that has cooled 180°F (100°C) or more develops a yield strength and begins to resist pressure from the newer lava behind it.

RUN FOR YOUR LIVES

The next morning, small earthquakes caused the ground around the team to tremble. The team logged ten such earthquakes at the Pu'u'O'o vent. They then called the volcano observatory. They knew that in a system like Pu'u'O'o's, where the conduit or lava passageway had remained free and open for three years, there should be no need for magma in the plumbing system to generate earthquakes. These earthquakes indicated that the lava was trying to find a new pathway, instead of following the established one. The team members were worried.

Over the crackling sounds of the radio they heard the words they had hoped never to hear: "Get off of Pu'u'O'o and the rift zone ASAP. A seismic swarm is in progress!"

Instantly, as their worst fear came true, every member of the team went into action. Now all that was left to worry about was their lives. Suddenly it had become very clear to everyone not only that Pu'u'O'o was erupting, but the entire mountainside under their feet was about to open and vigorously spew lava.

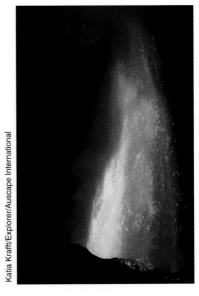

Katia Krafft/Explorer/Auscape International

WHEN MAGMA IS CHARGED *with substantial quantities of gas, the result is a spectacular fountain of fire, spewing lava and molten rock several hundred feet into the air.*

Robert Yonover

A WARY GEOLOGIST OBSERVES *the opening stages of a fountaining episode. Using lasers and the information provided by satellites, researchers can measure to an accuracy of an inch or so minute changes in the shape of the volcano. The results can be used to deduce the timing and severity of eruptions.*

F. A. Trusdell

PU'U'O'O ERUPTS ON THE SLOPES *of Kilauea. Researchers estimate that a total of about ½ cubic mile (2 cubic kilometers) of molten material has been ejected by Kilauea since its eruption began in 1983. Since then lava has spread over an area of about 39 square miles (100 square kilometers) and, flowing into the sea, added 295 acres (120 hectares) of new land to the island.*

Katia Krafft/Explorer/
Auscape International

A LAVA STREAM SPREADS ACROSS *a road near Kilauea. There is little choice but to abandon property and structures threatened by lava flows.*

➤ **RESEARCHERS KEEP WATCH** *through the night in their careful study of an eruption, timing its oscillations and measuring the height of the incandescent geyser.*

Speed was everything. Leaving behind most of the equipment, the team literally ran 500 feet (150 meters) down the cone to its base. At the bottom, the tremors they had felt earlier were even more noticeable. Slowly and cautiously they began to pick their way out of the rift zone. They had no way of knowing where lava might erupt next.

The rift zone of a volcano is a structural point of weakness on its flanks. Think of it as a small, hardened crust covering a lake of molten lava. The team knew that in an eruption of the magnitude they were expecting, lava can rise up anywhere in the rift zone.

Pu'u'O'o is located in the central portion of Kilauea's rift zone. The team had about 1 mile (1.5 kilometers) to walk to safety. The challenge they faced was to avoid any sudden bursts of lava into the rift zone and to keep away from the areas where the hardened lava crust had become thin and weak. No one wanted to think about what might happen if they made a careless step and broke through the crust.

They walked about 650 feet (200 meters). Suddenly the ground behind them unzipped. First a small crack appeared, then with surprising quickness the crack widened and lengthened. Luckily the other end of the crack spread away from the group.

The group stopped walking and stood still, spellbound. The side of the crack closest to them began to widen. Eventually a bluish-tinted smoke appeared from it. Shortly after that lava sputtered to the surface. Though it was time to get out, the team was reluctant to leave.

The scenario repeated itself over and over as the crack extended further and further away. At its maximum length, the fissure grew to be about ½ mile (800 meters) long. The spectacular curtain of fire that spread down its length reached 100 feet (30 meters) into the air.

This fissure was on the southwest side of Pu'u'O'o. Another very similar fissure opened up on the northeast side. The second fissure attained a length of about ¾ mile (1.2 kilometers) and also sent a curtain of fire 100 feet (30 meters) into the air.

Miraculously the team made it to safety. Eventually, the two curtains of fire localized into one eruptive center, and was named Kupaianaha. Over the next six years, Kupaianaha grew into a lava shield 180 feet (56 meters) high, erupted 19.5 billion cubic feet (550 million cubic meters) of lava, covered 15½ square miles (40 square kilometers) of land, and destroyed 165 homes and buildings. The property loss totals millions of dollars. The eruption still continues.

F. A. Trusdell

The Fire Goddess Pele

Hawaiians once believed that inside a volcano is a goddess whose name is Pele. She is just one member of the fire god family and she rules over lava flows.

According to Hawaiian mythology Pele arrived from a mythical land called Kahiki. When she first appeared in the islands, she landed on Kauai. Unsuccessful at establishing a permanent home there, she moved down the island chain establishing temporary residences on the other islands. Eventually, pleased with what she saw on the island of Hawaii, she decided to take up permanent residence there.

Interestingly enough, Pele's story parallels what we know about the geologic ages of the Hawaiian islands. Kauai, the oldest island in the chain and Pele's first home, is approximately 4 million years old. The newer islands, following Pele's restless movements as she searches for a permanent home, occur in a south-easterly direction. The newest island in the chain is the island of Hawaii itself. Of course, as it is Pele's permanent residence, Hawaii is the only island in the chain which has an active volcano.

PELE TODAY

There are some Hawaiians who still claim that if you are present during a volcanic eruption, or if you spend much time in and around volcanoes, you will see Pele.

Ironically, some of the people who recently have lost homes or property to the Kupaianaha lava shield speak of Pele in very bitter tones. Pele, they say, is showing her displeasure at the current state of affairs in and around Hawaii. But these are people who clearly know very little about volcanoes. For what they forget to take into consideration is that without Pele and her generous gift of lava, the land on which they live would not be there at all.

Even today Pele is worshipped in some places in Hawaii. Several different Hawaiian families claim to be descendants of the Pele clan and therefore by birthright the goddess's protectors. Undaunted by modern progress and ideas, they carry on many of the ancient rites and traditions that their ancestors associated with Pele.

Moreover, they frown upon any activity that can be construed to deplete or diminish Pele's liveliness. For example, Pele worshippers are very much against geothermal development, which would harness the volcano's heat to generate electricity. They argue that to take Pele's steam is essentially to steal her life blood. Without it, they say, Pele will wither and die.

HAWAIIAN FLORA AND FAUNA

Even the diversity and uniqueness of the flora and fauna found in the Hawaiian islands is attributed to Pele.

It is true that Hawaii's flora and fauna is even more diverse and unique than that found in the Galapagos islands. And in large part this is due to recurrent volcanic activity.

With the landscape being constantly paved over by lava, the forest develops a diverse mosaic of plants and insects. This in turn has spawned tiny microcosms allowing the further development of many unique species of plants and insects.

Hawaii Volcanoes National Park

D. H. HITCHCOCK'S PAINTING DEPICTS PELE, THE FIRE GODDESS, *who according to Hawaiian mythology roamed across the Hawaiian islands looking for a home. She finally selected Halemaumau ("house of the everlasting fire"), the crater at the summit of Kilauea, as a suitable abode.*

Katia Krafft/Explorer/Auscape International

PU'U'O'O ERUPTS. CONTINUING VOLCANIC ACTIVITY ON THE ISLAND *of Hawaii is taken by some Hawaiians as a sign of the presence of Pele.*

The Eruption Stages of Pu'u'O'o

Pu'u'O'o is a cone on the slopes of the Hawaiian volcano Kilauea. Eruptions on Pu'u'O'o follow a 25 day cycle.

During Stage 1, molten lava begins to accumulate in the magma chamber of Kilauea, and in the conduit leading to Pu'u'O'o's vent. Magma rises from the depths of the earth at a constant rate throughout the cycle. From days 7 to 20 the magma chamber gradually fills.

By day 20 the chamber is filled. It exerts pressure on the earth around it and earthquakes begin to occur. The tilt of the volcano's flanks increases due to pressure from

the magma chamber below, and Pu'u'O'o's vent is full. The older lava resists pressure from the newer lava behind it. It acts as an oscillating cork, blocking the opening.

By day 25 the pressure of the magma accumulating becomes so great that the "cork" is literally blown out of the vent and Pu'u'O'o erupts. A fire fountain carries molten rock hundreds of feet into the air. This reduces the magma chamber's contents and, with the pressure removed, the volcano's flanks revert to normal. The number of earthquakes decreases.

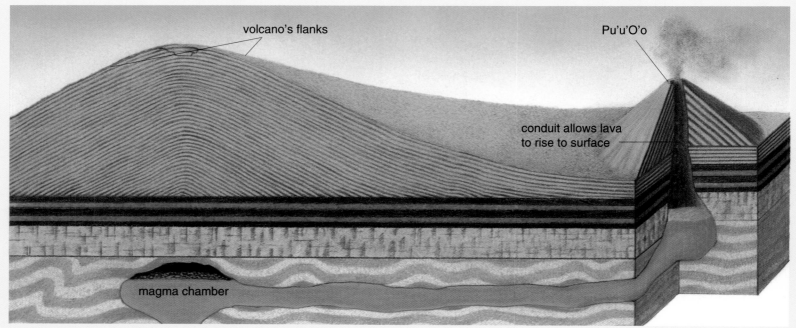

Stage 1 (days 0–7) The volcano accumulates magma.

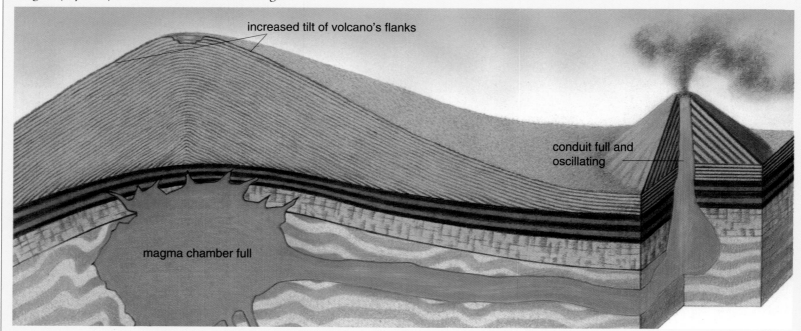

Stage 2 (days 20–25) The volcano's magma chamber is filled to capacity.

fire fountain

tilt of flanks reverts to Stage 1

level of magma reduced

Stage 3 (day 25) Pu'u'O'o erupts and the magma chamber deflates.

Katia Krafft/Auscape International

Tom and Pat Leeson/
Photo Researchers Inc.

AT 8:32 A.M. ON SUNDAY, *18 May 1980, Mount Saint Helens in the northwestern United States erupted in an awesome explosion that killed 61 people, blew apart the top 1,300 feet (400 meters) of the mountain, destroyed hundreds of square miles of forests, and caused at least $1 billion dollars worth of property damage.*

FOUR YEARS AFTER THE MOUNT *Saint Helens eruption, only fireweed relieves the stark desolation of the blast zone. Common across much of the northern hemisphere, the fireweed* Epilobium angustifolium *is often the first plant to colonise areas laid waste by fire or other disaster.*

M. Garcia

LAVA UNDER THE MICROSCOPE. *Microscopic examination and chemical analysis of lava samples yield valuable clues to the anatomy and behavior of an active volcano.*

THE LABORATORY

While there is no question that fieldwork is an important part of a geologist's life, it is not the only part. Once the work in the field is completed and geologists have collected their samples, they must go to the laboratory to investigate further. Here, using geochemical analytical techniques, geologists can study the samples they have brought back.

Consider the geologists who made up the team on Pu'u'O'o. When they returned with the few samples they were able to carry out, they wanted to know everything they could about these samples—what they were made of, how old they were, and many other questions as well. They hoped that the answers to these questions would help them to learn more about the volcano—how it evolved, what triggers an eruption, and whether eruptions can be predicted with more accuracy. They dreamed of unlocking some of the secrets of the fragile planet on which we live.

THIN SECTIONS

In the laboratory, after the lava samples have been catalogued, the first order of business is to cut the samples into slices $1/1000$ inch (25 micrometers) in thickness. This is so thin that light is easily able to pass through the sample, which is mounted on a glass slide and called a "thin section." To determine what minerals are present, the thin section is examined under a transmitted light microscope.

When a geologist looks at the thin section through a microscope, the orientation of individual mineral grains can be seen. These grains tell a story. They reveal the nature of the

lava flow, whether it erupted slowly or quickly, and the fluidity and gas content of the sample.

When light passes through the minerals under the microscope, the minerals are brilliantly colored. This contrasts with the dull appearance of the black-colored lavas in the field. The variation in colors is a function of the chemical composition of the minerals.

As various minerals and textures are identified, the geologist gets information about the composition of the parent magma and nature of emplacement of the lavas. For instance, lavas which display numerous large crystals are indicative of a slow ascent to the surface and/or a long storage period in a magma chamber.

GLASSY SAMPLE

Another section of the lava that geologists analyze is referred to as the "glassy" sample. This is a lava chip that is carefully cut out of the unweathered portion of the original sample. It is polished and mounted on a disk for analysis in an electron microprobe. Bombarding the sample with electrons emits radiation that accurately reveals the chemical composition of the lava.

Typical Hawaiian lavas, for example, are composed predominantly of silica, magnesium, iron, and calcium. Many past and present civilizations have settled near volcanoes, because the surrounding soils are rich in these types of chemical nutrients. Nutrient-rich lavas also explain why the lands surrounding an active volcano are able to regenerate life so quickly after an eruption.

The chemical composition of a lava provides clues about its genesis. For example, high magnesium lavas are indicative of primitive lavas derived from great depths within the earth. These lavas remain relatively unaltered and maintain high temperatures as they ascend to the surface. Chemical composition can also reveal the particular stages of the volcanic eruption. For example, high magnesium primitive lavas can be a sign of a new pulse of magma and a new eruptive phase.

SILICA CONTENT OF THE LAVA

Silica, another "indicator" element in lava, is directly related to the explosivity of a volcano. In general, the higher the silica content in a magma, the more explosive the volcano. This is because the strength of the silica enables magma pressure to build up until an explosion results. Vesuvius and Mount Saint Helens are examples of volcanoes with a high silica content in their lava. In contrast, low silica magmas tend to flow easily as liquids. The lava content of early Hawaiian volcanoes is relatively low in silica.

The degree of explosivity determines what the land looks like around a volcano. For instance, the early island-forming volcanoes of Hawaii were typically very fluid and non-explosive. The land mass around these volcanoes looks similar to a giant layer cake. But the lava of some of the later Hawaiian volcanoes has a higher silica content. The land mass around these volcanoes is cone-like. In contrast, volcanoes in New Zealand have a silica-rich lava and are highly explosive. Their violent eruptions obliterate the entire cone structure around them and leave only a lake or depression when the fireworks are finished.

FLUID INCLUSIONS

During the initial formation of the minerals found in lavas, small volumes of the parental magma called "fluid inclusions" are trapped in the growing mineral. These are like air bubbles in a freezer ice cube tray. They effectively "freeze in" the actual chemical composition of the magma as it occurred deep inside the earth in the magma chamber. Using laser and other electron/ion beam techniques to analyze these fluid inclusions, geologists are able to describe the parental source magma in the earth's interior.

But what is the earth's interior really like? Geochemists know that there are gases there. Yet as the gases find their way to the surface, they change. They interact with groundwater, the atmosphere, and other elements, altering their chemical composition.

But by vaporizing fluid inclusions in a vacuum and analyzing the released gases, geochemists have been able to re-create the gases as they exist in the earth's mantle. Typically the chemical composition of these gases is like carbonated water: mostly water, with a little carbon dioxide.

A WINDOW INTO GEOLOGIC HISTORY

Hawaiian volcanoes provide a window into geologic history. They tell us about the formation of the earth and our solar system. In chemical composition they are very similar to the moon. In studying these volcanoes geologists hope to contribute to the overall knowledge of volcanoes, and to provide useful information to those who live near them whose lives are threatened by their potentially lethal eruptions.✪

Types of Volcanoes

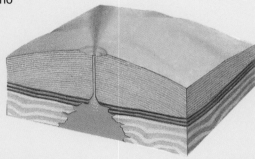

There are three types of volcanoes. Caldera volcanoes are the most explosive, then composite, with shield volcanoes the least explosive.

shield volcano

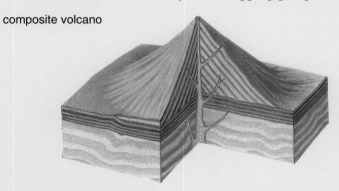

A shield volcano is built up from accumulated lava flows. The Hawaiian Islands are formed by an overlapping group of these.

composite volcano

A composite volcano is formed from layers of lava flows and other volcanic products (rocks, ash, and dust). Mount Saint Helens in the US and Mount Fuji in Japan are examples of composite volcanoes.

caldera volcano

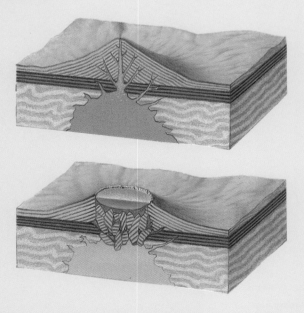

A caldera volcano is created by the collapse of the summit into the magma chamber after a violent eruption. A lake commonly forms in the caldera. Valles Caldera in New Mexico, in the US, is an example of this type of volcano.

ASTRONAUT ROBERT L.
*Stewart rides a lonely orbit high
above earth, the water planet, the
only home—as far as we know—of
all the life there is. High on the list
of NASA's priorities is its Mission
to Planet Earth, a detailed survey of
our own planet. Apart from scientific
research, a wide range of global
"housekeeping" chores, such as
weather-forecasting, mapping,
agricultural monitoring, and land-
use planning can be done most
effectively from the vantage point of
space. NASA's other goals include
preparations for the space station
Freedom, studies of the sun and
distant galaxies, and experiments
in advanced materials technology.*

➤ PROVIDING A SKIN CAPABLE
*of withstanding the furnace heat
of re-entry was one of the greatest
challenges confronting the space
shuttle's designers. Here a Cray-2
supercomputer models the shuttle's
heat-resistant characteristics.*

Astronauts of the Future

MAE C. JEMISON

At the Lyndon B. Johnson Space Center in Houston, Texas, a new generation of astronauts is being trained. Their missions are to study the earth, to experiment in space laboratories, to develop new materials, to launch and repair satellites, and to prepare a space station for human residence. Dr. Mae C. Jemison is the first woman of color in the world to go into space. In a laboratory that circled the earth for eight days, she tested human physiologic response to weightlessness, conducted experiments on animal reproduction and growth, as well as developing new techniques for the manufacture of semiconductors and other materials. These studies will be used one day to support a population living in outer space.

Dale K. Boyer/Stock Photos

NASA

GOBBLING FUEL AT AN AMAZING *rate, the space shuttle* **Atlantis,** *seen a few seconds into mission STS-45, on liftoff from Kennedy Space Center on March 24, 1992.*

➤ **THE ATLAS** MISSION CREW *gather on the flight deck of* **Atlantis** *for the traditional inflight group portrait: in front, Kathryn Sullivan, payload commander, and Charles Bolden, mission commander; behind (left to right), David Leestma, Brian Duffy (pilot), Byron Lichtenberg, Dirk Frimout, and Michael Foale.*

O n Tuesday, March 24, 1992, at the Kennedy Space Center, Florida, Commander Charles Bolden and his crew of six awaited ignition of the space shuttle *Atlantis'* three main engines and solid rocket boosters. More than 6 million pounds (2.75 million kilograms) of thrust—the equivalent of over 44 million horsepower—would carry them and their ATLAS laboratory into orbit. Their mission is dedicated to the study of the earth's atmosphere and the sun, and is part of the National Aeronautics and Space Administration (NASA) program Mission to Planet Earth.

THE ASTRONAUTS

The astronauts aboard had prepared for this mission during years of advance training in the simulator and test chambers of the NASA

Centers in Houston and Huntsville and scientific laboratories all around the world.

Atlantis' commander, a colonel in the United States Marine Corps, is a veteran space traveler. He is a test pilot who flew more than a hundred sorties in Vietnam. He and the flight crew of the mission, responsible for maintaining and piloting the shuttle in space and when landing, all have undergraduate degrees from military academies. In training and ability they harken back to the early days of NASA—the days of Mercury and Gemini, first of the moon flight programs.

The payload (cargo) commander is Dr. Kathryn Sullivan, the first US woman to walk in space. She is a geologist, who along with fellow career astronaut Mike Foale, a British born astrophysicist, will ensure as much scientific data as possible is collected. They are joined by payload specialists: a physicist from Belgium and a US biomedical engineer.

These astronauts represent a NASA space program that is in transition. NASA's goal in the early years—the early 1960s—was to prove that people could travel in space. After numerous space flights of satellites and space probes, NASA began human flights. The launch of Alan Shepard on May 5, 1961, proved that the United States was capable of putting a person in space. By 1969, when *Apollo 11* landed the first human beings on the moon, NASA's major goal had been accomplished. Now new goals are being set and human beings will take on a new role, as a space-faring species.

SCIENTISTS IN SPACE

Today's space shuttle program provides the opportunity to launch large crews into space to study an ever-widening range of phenomena: from the ozone layer to crystal growth, to pollution patterns, to animal and human adaptation to weightlessness. No longer exclusively the

An Experiment in Space

Space travel and stays of more than a few months will become more practical if methods can be found for producing food in the space environment. Growing plants and animals is one obvious means. Many look forward to the day we build colonies, live, and raise families in space. Producing food and raising families brings up the question of how the lack of gravity will affect reproduction and embryologic development. The NASA Ames Research Center in Mountain View, California, is attempting to find some of the answers to this question with the Frog Embryology Experiment (FEE). FEE was performed on the space shuttle *Endeavor* mission, Spacelab J, which was launched in fall 1992.

For years, biologists have noted that the eggs of frogs and other amphibians have a preferred orientation to gravity. The eggs, which have two distinctly colored hemispheres or halves, rotate after fertilization so that the dark or animal pole faces up. If this rotation is inhibited, the resultant embryos have mutations and generally do not develop into tadpoles.

On Spacelab J, a cooperative mission between Japan and the United States, astronauts studied the development of embryos and tadpoles of the African clawed frog (*Xenopus* sp.) in weightlessness. The experiment is the first to fertilize vertebrate eggs in space and follow the development to tadpoles. On the first day, four adult female frogs were injected with a hormone to cause ovulation. After fourteen to sixteen hours, when the frogs started shedding eggs, the eggs were harvested and fertilized with sperm. The eggs were preserved at various stages of development so that the earthbound investigators could evaluate the microscopic anatomy of the space conceived embryologic stages.

The astronauts also monitored the swimming behavior in orbit of earthborn tadpoles alongside spaceborn. The behavior of the live adult frogs and earthborn tadpoles was studied for changes following the space flight. Live spaceborn tadpoles were returned to earth and studied for their swimming behavior and will be allowed to grow to adulthood and reproduce.

BABIES MUST BE BORN IN SPACE IF HUMANKIND IS TO EVER THRIVE *there, but nothing is known of the effects of zero gravity on animal reproduction, embryology, or growth. The African clawed frog has played a key role in a study of the development of embryos and tadpoles in space.*

Jane Burton/Bruce Coleman Limited

NASA/B.Bauer/Explorer/Auscape International

NASA

ON JUNE 3,1965, *GEMINI 4*
pilot Edward H. White II became
the first American to maneuver freely
in space, duplicating the Russian
cosmonaut Aleksey Leonov's pion-
eering feat of three months earlier.

NASA'S APOLLO PROJECT HAD
only one aim—to put a man on the
moon and bring him safely back.
Here astronaut John Young salutes
the flag during mission Apollo 16
in 1972, fifth of six successful US
landings on the moon.

domain of test pilots and an occasional scientist, shuttle crews now include mission specialists whose backgrounds are in science and engineering and payload specialists with expertise specific to the experiments to be conducted on board. They include astronomers, physicians, pilots, schoolteachers, geologists, and senators. They come from different nations—Japan, Italy, England, Switzerland, Saudi Arabia, Germany—and represent different races and cultures.

NASA's four reusable space shuttles can carry their crews into orbit around the earth for more than two weeks. The astronauts may release satellites into earth orbit where they may continue circling the earth for tens of years. Or they may launch space probes to the planets. Satellites can be retrieved, repaired, and re-deployed from the shuttle's cargo bay. Or entire space shuttle missions, like Spacelab J, may be dedicated to scientific and medical experiments.

NASA TODAY

The cornerstones of the present space program include Mission to Planet Earth, which uses space as an observation platform for viewing the earth. From the space shuttle, astronauts can check the earth's atmosphere and weather, land masses, and geologic formations like volcanoes and earthquake fault zones. The oceans can be observed for biologic activity of plankton and the effects of pollution.

Then there is the program for the construction of space station *Freedom* which aims to have a permanent crew on board by 1998. Once *Freedom* is built, an international crew is initially scheduled to remain in space for ninety days.

The Life Sciences programs test the laws of biologic nature in space. Astronauts research the growth of and adaptation to weightlessness of plants and animals and humans. When the space shuttle *Endeavor* launched Spacelab J, Jemison and other astronauts tested techniques, including biofeedback, for keeping the human body healthy.

To explore the laws of the universe, the Great Observatories programs use instruments such as the Hubble telescope. By taking pictures of the stars at the edges of the universe, these instruments may one day reveal the potential for life in other places. And by studying the data from telescopes collecting gamma rays and x-rays in space, physicists may find answers to how the universe was formed.

The Materials Development programs include research into the techniques to manufacture semiconductor chips, ceramics, plastics, and foams in the weightlessness of space. It also tests basic principles of material engineering without gravity problems. Each country participating in space exploration is looking for commercial applications for the technological advancements made in space flights.

The term "spinoff" is used by NASA to describe an earthbound use for technology that was originally designed solely for space science. Magnetic resonance imaging was developed from computer algorithms designed to analyze data from the *Landsat* satellite's space photographs of planetary mountain ranges. Satellites which were designed to collect data on atmospheric conditions now can be used to follow the trails of migrating whales and elephants. From the need for miniaturized equipment in space came the heart pacers. Systems that are now commonly used in hospitals for monitoring patient responses were originally developed for astronauts. Digestible toothpaste was developed because in the weightlessness of space astronauts cannot "swish and spit." And from the visual scanners used for processing satellite images come new specially designed goggle-eyeglasses that provide a greater visual field for people with limited vision.

TELECOMMUNICATIONS

Yet it is through communication satellites that space exploration has had its most profound effect. Communication satellites have changed our perception of the world. They have en-

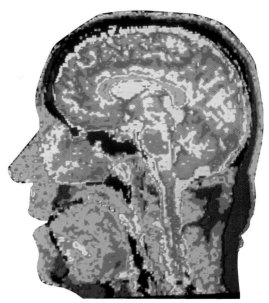

Science Photo Library/The Photo Library, Sydney

hanced the ability to transmit information from one country to another. So now what happens in China and South Africa becomes the staple of the United States evening news. Conversely, what happens in the US is transmitted to other nations around the world. The people of this planet have come to see the world more and more as a global village.

Space exploration and satellites allow us to more accurately forecast weather. We can clear threatened areas prior to the onslaught of hurricanes. We can monitor the adherence to arms control treaties with satellites. We can watch pollution as it crosses the borders of countries. And we can see the changes that result from dam constructions and the dumping of garbage in the shipping lanes of our oceans.

Space exploration has been invaluable in focusing our attention on our responsibility for

NASA/Science Photo Library/The Photo Library, Sydney

NASA/Science Photo Library/The Photo Library, Sydney

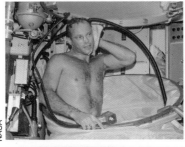

NASA

NASA

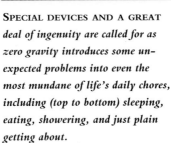

NASA

SPECIAL DEVICES AND A GREAT deal of ingenuity are called for as zero gravity introduces some unexpected problems into even the most mundane of life's daily chores, including (top to bottom) sleeping, eating, showering, and just plain getting about.

NASA

A DISTANT GALAXY, NGC 6946, lies conveniently face-on to earth, laid out for our scrutiny. This open spiral nebula can be seen much more clearly from space than from earth.

RAINFOREST IN WESTERN BRAZIL
photographed by Landsat's *thematic
mapping image cameras in 1988.
Virgin rainforest shows red; "slash
and burn" clearing shows blue.*

ALL ONE WORLD, WITH NO
*national boundaries visible: a view
of earth beyond a lunar landscape.*

the world and its future. It is now clear that
though the earth has an abundance of resources
and seems to have eternal life, it can be made
into a toxic wasteland.

As the space probe *Voyager* traveled through
the solar system photographing planets such as
Saturn, the diversity of the universe in which we
live made itself known. Knowledge of our
fellow planets can be used to better care for the
planet on which we live and depend for our
sustenance. When the *Apollo* crews visited the
moon, they saw the earth as a shining sphere
with a thin, gentle layer of blue as our shared
atmosphere. When looking back at the earth,
all the astronauts say they see no boundaries.

Although they can recognize geography and
geologic formations, they cannot differentiate
countries. There does not seem to be a need.

All the crews of the space shuttles report a
deterioration of the planet. They note each year
that Lake Chad in Saharan Africa is shrinking.
They view the burning rainforests of South
America, the burning mangroves of Africa.
They also report how the brilliant lights of
civilization outline the continents, especially the
industrialized nations. These city lights represent
an enormous use of energy, some efficient and
cleanly produced, but most from nonrenewable
resources and highly polluting fossil fuels.

ASTRONAUTS OF THE FUTURE

Many of the astronauts of the future are already
with us today. Some of them are current members of the astronaut corps who are in their
thirties, often the age of astronauts first accepted
in the program; they will become the veteran
space explorers of tomorrow.

Some of the astronauts of the future are
children in school who attentively follow the
progress of each and every space launch. They
will astound us with their exploits in the
twenty-first century.

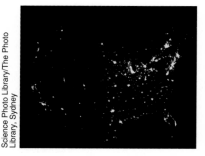

THE NIGHT-TIME CITY LIGHTS OF
the UnitedStates as seen from space.

THE *VOYAGER* PROBES
*successfully completed a twelve-year
mission to photograph all the outer
planets, except Pluto, and their
satellites. Launched in 1977, and
now in deep space, the* Voyager
*bristles with antennae, sensors,
and cameras.*

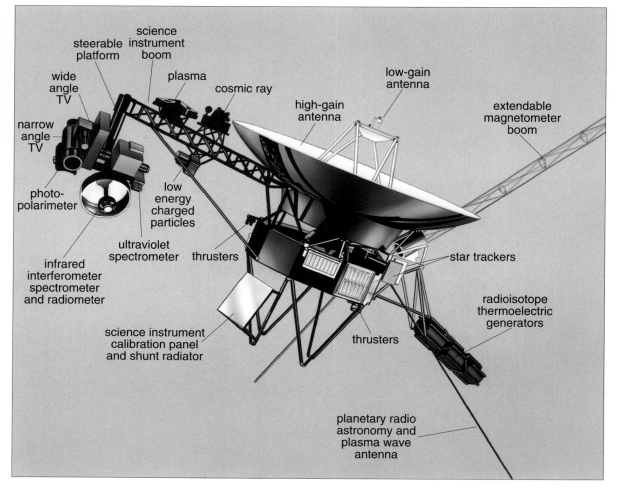

science
steerable instrument
platform   boom
wide
angle   plasma
TV   cosmic ray
narrow
angle
TV
photo-
polarimeter
low
energy
charged
particles
ultraviolet
spectrometer   thrusters
infrared
interferometer
spectrometer
and radiometer
science instrument
calibration panel
and shunt radiator
low-gain
antenna
high-gain
antenna
extendable
magnetometer
boom
star trackers
thrusters
radioisotope
thermoelectric
generators
planetary radio
astronomy and
plasma wave
antenna

Spacelab

NASA

Spacelab is the first purpose-built space laboratory. Fully integrated with the space shuttle, it amounts to a container built to conform to the shuttle's cargo bay dimensions. With a maximum permitted weight of 32,000 pounds (14,500 kilograms), the unit may take any one of three configurations: module only, module plus pallet, or pallet only. The module is fully pressurized to allow personnel to work within it. When off-duty, they live in the shuttle itself. Almost any experiment that will fit within the weight and volume restraints can be catered for. Standard items of equipment include a controlled-environment bay for computers and other sensitive equipment, and a sophisticated Instrument Pointing System (IPS). Other systems include power, communications, data links, and control links with the shuttle's flight deck.

ONCE IN ORBIT, THE SPACE SHUTTLE'S CARGO DOORS ARE LEFT OPEN *to allow surplus heat to radiate away. Over 60 feet (20 meters) long and crammed with tons of hi-tech gear, the payload space allows a variety of experiments, exploiting the conditions of no heat, no air, and no gravity.*

A truly international enterprise, Spacelab was developed by the European Space Agency for use by any of its member states or—under appropriate arrangement—any other scientific or technological body. Developed during the 1970s, it was first launched aboard *Columbia* on November 28, 1983, on a proving mission lasting 10 days.

Spacelab's greatest contribution lies in its flexibility. Designed for up to fifty flights, its reusability means that the equipment or experimental apparatus it carries can be redesigned or modified as needed back on earth for return to space on a subsequent flights.

A New Type of Astronaut

MAE JEMISON IN TRAINING TO REALIZE A DREAM THAT BEGAN WHEN SHE *was a child in Chicago, daydreaming of space travel.*

AN ASTRONAUT'S BACKGROUND

Although scientific discovery colored her childhood dreams, Mae Jemison may not have what people think of as a typical astronaut's background. She is a dancer trained in ballet, modern, jazz, Brazilian, and African dance. She has studied several foreign languages including Russian, Swahili, and Japanese, and her penchant for art is expressed in block and silk screen printing. Yet when she graduated from Stanford University in 1977, with degrees in African Studies and Chemical Engineering, she still knew she would apply to the astronaut program. But there were other roads to travel first.

There was Cornell Medical School and work in Kenya with the Flying Doctors and in Thailand at a Cambodian refugee camp. And then the Peace Corps in Sierra Leone and Liberia, West Africa, where she was the Area Medical Officer. Although her work experiences in the isolated health care environment of developing countries did not seem applicable to space exploration, she found that many of the qualities she developed during her work in these countries—resourcefulness, responsibility, the ability to work in a team of individuals with disparate skills, and self-motivation—were just the characteristics for which the astronaut selection committee was looking.

THE ASTRONAUT PROGRAM

When Mae Jemison finally did apply to be an astronaut, she was among 2,000 other qualified applicants. The selection process then winnowed her to one of 100

applicants brought to the Johnson Space Center in Houston, Texas, for interviews and physical examinations. Applicants spent one week learning about the astronaut program and having NASA learn about them. All applicants were poked and prodded to be sure there were no significant abnormalities of the gastrointestinal tract, brain, heart, eyes, skeletal musculature, sinuses, and psyche. The highlight of that NASA week was having John Young, whom she had watched in the Gemini and Apollo programs as a child, on her interview board.

Once she was accepted to the program, she had a new journey before her, and a new occupation. Her primary role would change from taking care of patients to learning and training for the world of the astronaut. The two women and thirteen men in the 1987 Astronaut Candidate class began a training curriculum that taught them about supersonic vehicles that fly at twenty-five times the speed of sound, about portable life support systems able to withstand the vacuum and thermal extremes of space, and about survival training that included lifesaving parachuting skills and water survival techniques. For all NASA's astronauts, training for space survival and for upcoming missions is a continuous process.

Dr. Jemison had entered an astronaut program that had undergone fundamental changes since she had seen her first space launch. Civilians and scientists were a growing part of NASA programs. There were international missions. There were routine missions devoted to scientific discovery. Dr. Mae Jemison was to be among them, one of the class of astronauts likely to work and live on the Space Station *Freedom*. One of the astronauts of the future.

DR. JEMISON'S BACKGROUND HELPED LAY A BASE OF *resourcefulness, responsibility, and teamwork.*

To define the astronauts who will travel to space in the next ten, twenty, or thirty years, is to define the direction of space exploration today. The space program is geared to making travel into space and the exploitation of its resources commonplace. Building a space station with people permanently aboard, returning to the moon and establishing a moon base, and journeying to Mars are national goals. Industrial facilities in space will manufacture semiconductors to make computer chips that are far superior to those that can be produced here on earth. Space research will capitalize on zero gravity to study animal development and solve fundamental problems in physics. Scientists working on board the space station *Freedom* will design alternative, on-the-spot experiments to resolve newly raised questions. The crew members will look at the earth and will be able to make minute-to-minute weather forecasts as they view an entire hemisphere. Space will continue to represent our dreams and aspirations, and those who venture into space will be representative of all humanity.

Astronauts of the future will be scientists and specialists. They will come from a wide range of disciplines. They will be construction workers who will build the facilities of the moon's Tranquility base. They will be generalists who maintain the facilities on the moon and Mars. They will be the individuals who travel to

Tony Stone Worldwide/The Photo Library, Sydney

space and heighten the experiences of the earth-bound by bringing back pictures, poetry, and stories of what it is like to be surrounded by the red dust of a Martian windstorm. They will be geologists who study the planets and then, like cosmologic physicians, offer a prescription to maintain the health of the earth.

Perhaps the dreams of the astronauts of the future can best be summed up by seven-year-old Apolinar Jimenez of Dallas who wrote:

"I am ready to fly to the sky to see the stars. For every star that I would count, I would put it in my pockets. When my pockets are full, I would bring them to the earth. I would give every child a star to make a wish." ✪

EQUIPPED WITH A REMOTE *manipulator arm, the space shuttle was designed to carry out a variety of tasks in space, such as repairing, retrieving, or redeploying malfunctioning satellites like this one.*

NASA

AN ARTIST'S CONCEPT OF A *proposed lunar habitat module designed to house a dozen people living and working on the moon's surface for extended periods. Energy, mineral resources, and specialized industrial facilities are likely to be the first "hard" benefits of space exploration. The establishment of a permanent lunar base is seen as a vital first step in achieving this.*

Space Station *Freedom*

Alan Chinchar/NASA

NASA has studied the feasibility of setting up a space station since the 1960s, especially following the success of the impressive Russian *Salyut* and *Mir* space stations. However, it was not until 1984 that NASA was committed to such a project and the concept of *Freedom* was born. *Freedom* is being developed with the active participation of Japan, Canada, and the European Space Agency.

The original plans called for five modules: a command unit, a living unit for six to eight crew, two laboratory units, and a storage module, all arranged along a girder 400 feet (122 meters) in length. The total assembly would weigh around 250,000 pounds (113,400 kilograms). The major design aims were to provide facilities for conducting research, servicing satellites, and preparing other craft for deep space missions.

Now much modified by budgetary constraints, *Freedom* has a planned service life of thirty years. Assembly will begin in 1995, for completion in 1998, at a total cost of about 30 billion dollars.

FACILITATING A RANGE OF SCIENTIFIC AND TECHNOLOGICAL ACTIVITIES, Freedom*'s design provides for US, European, and Japanese laboratory modules as well as a habitation module for its crew. Three sets of solar arrays provide more than 65 kilowatts of electrical power.*

AN ARTIST'S CONCEPT OF NASA'S PROPOSED SPACE STATION FREEDOM *in its permanently manned configuration, scheduled for completion late in 1998. Looming symbolically close, images of the moon and Mars underline the station's importance as a vital stepping stone to a permanent lunar base and to the landing of astronauts on Mars.*

MOST GARBAGE CURRENTLY GOES to landfills, like this one in Florida, but everywhere these are overflowing, and new sites are hard to find. Ironically, some of these sites are by far the largest objects ever built by humans. If not properly managed, landfills can attract scavengers such as birds and rodents.

➤ ONE PERSON'S TYPICAL street litter is merely an eyesore. But multiplied by that from millions of other urban dwellers and added to all the rest of our domestic, commercial and industrial garbage, the result is one of the most intractable problems of our age.

Eric Meola/The Image Bank

Where Does Our Garbage Go?

M A R T I N   V .   M E L O S I

I n his book *Garbage in the Cities*, Martin Melosi noted that historians generally concede that *laissez-faire* capitalism began in the late eighteenth century with the mass migration of European populations to cities. Ironically, historians also can point to this period as the beginning of "municipal socialism." For it was the Industrial Revolution that forced cities, for the first time since antiquity, to shoulder responsibility for such duties as public safety and sanitation. Currently Dr. Melosi is a professor of history at the University of Houston and one of the world's acknowledged experts on the debris and rubble that civilizations leave in their wake.

Jenny Mills

Dick Kraus/Newsday

NEW YORK'S GARBAGE PROBLEM *is so critical that much of its refuse must be exported. But few destinations will accept it. The refuse barge* **Mobro** *shown here is a notorious example of one such cargo that was rejected by five states and three countries before the* **Mobro** *was finally forced to return to its home port of New York with its cargo still undischarged.*

A NEW YORK STREET SCENE *from the 1950s shows that municipal authorities have wrestled with the litter problem for decades.*

Philadelphia is the fourth-largest city in the United States. It boasts a population of over three million people and a history so rich that historians often refer to it as the birthplace of American democracy. It has a world-class philharmonic orchestra. It has museums renowned for their treasures and art. It has great universities, restaurants, theaters, and bookstores. In short, Philadelphia has many of the amenities that we have come to expect of a modern metropolis at the end of the twentieth century.

But Philadelphia, like New York, Rome, London, Paris, and the other great cities of this century, also has something else—a serious garbage problem. To put it in the simplest terms, Philadelphians create more waste and garbage than they know what to do with.

THE STRANGE VOYAGE OF THE *KHIAN SEA*
Probably the most telling example of Philadelphia's garbage predicament is the 1987 voyage of the *Khian Sea*. The saga of this voyage begins with the stench and ugliness of an ever-growing mountain of ash residue piled near Philadelphia's main incinerator. It united in common cause the citizens of Philadelphia, who sued to have it removed. The only question that remained was what to do with the ash.

New Jersey, the next state over, didn't want it. Neither did Virginia or Ohio, where residents formed a human chain to block trucks carrying the ash. So, having failed in this method of disposal, the citizens of Philadelphia settled on another method. They loaded the ash, 14,000 tons (12,700 tonnes) of it, into the hold of a seventeen-year-old freighter, the *Khian Sea*.

The Bahamas was the *Khian Sea*'s first port of call. Its cargo was rejected straightaway. The next stop was Panama. There, environmental activists informed the authorities that the ash contained dioxin, a known carcinogen. Again the freighter was asked to leave. The next stop was Haiti where the military oligarchy agreed to let the *Khian Sea* dump the ash on a beach near the port of Gonaïves. Haitian dock workers, who were to unload the ash, were told that it was fertilizer. This might have worked, had activists not stepped in once again and told the dock workers what it was they were unloading. Again the *Khian Sea* was forced to leave with its cargo (lightened by several tons) largely intact.

Thus it was that in late 1987 and throughout much of 1988 the *Khian Sea* made many voyages across the Caribbean, and sailed to Africa, on into the Indian Ocean, to Sri Lanka, and finally to Singapore. During the course of

hunter-gatherer stage, people simply moved too often and too quickly for garbage to be much of a problem. It wasn't until humans began abandoning their nomadic life for more permanent settlements that they began to think about what to do with the material they were discarding. Even then their first thoughts could be described only as rudimentary.

In the ancient city of Troy, for example, garbage was simply thrown out into the streets or left in the house on the floor. When the stench became unbearable, or the mess in the home caused people to stumble, the garbage was covered with fresh layers of dirt. The earthen floors in the homes of the Trojans literally rose underneath their feet. When the level reached the point where it prevented the people of Troy from opening their doors, they came up with another solution. They simply sawed off the bottoms of the doors. Eventually, as layer upon layer of dirt was built over their garbage, it was inevitable that the ceilings would close in on them. When this happened, the Trojans hit upon another strikingly simple solution. They raised their roofs. When Troy

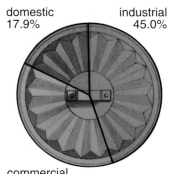

domestic 17.9%   industrial 45.0%

commercial 37.1%

INDUSTRIAL WASTE CONTRIBUTES *nearly half to the overall garbage total. Shops, restaurants, offices, and other commercial enterprises contribute just over a third, while the remainder comes from the ordinary family home.*

the *Khian Sea*'s lengthy and seemingly aimless odyssey, it was sold several times to new owners and renamed twice. The freighter's last owner alerted officials in Philadelphia that the freighter's cargo had been discharged. Philadelphians were advised: "Owners will not reveal location." It is widely believed that the ash was dumped somewhere in the Indian Ocean.

This is not the only example of such a problem. There is a similar story about a garbage barge by the name of *Mobro* that left Islip, New York, also in 1987. Five states and three countries banned the *Mobro* from unloading its unwanted cargo. Eventually its captain was forced to return to New York, the *Mobro*'s home port, where there, too, was no room for the *Mobro*'s cargo.

Picture an old vessel set to sail in the open ocean, laden with the filth and waste of a modern city. Wherever it goes it finds itself notorious. Its cargo is unwanted. Its captain and crew have nowhere to hide it. Is there a better metaphor for garbage in the twentieth century?

GARBAGE IN THE ANCIENT WORLD

Garbage was not always the problem that it is today. Before 10,000 B.C., when human populations were relatively small and still in a

IN THE NEWLY INDUSTRIALIZED *world of the nineteenth century many people made their living scavenging in refuse dumps for materials to resell and reuse, as shown in this print published in 1836.*

MUNICIPAL GARBAGE REMOVAL *services began in North American cities in the latter part of the nineteenth century. Here a horse-drawn cart and a clean-up crew work their way through the streets of New York in the 1890s.*

STRAY DOGS AND CATS STILL *scavenge in street litter bins and garbage cans, but in earlier times the list of common animal scavengers included kites, chickens, pigs, and other wild and domestic livestock. This pig was photographed in the streets of New York in 1896.*

WELL INTO THE NINETEENTH *century in most places, raw sewage, litter, and garbage of all kinds were left in the street to rot, constituting an ideal breeding ground for such dread diseases as cholera. This threat was widely recognized even at the time, as the title of this print, "A Court for King Cholera", indicates. It shows London slums in 1852.*

a plebeian foreman and a horde of riffraff newly arrived from the provinces. It was almost a daily sight in Rome to see burly men in tunics and leather aprons walking next to horse-drawn wagons collecting the city's refuse to take it to dumps outside the city boundaries. As Rome made its influence felt across Europe, it was natural that its population would increase. During the heyday of the empire the daily accumulation of refuse and waste in Rome

became such a problem that all over the city signs were posted which read: "Take your refuse further out or you will be fined."

From time to time in the ancient world, some cultures grasped the importance of finding solutions to the waste problem. Ancient Babylon had an effective sewage system. Chinese records from the second century B.C. note that forces of "sanitary police" were responsible for collecting and removing dead animals, while "traffic police" were responsible for sweeping the streets. Similar advances could be found in Egypt, Crete, and Jerusalem.

THE INDUSTRIAL REVOLUTION

With the decline of Rome's power, Europe no longer had a center. And Europeans no longer had an incentive to travel. By and large they stayed at home, isolated in small towns and cities that were surrounded by acres of countryside. In this setting garbage was not the problem it had been in a great cosmopolitan city such as Rome.

So it is not surprising to find that it wasn't until the end of the nineteenth century that cities once again would feel a responsibility to

produced refuse in one year "equal in volume [to] a cube about one-eighth of a mile on an edge. This surprising volume is over three times that of the Great Pyramid of Giza, and would accommodate one hundred and forty Washington monuments with ease."

CHANGING PATTERNS

Throughout the nineteenth and most of the twentieth centuries, garbage was collected from within cities and taken to sites outside the city limits to be dumped. These dump sites are the forerunners of modern-day landfills.

But this method of collecting and disposing of garbage only accounts for garbage produced by modern cities. It fails to take into account a whole range of garbage—the industrial wastes generated by the great manufacturing plants and factories of the nineteenth and twentieth centuries. Until very recently the traditional method of disposing of this waste was either to dump it into rivers and lakes or to burn it off into the air. In fact, even today in many parts of the world, these are the primary methods of disposing of industrial waste.

G. A. TRAVER'S DRAWING FROM *about 1890 illustrates one method of garbage disposal in vogue during the late nineteenth century: using tugs to tow barge-loads of rubbish out to sea for dumping.*

collect the garbage of their citizens. This is important because it illustrates a simple but very telling point: an increase in garbage is directly proportional to an increase in population density. The more people you have, the more there is to discard. The Industrial Revolution drew the population from the country into cities, which grew at enormous rates.

Soon cities, which by twentieth-century standards had been scarcely more than country villages a generation before, teemed with people. These citizens produced mounds of garbage, and the municipal fathers were forced to contend with this. And so we see what had not been seen since the time of Rome in its heyday—the systematic collection of garbage.

But things are never quite as simple as they seem. The Industrial Revolution was fed by new technologies. As technologies matured and still newer technologies developed, there was demand for more sophisticated raw materials, which resulted in ever more sophisticated garbage.

Coal mines left hills of slag. Factories spewed out smoke and polluted the air. By 1912 one writer noted that New York City alone

We Discard Each Year

These are the approximate quantities discarded annually by the average family in the United States.

640 cans of food and drink

8 trees worth of paper

430 glass bottles and jars

400 pounds (180 kilograms) of plastics

In the United States, especially since the Second World War, we have made enormous progress in understanding the content of our garbage and the implications it has. While the discards of our grandparents' and great-grandparents' times were largely food wastes, wood and coal ash, rubbish, and horse manure, our discards today are much more complex and often far more lethal to the environment.

Today our own garbage, or "solid waste," is a mixture of paper, plastics, cans, food discards, rags, leaves, wood and yard trimmings, glass, dead animals, abandoned cars, and sewage. Paper makes up the largest share of what we throw away, taking up at least half the space of all landfills. Of all current discarded items, paper, plastics, and aluminum have grown the most steadily. The use of these materials reflects a substantial increase in packaging waste and a wide variety of additional uses for paper in what some people call our "throw-away" society.

LANDFILLS

Landfills, incineration, ocean dumping, recycling, and source reduction—these are the basic methods of dealing with garbage.

Of all the problems associated with waste disposal in recent times, none raises the cry of "garbage crisis" like the issue of shrinking landfill sites. This perceived lack of landfill space is becoming an important issue in many regions of the world, which do not care to make room for the garbage of populations who live hundreds and even thousands of miles from them. Compounding this lack of space is perhaps an even greater problem. The nature of our garbage has changed along with the nature of our world. Today many of the items we discard are toxic. Other items tend to survive largely intact, not just for decades, but for centuries. Perfectly readable newspapers, for example, have been unearthed after thirty years inside a landfill. So constructing a landfill site today is nothing like it was for the Romans two thousand years ago. Building a landfill now is creating a product of science and high technology.

Modern sanitary landfills originated in Great Britain in the 1920s. American versions were first attempted in the 1930s in New York City and Fresno, California. Through the 1950s and 1960s engineers and solid waste managers believed that sanitary landfilling was the most economical form of disposal and also offered a method which reclaimed land.

CRUSHED INTO SQUARE BALES *for efficient transport, aluminum drink cans are easily recycled. Recycling an old aluminum drink can uses much less than a tenth of the total electrical energy needed in starting from scratch with bauxite.*

Steve Niedorf/The Image Bank

WMX Technologies, Inc.

By the 1970s some experts began to question whether sanitary landfills could serve the future needs of cities without other alternatives being required. They questioned the serviceability of sanitary landfills because some of these dump sites do not live up to their name. When not operated properly, they can become havens for birds, insects, rodents, and other animals that can spread diseases to humans. If not properly lined with clay or plastic, they threaten groundwater and surface water, especially through the leaching of rainwater, melted snow, and other liquids which have seeped through the waste. Other concerns relating to landfills include the production of methane gas from the decomposition of organic wastes that are dumped in the landfills. Methane gas is flammable and can explode when mixed with a certain amount of oxygen, thereby raising a safety concern.

IN THE DAILY ROUTINE OF *modern landfill management, incoming dump trucks spread their loads of garbage, which are then compacted by heavy tractors (here one is just barely in view behind the trucks) to crush air spaces and reduce volume. A scraper (left) then covers the area with a 6 inch (15 centimeter) layer of soil to suppress odor and discourage vermin. The surrounding grassed areas control erosion and also absorb rainfall.*

Getting Rid of Garbage

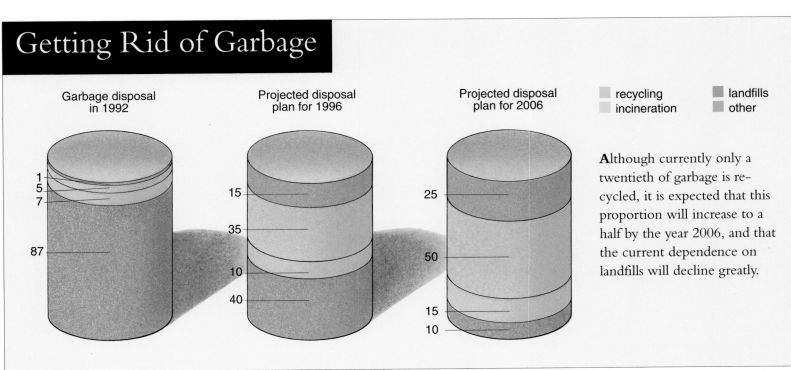

Garbage disposal in 1992

1
5
7

87

Projected disposal plan for 1996

15

35

10

40

Projected disposal plan for 2006

25

50

15
10

■ recycling   ■ landfills
■ incineration   ■ other

Although currently only a twentieth of garbage is recycled, it is expected that this proportion will increase to a half by the year 2006, and that the current dependence on landfills will decline greatly.

215

Trash to Energy

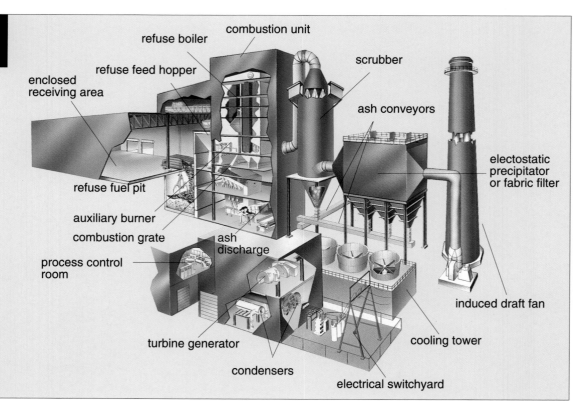

combustion unit
refuse boiler
scrubber
refuse feed hopper
ash conveyors
enclosed receiving area
electostatic precipitator or fabric filter
refuse fuel pit
auxiliary burner
combustion grate
ash discharge
process control room
induced draft fan
turbine generator
cooling tower
condensers
electrical switchyard

Trash-to-energy systems across the US process thousands of tons of garbage each day, and produce hundreds of megawatts of electric power. In this system the garbage is transferred by crane to the feed hopper of the combustion unit. A boiler above the combustion grate area produces superheated steam which drives a turbine generator, producing electricity. The electro-static precipitator thoroughly cleans the furnace emissions.

GARBAGE REMOVAL BY *incineration was widespread until the development of the sanitary landfill in the 1920s and 1930s. Here a mobile incinerator operates in the streets of Chicago in the 1890s.*

Mary Evans Picture Library

Statistics paint a gloomy picture of the phasing out of sanitary landfills. Approximately half the United States' 6,000 landfills have less than five years of life left and cities that have relied on them do not know where the next facilities will be.

INCINERATION

Incineration poses equally demanding chal-lenges, if only because we have become so aware of the air we breathe and how vulnerable it is to the pollutants we put into it.

The first "cremators" were built in the United States in 1885. These cremators were actually large vats in which wet garbage and

➤ AIR POLLUTION PRODUCED BY *industrial furnaces of all kinds is a serious problem. When garbage is burnt special precautions must be taken to filter the furnace emissions.*

dead animals were stewed to produce grease and residuum. The grease was sold for use in the manufacture of soap, candles, perfume, and lubricants; the residuum was sold for fertilizer. These plants, however, emitted strong odors and run-off. By the 1920s they were shut down. Incinerators, as waste burners, made a brief comeback in the 1930s. But they were no match for the enthusiasm for landfills. It wasn't until the 1970s and the "energy crisis" that incinerators returned with new status as "resource recovery plants."

Two types of incinerators operate today. The first type is a "mass burn" unit that can devour up to 1,000 tons (900 tonnes) of waste per day, or more depending on design. The second type, a "waste to energy" unit, burns waste as fuel to generate steam and electricity. Both types reduce the volume of garbage by as much as 90 percent. In the future approximately a quarter of American and European garbage will be treated by some incineration method.

Beyond their enormous expense, the prob-lem with incinerators is the emissions from the plant stacks and the ash itself. Studies of ash samples trapped in the incinerators' air pollution control devices show toxic levels of lead and cadmium. In addition, carcinogenic dioxin is formed when chlorine compounds in plastic, bleached paper, table salt, and other materials are burned. Fear of their airborne health hazards make incinerators as unwelcome as any landfill.

Recycling Paper

Like glass and aluminum, paper is easily recycled, though printing ink and other dyes are difficult to remove and so limit the usefulness of the recycled product. Also, the strength of paper depends largely on the length of the fibers in the pulp from which it is made, and the average fiber length is inevitably decreased each time the material is recycled.

Waste paper is digested in pulper.

Pulp is washed to remove impurities.

Brightener is added.

continuous papermaking machine

Paper is despatched.

Paper is machine rolled onto reels.

Paper is flash dried and pressed.

Steam heated rollers dry the material.

WMX Technologies, Inc.

A COLLECTION TRUCK RETURNS *to a recycling center in the United States. It dumps a load of plastic onto the open floor of a materials recovery facility for subsequent inspection and sorting.*

WMX Technologies, Inc.

SORTING AT THE SOURCE IS A *key factor in effective recycling programs. Here the operator of a Recycle America truck works his suburban round, sorting aluminum, plastic, and glass into separate compartments in his vehicle as he empties each household bin.*

RECYCLING AND SOURCE REDUCTION

While recycling has emerged as an alternative to more traditional disposal methods, there are still many problems with recycling that need to be resolved. For example, what incentives should be used to get householders, businesses, haulers, and manufacturers to participate? Are mandatory recycling laws workable? And the biggest question of all: can markets be found for the ever-increasing volume of recyclables?

Before 1980 fewer than 140 communities in the United States had door-to-door recycling collection services. By 1989 more than 10,000 recycling centers were in operation. In the United States the Environmental Protection Agency called for a national recycling goal of 25 percent by 1992. Some communities claimed rates surpassing the 25 percent standard, but overall it was not met. Nevertheless recycling is gaining broad appeal because it conserves virgin materials and creates less pollution.

Source reduction also aims at conserving raw materials and creating less pollution. It can be thought of as a kind of preventive measure which seeks to reduce the amount of garbage we need to dispose of by reducing the amount of garbage we generate. For example, bulk distribution of large-volume items like motor oil, soap, and toxic or industrial materials falls within the category of source reduction. Also, reducing the use of some plastics would eliminate the problem of toxic byproducts from incineration.

Source reduction and recycling both hold out hope for the future. However today these methods are largely untried and immature. How we develop them depends largely on our willingness to work together.

INTO THE FUTURE

In some respects, the best we can do is to manage the garbage problem more effectively, rather than assuming that we can "solve" it. There will always be waste of some type. Con-

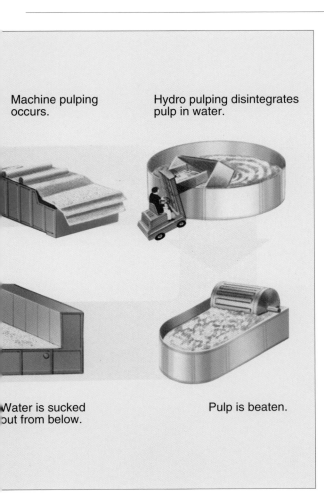

Machine pulping occurs.

Hydro pulping disintegrates pulp in water.

Water is sucked out from below.

Pulp is beaten.

fronting the problem requires cooperation from everyone. Consumers must shop wisely, selecting products and packaging that do not place an unnecessary burden on the waste stream. People can participate in one or several recycling programs in their communities. Producers of goods should also be good consumers of materials used in their businesses, and should manufacture products which take into account recyclability.

Providers of collection and disposal services need to consider the environmental implications of their decisions alongside questions of cost and efficiency. Government entities must provide a climate that protects the interests of all parties, while helping to set environmental priorities. If the community acts together, the solid waste problem need not reach crisis proportions.

One thing is certain. As we find our planet shrinking and as the idea of a global village becomes real for more and more of us, are we going to find more efficient, more productive ways of taking care of our garbage? Or are we one day going to look at our cities sprawled over our crowded little planet, and think, "Mud hovels, with their dunghills ... around them"? ✪

Bill Varie/The Image Bank

GLASS IS THE ULTIMATE *recyclable, and can be used over and over again without limit. Glass of different colors must be segregated because the dyes often used to color glass cannot be removed.*

COMPOSTING IS THE IDEAL MEANS *of handling the organic component in domestic and commercial garbage. Here a front-end loader is used to load yard waste into a tub grinder, which shreds the material to a standard consistency as the first step in the composting process.*

WMX Technologies, Inc.

Waste in the Community

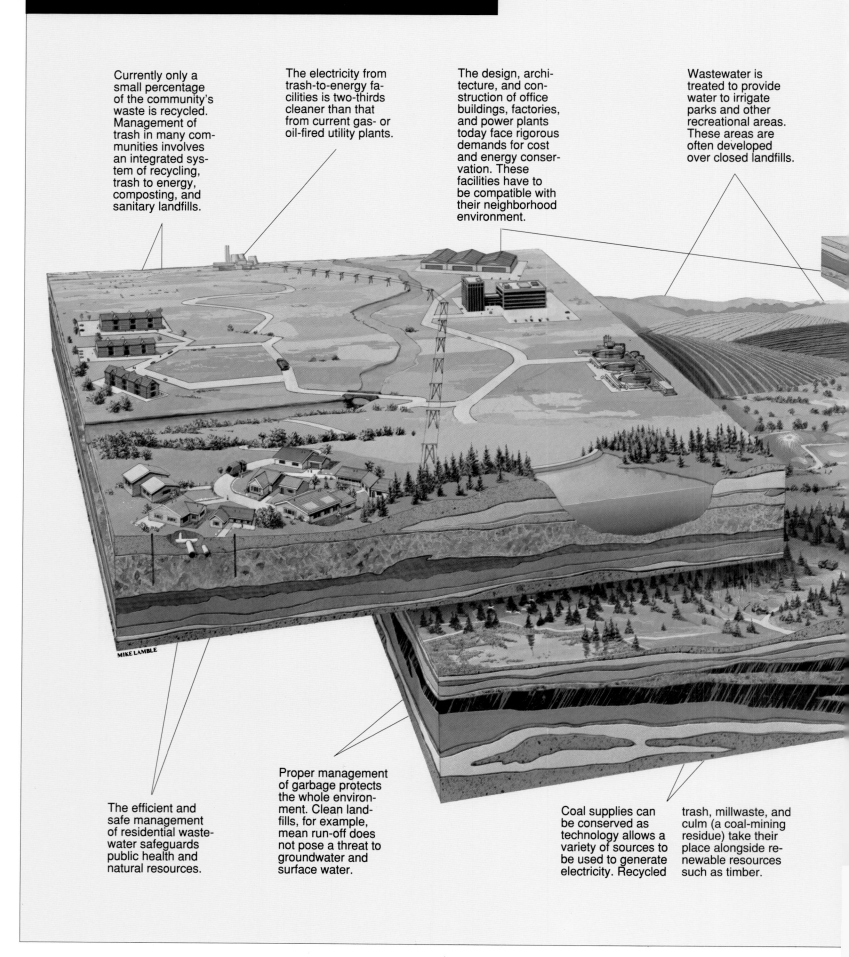

Currently only a small percentage of the community's waste is recycled. Management of trash in many communities involves an integrated system of recycling, trash to energy, composting, and sanitary landfills.

The electricity from trash-to-energy facilities is two-thirds cleaner than that from current gas- or oil-fired utility plants.

The design, architecture, and construction of office buildings, factories, and power plants today face rigorous demands for cost and energy conservation. These facilities have to be compatible with their neighborhood environment.

Wastewater is treated to provide water to irrigate parks and other recreational areas. These areas are often developed over closed landfills.

MIKE LAMBLE

The efficient and safe management of residential wastewater safeguards public health and natural resources.

Proper management of garbage protects the whole environment. Clean landfills, for example, mean run-off does not pose a threat to groundwater and surface water.

Coal supplies can be conserved as technology allows a variety of sources to be used to generate electricity. Recycled

trash, millwaste, and culm (a coal-mining residue) take their place alongside renewable resources such as timber.

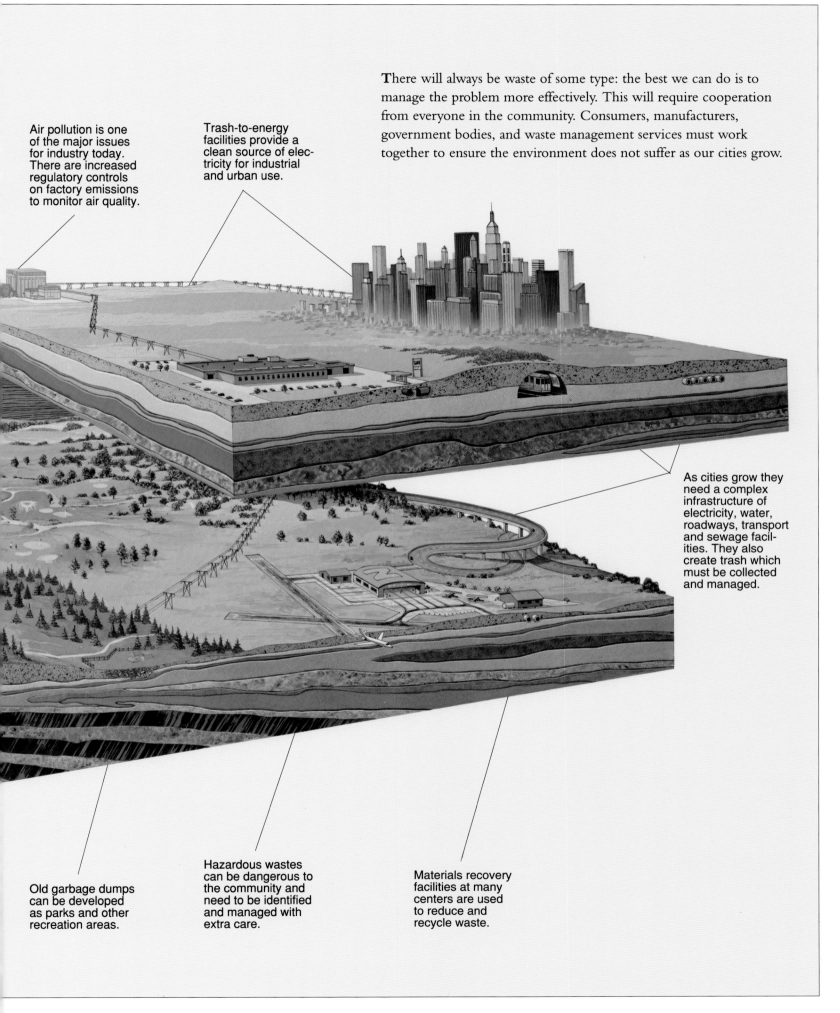

Air pollution is one of the major issues for industry today. There are increased regulatory controls on factory emissions to monitor air quality.

Trash-to-energy facilities provide a clean source of electricity for industrial and urban use.

There will always be waste of some type: the best we can do is to manage the problem more effectively. This will require cooperation from everyone in the community. Consumers, manufacturers, government bodies, and waste management services must work together to ensure the environment does not suffer as our cities grow.

As cities grow they need a complex infrastructure of electricity, water, roadways, transport and sewage facilities. They also create trash which must be collected and managed.

Old garbage dumps can be developed as parks and other recreation areas.

Hazardous wastes can be dangerous to the community and need to be identified and managed with extra care.

Materials recovery facilities at many centers are used to reduce and recycle waste.

221

VIBRANT WITH MALIGNANT HUES, *a heavily polluted river flows from an industrial site. Clean water is among the most vital of requirements for all life on earth. Yet since the dawn of the Industrial Revolution the world's waterways have been viewed as convenient drains for the dumping of unwanted materials of all kinds, many of them highly toxic. An innovative program now seeks to remedy this problem at its very source: community attitudes imparted to school students.*

> DRUMS OF INDUSTRIAL WASTE *symbolize the fact that disposal technology has lagged far behind other areas of industrial expertise. Many processes result in chemicals so toxic that there is no known way to dispose of them safely, leaving storage as the only alternative.*

Monitoring Rivers

WILLIAM B. STAPP

When scientists look for evidence of life on other planets the first thing they look for is water. Without water, life as we know it could not exist. It is one of the earth's most precious resources. Yet almost everywhere increasing amounts of organic waste and industrial pollutants threaten the planet's water supply. To fight this threat Dr. William Stapp is attempting to organize elementary and high school students around the world into a network of water monitors. The goal of this ambitious project is not only to improve water quality throughout the world but also to teach children about science and the immediate bearing it has on their lives.

Robbi Newman/The Image Bank

Water precedes life. According to the Bible, before there was light, before there was night and day, before there was dry land, before there was grass and herbs and yielding seed, there was water. This is not just an ancient religious belief, modern evolutionary science postulates that life began in water in the form of a single cell organism.

Ingrained in modern science is the principle that water is an essential ingredient of all life. From the least complex, single cell organism to all the so-called higher organisms, all forms of life require water.

WATER AND HISTORY

In a narrowly focused perspective, water means the difference between life and death for an individual organism. Yet this also is true in the larger sweep of things, where water determines life and death for whole civilizations. Consider the history of the ancient city of Sumer.

In the second half of the fifth millennium the Sumerians built huts in marshes alongside the lower Euphrates. Like their northern neighbors, the Sumerians were basically farmers. In their new land they planted date palms and herbs, and farmed barley and other grains.

But the enterprising and imaginative Sumerians grew tired of depending on rains or the unpredictable flooding of the Euphrates for water for their crops. They had the imagination to see that before life would get any easier they had to acquire a reliable source of water to sustain them through times of drought. So they built a series of dikes and canals to store water. In

the process they transformed a flat land of brown dust and mud into one of milk and grain.

Having gained a reliable source of water, the Sumerians found food plentiful and could devote themselves to activities other than farming. Not only did these remarkable people end up building what many historians argue was the world's first great civilization, they also made one of the greatest contributions to the advancement of civilization: the invention of writing.

The lesson of the ancient city of Sumer is that it could not have evolved without a reliable source of water. Moreover, this has been true for every civilization and city state since. It is an unvarying and immutable law of nature that when water is scarce, food is scarce, and an economy suffers. No country, however sophisticated its culture and technology, is exempt.

In ancient times city states were built along the banks of rivers. In more recent times, with improvements in technology for acquiring and storing water, countries and cultures have not been so dependent on a single source of water. Yet even today 85 percent of the people in the world live along rivers and waterways.

AN AERIAL VIEW OF THE TEMPLES *at Abu-Simbel, Egypt. The builders of these impressive monuments, inhabitants of a land where it seldom rains, forged one of humankind's most enduring civilizations, which prospered for three millennia. Yet these people and all their works were utterly dependent on a single source of water, the River Nile.*

MANY PEOPLE TODAY STILL *obtain their water for domestic use directly from rivers and other waterways such as this Bangkok klong.*

SOME LEVEL OF POLLUTION *from industrial, commercial, or domestic sources now degrades virtually every important waterway on earth, and very few rivers retain the pristine qualities of this foaming torrent in New Zealand's Fiordland.*

◄ LAKE WENATCHEE, *Washington, shows the natural beauty of large expanses of clean water. Such waterways can be of great recreational value.*

AIR AND WATER POLLUTION ARE *intertwined: the toxic fumes from these smouldering drums of chemicals in a Taiwanese dump may well be washed immediately back to earth in the next shower of rain, the resulting run-off adding to the toxic burden of nearby rivers and streams.*

William B. Stapp

THREATS TO THE WORLD'S WATER SUPPLY

Knowing that water is one of the earth's most precious resources makes it all the harder to understand why today we are allowing organic and industrial pollution to threaten this supply on a global scale. Perhaps the answer lies in the fact that until very recently remarkably few of us actually appreciated how fragile and small is the planet we all share. It only has been in the last decades that we have been able to see the earth as a closed system run by radiant energy from the sun. Viewed in this perspective one readily sees that packed into the earth's structural design are all the resources we shall ever have.

The other part of this new perspective on the earth's design is that the planet is also smaller than most of us once imagined. We are only beginning to appreciate that when it comes to using the earth's resources, actions in one part of the globe frequently affect people who live in another part. For an example we need to look

Michael Melford/The Image Bank

SWATHED FROM TOP TO TOE IN *protective gear, a worker inspects a toxic chemical dump in New Jersey in the United States.*

UNSIGHTLY FROTH BETRAYS *serious detergent pollution. At least until the emergence of the now familiar "biodegradable" label on our laundry liquids, detergents were a major source of severe pollution in many waterways.*

David Sutherland/The Photo Library, Sydney

Pete Turner/The Image Bank

no further than acid rain. Industrial pollutants discharged into the air affect areas hundreds, even thousands, of miles from where they were originally released.

The sad truth is that human beings have developed both an economic system and a technology to go with it that consumes vast amounts of resources while creating rapid environmental changes and overloading the environment with wastes. The earth's limited resources are threatened as they have never before been threatened. Most earth scientists and environmentalists agree that if something isn't done to remedy this situation, we could end up inflicting irreparable injury on the limited resources our planet offers us. Moreover, in the process of destroying these resources we are also sure to destroy ourselves.

Every day the world's water supply is becoming more and more contaminated. Today in the Third World people with waterborne disease occupy four out of every five hospital beds.

Jenny Mills

THE GANGES RIVER BANK AT THE *sacred city of Varanasi, or Benares, has been fashioned into stairs, called ghats, of great religious significance. At burial ghats, the ashes of the dead are scattered on the waters to ensure a favorable reincarnation, while at bathing ghats pilgrims wash to gain spiritual purification. This latter practice, however, exposes them to the risk of waterborne diseases.*

FLUSHED FROM STORM SEWER *systems during heavy rain, street litter pollutes many city waterways in what seems the ultimate insult.*

Acid Rain

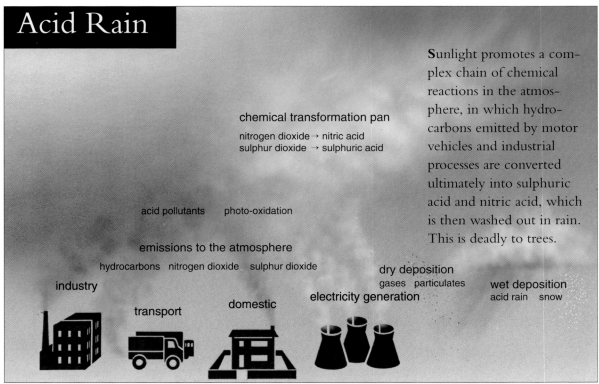

chemical transformation pan

nitrogen dioxide → nitric acid
sulphur dioxide → sulphuric acid

acid pollutants   photo-oxidation

emissions to the atmosphere

hydrocarbons   nitrogen dioxide   sulphur dioxide

industry

transport

domestic

electricity generation

dry deposition

gases   particulates

wet deposition

acid rain   snow

Sunlight promotes a complex chain of chemical reactions in the atmosphere, in which hydrocarbons emitted by motor vehicles and industrial processes are converted ultimately into sulphuric acid and nitric acid, which is then washed out in rain. This is deadly to trees.

Stephen Studd/The Photo Library, Sydney

ACID RAIN HAS IMPORTANT *political and diplomatic ramifications, because the forests it injures are often located far beyond the national boundaries of its source.*

227

Tony Stone Worldwide/The Photo Library, Sydney

HEADQUARTERS FOR THE "BIG Three" American car manufacturers (Ford, Chrysler, and General Motors), Detroit has been a major industrial center for more than a century. Before recent vigorous attempts at clean-up, the Rouge River flowing through Detroit was badly polluted.

THE MAP SHOWS THE ROUGE River watershed and its tributaries. The colored circles identify the points at which Dr. Stapp's student monitors tested the water quality.

THE ROUGE RIVER

The Rouge River is a 126 mile (203 kilometer) long waterway that runs through Michigan's Great Lakes Basin. Its route follows what often is called the "cradle of industry" in the United States. Past schoolyards and underneath bridges, through housing projects and around office buildings, the Rouge flows directly into the heart of Detroit where it joins the Detroit

River. Approximately 1.5 million people live within its urban watershed.

Yet for all its importance, in 1985 the heavily industrialized lower Rouge resembled a concrete-lined open sewer. Decades of industrial pollution and neglect had left it polluted and smelling bad. The International Joint Commission (IJC), an independent agency jointly supported by the US and Canadian governments, identified it as the worst of 43 hotspots in the Great Lakes Basin.

Soon after the Commission published its report, a non-profit citizens group was formed to study the Rouge and develop ideas to save it. These "Friends of the Rouge" learned of a nearby water quality monitoring project that had begun in 1984 on the Huron River. This project was the product of the creative imagination of new explorers at the University of Michigan's School of Natural Resources.

Reflections on the Rouge River Project

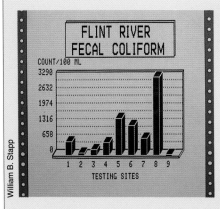

William B. Stapp

PREPARED BY STUDENTS, A *computer printout shows fluctuations in disease-carrying potential of polluted water at one site in the Rouge River drainage.*

The Rouge River Project is based on the principle that public attitudes must change for environmental action to be effective, and that the best place to work on changing attitudes is in the schools. Not only an innovative way to monitor water quality, the Rouge River Project is also an attempt to transform the way we see the environment.

REDEFINING THE CLASSROOM

Teachers are traditionally conveyers of accumulated knowledge from a curriculum which is based in text-books and lectures.

The new curriculum that Dr. Stapp and his colleagues proposed sought to alter this. In Dr. Stapp's classroom a teacher's first and most significant function was to involve students in the learning process. By leading the students in discussions and by encouraging them to immerse themselves in the issues they were confronting, the teacher can transform students into active learners. The premise here is that students can only truly understand what they learn for themselves.

IMPACT OF COMPUTERS

Once students had grappled with issues and raised fundamental questions, it was time for them to compare their ideas with the ideas of others. Here they benefited from textbooks and papers that dealt with similar issues. This written material gave students the opportunity to test their own ideas against the ideas of experts.

Yet for Dr. Stapp this was not enough. The Rouge River Project also sought to extend the physical boundaries of the classroom in other ways as well. Dr. Stapp wanted to link together diverse schools and communities and to involve them all in the same discussion. Computers made this possible. In the Rouge River Project these machines were more than just tools for storing and analyzing data. They provided an electronic forum in which students could raise questions, make observations, and share ideas. The Rouge River Project was the first educational endeavor in the nation involving computer conferencing for scientific, environment-related matters.

In the computer network, divisions based upon class and race were blurred because students were interacting through print on a screen and out of a common concern for the Rouge River. Moreover, computer conferencing softened the traditional power structures, which often depend on nonverbal, subconscious aspects of communication, such as impressive offices, layers of screening by subordinates, or commanding body language. The common ground of Rouge River Project's computer network helped foster independence, equality, and cooperation among students.

William B. Stapp

A TEACHER COACHES A YOUNG STUDENT IN PROPER WATER *sampling techniques.*

229

ONE OF THE MAJOR CAUSES OF *water pollution is the dumping of waste into drains which then discharge into natural waterways.*

DEVELOPING ENVIRONMENTAL ACTIONS

At the School of Natural Resources and Environment Dr. William Stapp and his colleagues recognized that humans, almost unawares, had developed the potential to destroy the fragile, limited natural resources of their environment. According to Dr. Stapp, we are in the process of doing exactly this. The only thing that will save us is strong environmental action.

Strong environmental actions, however, depend on finding some way to change our attitude towards the planet on which we live and the precious resources that make life possible. But psychologists tell us that attitudes are generally formed early in life and can only be changed with great difficulty. Thus Dr. Stapp saw that the foundation for strong environmental actions rested in the environments where our attitudes are first formed and developed—namely, in our homes, schools, youth programs, churches, communities, and media.

Clearly we have to pay considerably more attention to environmental problems such as water and air pollution, urban decay, indiscriminate use and disposal of hazardous material, housing problems, health issues, and the lack of institutional arrangements needed to cope with these issues. And clearly, according to Dr. Stapp, the place to begin doing this is in our schools.

A STUDENT GROUP SAMPLES *water quality. Water quality tests are easily carried out by anyone with a minimum of simple equipment after a few days of instruction, and high school students also benefit from the resulting sense of direct participation in matters of science and technology.*

EDUCATING CHILDREN

In 1984, realizing that it was time to try out their theories, Dr. Stapp and his colleagues began to develop what has become one of the most innovative environmental programs in the world today: the Interactive Rouge River Water Quality Monitoring Program. The program had a modest start in a high school science class at Huron High School in Ann Arbor, Michigan. Huron High School was chosen because it was near Gallup Park on the Huron River, and because students windsurfed from Gallup Park and jumped from its bridges. Over the years windsurfers from Huron High School had reported ear infections and diarrhea, and at least one had fallen ill with hepatitis A.

Initially Dr. Stapp's program had two goals. The first was to teach students about science and their environment, and the process of solving environmental problems. The second was to set up a watershed

DAY FIVE OF DR. STAPP'S TWO-week training course is devoted to on-site sampling after several days of practice in the classroom. Results are then analyzed, followed by brainstorming sessions to isolate problems and explore solutions.

Student Sampling Parameters	• Dissolved oxygen • Fecal coliform • pH • BOD • Temperature • Total phosphorus • Nitrates • Turbidity • Total solids

POLLUTION EXPERTS ARE AGREED that a useful concept, called the Water Quality Index, can be calculated from the results of testing for the nine basic variables listed.

WATER QUALITY ADVISORY
DUE TO STORM WATER RUN-OFF FROM RECENT RAINS, BACTERIA LEVELS IN THE WATER HERE EXCEED STATE WATER QUALITY STANDARDS.
FULL BODY CONTACT IS NOT RECOMMENDED.

AFTER TESTING FOR POLLUTION, the next step is the posting of warning signs to indicate problem spots, then brainstorming and consultation in search of solutions.

monitoring program designed to improve water quality in their immediate area.

Through such a program Dr. Stapp hoped to break out of the traditional role that calls for the student to sit passively in front of a teacher and take notes. Instead he wanted to involve them in the learning process itself. By having students directly monitor the quality of local water, he sought to develop in them a vigorous appreciation for scientific method, for collecting accurate data and analyzing it, for thinking critically, for testing their assumptions, and trusting the results of their own thinking.

Dr. Stapp's program had other even more ambitious goals. He also wanted to teach the students about the importance of cooperating amongst themselves and to show them the results they could achieve by doing so. He wanted the program to show students that by working together, by respecting each others' ideas and needs, by taking into account the ecological, economic, social, technological, and political

issues of their communities, they could bring about useful and important changes.

Dr. Stapp began by teaching science classes how to perform the nine water quality tests that constitute the National Sanitation Foundation's Water Quality Index. Students learned how to safely and accurately test for dissolved oxygen, fecal coliform, pH, biochemical oxygen demand, temperature, nitrates, total phosphates, turbidity, and total solids.

These tests became the data that the student monitors collected and analyzed. Eventually, as the results of their testing began to accumulate, students began to suspect that storm sewers upriver from Gallup Park were the primary source of the fecal coliform bacteria which they were finding in the river where they wind-surfed. When they were sure that they had confirmed this hypothesis, they started a letter campaign to the local newspaper, to the City Council, to the County Health Department, and to anyone else in authority.

Kathleen O'Donnell/Stockphotos/The Image Bank

THE PURELY ESTHETIC resources embodied in clean rivers have been too long neglected. There seems no good reason why all waterways should not flow as pure and clean as this stream in the Great Smoky Mountains National Park in the United States.

William B. Stapp

DURING THE TRAINING PROGRAM, students learn to use the techniques of water testing.

William B. Stapp

THESE THREE KENYAN STUDENTS running tests on their local water source are part of the Global Rivers Environmental Education Network.

STUDENT WATER QUALITY MONITORS

Hearing of this unusual program at Huron High School in Ann Arbor, the Friends of the Rouge asked Dr. Stapp to set up a similar program for their high schools in Detroit.

Dr. Stapp began the Rouge River Project with 16 high schools. By the end of the second year the number of schools participating in the program had doubled. And by the end of 1992 about 55 high schools were participants.

The program is short—it takes only two weeks to complete. The first day is devoted to orientation. Students discuss what the program is about, look at maps of the areas in which they will be testing, watch videotapes of these areas, and in general learn what they can of the area's history. Days two through four are devoted to practicing the skills required for water testing. On day five the students travel to the monitoring site and perform the tests. On day six students convert the raw data into a single number—a Water Quality Index (WQI)—that represents the water quality of the site they visited the day before.

On days seven and eight students upload the data they have collected onto a computer network that links all the schools participating in the project. At the same time students download data from the other schools. Day nine is devoted to brainstorming about possible water quality problems as reflected in the data. And days ten

and eleven are spent clarifying problems that students want to know more about. These are some of the questions students raise. Who are the appropriate people to ask for more information? What government agencies should be informed of the problems with water quality that the students may have found? And what kind of action strategies can the students develop?

ROUGE RIVER STUDENT CONGRESS

On May 14, 1988, the first Rouge Student Congress was held at Martin Luther King Jr. High School in Detroit. Nearly 270 students, teachers, water resource professionals, and university resource people participated. It was a rare opportunity for students and teachers from very different backgrounds to meet in search of solutions to a common problem—the loss of the Rouge River.

Students from 32 schools formed working groups to discuss water quality data at their sites. In these discussions they identified many problems, shared observations and opinions about land use, and even came up with specific recommendations for solving shared problems along a particular river branch.

EXPANDING THE DREAM

Will this small planet of fragile, limited resources survive? As shocking as it may seem, to many earth scientists and environmentalists the answer to this question is doubtful. At the moment, if strong environmental actions aren't taken, it seems that we are headed for extinction.

But how do we know what specific environmental actions are required of us? And once we find out, how can we convince ourselves and others to deal with them?

On a small scale the Rouge River Project was a start. It demonstrated that at a grass roots level there are resources to make environmental changes. Recruiting local students from different backgrounds and cultures, the Rouge River Project taught these students to monitor the quality of water in their own neighborhoods. By giving them access to computers it taught them to share what they had learned. It showed them how to join in collective action in a student congress. And finally it taught students the greatest of all lessons: that they themselves had the power to transform their environment.

But Dr. Stapp and his colleagues never intended their work to end with a small river in Michigan's Great Lakes Basin. They shared a much larger vision. They were designing a model for an environmental action program that could be carried out on a global scale.

In the winter of 1989 they took the next step towards achieving this dream. Sponsoring twenty-two workshops on five continents they expanded the Rouge River Project into GREEN—the Global Rivers Environmental Education Network.

The idea of inviting schools to incorporate water studies into their curricula was greeted with remarkable enthusiasm. In just three years GREEN has attracted members from 130 nations. In regions all over the globe—from Africa, Asia, Europe, South America, the Middle East, to North America and Oceania—high school teachers are recruiting tens of thousands of students to monitor water quality.

As the program enters the international arena other components have been added. Students now also test for heavy metals. They use EcoNet, a computer network that spans the globe. Researchers are developing international, cross-cultural partner programs. And they are extending the program into other areas of the school curricula.

If the future depends on our finding some way to change our attitudes towards the planet on which we live and the precious resources that make life possible, then this future rests with programs like GREEN.☮

oceans 97%

freshwater 3%

icecaps and glaciers 79%

groundwater 20%

easily accessible surface freshwater 1%

lakes 52%

soil moisture 38%

atmospheric water vapor 8%

water within living organisms 1%

rivers 1%

William B. Stapp

OF THE GLOBAL WATER SUPPLY, only about one ten-thousandth flows in rivers and streams at any one time. Most lies in the oceans or is locked up in the polar ice caps.

Global Rivers Environmental Education Network

Red Global de Educación Ecológica de los Rios

IN THE FIRST THREE YEARS AFTER its inception in 1989, GREEN had attracted members from 130 countries, and now involves tens of thousands of high school students worldwide.

FROM A MODEST START, THE student network first established to involve local communities in the search for solutions to pollution in a minor waterway in the central United States has now achieved encouraging success and a global membership. Here a group of Japanese students is being taught to apply the same techniques to their own waterways at Minamata, Japan.

William B. Stapp

The Contributors

GEORGE ARCHIBALD
Dr. Archibald completed his Ph.D. in ornithology at Cornell University. In 1971 he met Ron Sauey and together they established a foundation dedicated to the study and preservation of cranes, the International Crane Foundation. One of Dr. Archibald's first achievements was the discovery of red-crowned cranes nesting on Hokkaido, and the subsequent campaign to protect them. He has received many awards recognizing his important contributions in the field of international conservation diplomacy.

RANDALL L. BRILL
Dr. Brill has worked with marine mammals for twenty years. He has written a number of popular and technical articles, twice served as President of the International Marine Animal Trainers Association, and chaired the Marine Mammal Interest Group. At the Brookfield Zoo (Chicago Zoological Park) near Chicago, Dr. Brill coordinated marine mammal training, research, and education. It was there that he conducted his doctoral research, which demonstrated important aspects of dolphin echolocation processes. He is currently a scientist in the United States Navy's marine mammal program.

LEONARD J. CERULLO
Dr. Cerullo received his medical degree from Jefferson Medical College. He served his residency in neurosurgery at Northwestern Medical School and was awarded a Master of Science degree in surgery. With the opening of the Chicago NeuroSurgical Center at Colombus Hospital in 1987, he realized his dream of creating a center of excellence in the field of neurosurgery. Dr. Cerullo has been at the forefront of neurosurgical advances that have increased the odds for recovery. The application of high technology in neurosurgery has been his abiding interest.

CHRISTOPHER JOHN CHIAVERINA
Chris Chiaverina holds an M.S.Ed. in physics from Northern Illinois University and has taught physics on the secondary school level for twenty-three years. He is co-founder of the Science Place, an interactive science museum in Barrington, Illinois. In addition, he has written ten articles on physics education, is co-author of three textbooks, and is a member of the editorial board of *The Physics Teacher* magazine. Chiaverina is involved in the organization of the annual Six Flags Great America's "Physics Day," an event that encourages over 13,000 physics students to explore the laws of physics. He is currently physics teacher at New Trier High School in Winnetka, Illinois.

BETSY L. DRESSER
Dr. Dresser is Director of Research at the Center for Reproduction of Endangered Wildlife at the Cincinnati Zoo and Botanical Garden, the research program she founded in 1981. Dr. Dresser is Research Associate Professor in the Department of Obstetrics/Gynecology at the University of Cincinnati College of Medicine. Her specific research involves artificial insemination, embryo transfer and micromanipulation, *in vitro* fertilization, and gamete cryopreservation with wildlife species. She has written many scientific publications. Dr. Dresser holds a K.S. and Ph.D. in Animal Reproductive Physiology.

JOHN W. FITZPATRICK
Dr. Fitzpatrick received his Ph.D. from Princeton University in 1978. From 1974 through 1988 he was Curator of Birds and Chairman of the Department of Zoology at the Field Museum of Natural History, Chicago. He has discovered and described seven new bird species and is co-authoring a book on the ecology and conservation of tropical American birds. He received the William Brewster Award of the American Ornithologists' Union in 1985 for his work with Dr. Glen Woolfenden. In 1988 he became Executive Director of Archbold Biological Station in Florida and maintains an adjunct position at the Field Museum. He has written over sixty scientific publications.

STEVEN P. FRENCH
Dr. French first became interested in grizzly bears by treating victims of grizzly bear attacks. Combining his curiosity about grizzly–human relationships with his scientific background in engineering and medicine, he embarked upon a long-term study of grizzly bear behavior in the Yellowstone ecosystem in 1983, and is co-founder of the Yellowstone Grizzly Foundation. He has since expanded his studies into the areas of hibernation physiology and the use of molecular genetics to investigate social dynamics and genetic diversity. Dr. French is an Adjunct Assistant Professor at Montana State University.

MARILYNN GIBBS-FRENCH
Marilynn Gibbs-French has spent the past ten years studying grizzly bear behavior in the Yellowstone ecosystem. As the co-founder of the Yellowstone Grizzly Foundation she has pursued grizzly bear conservation by combining her research findings with a vigorous education program. She lectures widely across the United States. She received the Department of Interior's Take Pride in America Award in 1987, and in 1991 she received the Department of Agriculture's Regional Forester's Award. Gibbs-French is a member of the IUCN-SSC Bear Specialists Group and is working on a book about her research.

JAMES W. GRIER
Dr. Grier has been a professor at North Dakota State University since 1973, teaching courses in general zoology, animal behavior, animal population dynamics, herpetology, and research principles. His main research areas are eagles and other birds of prey, animal populations, computer modeling, and biostatistics. He has worked with bald eagles since 1959 and was the first person to successfully breed eagles in captivity using artificial insemination. He is team leader for the Northern States Bald Eagle Recovery Team. Dr. Grier has over eighty publications in scientific, technical, and popular media. He has presented numerous seminars and talks at schools, universities, and institutions.

JAMES L. HICKS
Dr. Hicks has been a physics teacher at Barrington High School in Illinois for the past twenty-seven years. In 1980 he received the Outstanding Educator Award given by the *Chicago Tribune*; in 1985 he won the Kohl Educational Foundation Award for Exemplary Teaching; and in 1991 the Illinois Section of the American Association of Physics Teachers named him Outstanding Physics Teacher (state of Illinois). He has conducted numerous workshops in physics education for elementary, secondary, and college curricula.

MAE C. JEMISON
Dr. Jemison's background includes engineering and medical research. She has worked on many projects, including the evaluation of printed wiring board materials, magnetic disk production, computer programming, schistosomiasis, hepatitis B vaccine, and nuclear magnetic resonance spectroscopy. She served as the Area Peace Corps Medical Officer in Sierra Leone and Liberia for two and a half years. In 1980

she worked in Kao-I-Dang Cambodian Refugee Camp in Thailand. In 1992 she was the first Mission Specialist Astronaut with NASA, and was assigned to Spacelab J, dedicated to the accomplishment of the science objectives on the mission.

DANIEL KRAUS

Daniel Kraus has a broad background in caring for wildlife and the conservation of endangered species. In 1983, in West Africa, he assisted George Adamson and Tony Fitzjohn with their release programs for lions and leopards in Kenya's Kora Reserve. While working at Oregon's Wildlife Safari Park he met Laurie Marker and they joined forces in their concern for the survival of the cheetah. Together they are the founders and co-directors of the Cheetah Preservation Fund. In April, 1991, they moved their base to Namibia, Africa, to develop their long-term conservation program for the cheetah.

WALTER C. MCCRONE

After postdoctorate research at Cornell University, Dr. McCrone spent twelve years at the Armour Research Foundation of Illinois Institute of Technology. In 1956 he organized McCrone Associates to handle contract research in microscopy, ultramicroanalysis, and crystallography. In 1961 Dr. McCrone organized the McCrone Research Institute, a non-profit corporation devoted to fundamental research in, and teaching of, microscopy and crystallography. He has published over three hundred technical papers, contributed to books, and written twelve books of his own. Dr. McCrone has received numerous awards and honors for his services to the scientific world.

LAURIE MARKER-KRAUS

Laurie Marker-Kraus has worked with over 200 species of exotic animals, but her main interest is in the cheetah. During her fifteen years at the Wildlife Safari Park in Oregon, it established the most successful captive breeding facility for cheetahs in North America. In 1982 she became the Cheetah Studbook Keeper. Together, Marker-Kraus and her husband Daniel Kraus are founders and co-directors of the Cheetah Preservation Fund. In April, 1991, they moved their base to Namibia, Africa, to develop their long-term conservation program for the endangered cheetah.

MARTIN V. MELOSI

Dr. Melosi is Professor of History and Director of the Institute for Public History at the University of Houston. He received his Ph.D. in History from the University of Texas in 1975. His areas of research include urban environmental history, the history of technology, the history of energy, and public policy history. Among his publications are *Coping with Abundance* (1985), *Garbage in the Cities* (1981), and *Thomas A. Edison and the Modernization of America* (1990). He is now writing a study of the impact of technical systems on urban growth.

SY MONTGOMERY

Sy Montgomery is an author, columnist, and naturalist. Her work appears in magazines and newspapers including *Natur* and *GEO* (Germany), *Male and Femail* (UK), and *Lear's, Omni, International Wildlife,* the *New York Times,* the *Boston Globe,* and the *Los Angeles Times* (USA). Awards include the Ray Bruner Science Writing Fellowship given by the American Public Health Association. Her first book was *Walking with the Great Apes,* and she has another book in progress, "Tiger Magic," which will look at man-eating Bengal tigers, and the village people who share the tigers' territory.

PHYLLIS BURTON PITLUGA

Phyllis Burton Pitluga is Senior Astronomer at the Adler Planetarium and has been a member of the Astronomy Department for the past twenty years. She has a B.A. from the University of California, San Jose, an M.S. from the University of New York, Oswego, and is working toward a Ph.D. at the University of Chicago. Her specialty is the history of astronomy. For the past nine years she has been investigating the figures and lines of Nazca, Peru. She has received a Wenner-Gren grant and a Senior Fulbright Scholarship.

MARK J. PLOTKIN

For much of the past fifteen years, Dr. Mark Plotkin has focused his field research on the plants and peoples of the northeast Amazon. A popular account of his work, entitled "Tales of a Shaman's Apprentice," is planned for publication in August, 1993. Dr. Plotkin is the Vice-President of Conservation International and he is also a member of the Scientific Advisory Board of Shaman Pharmaceuticals.

MARLETA REYNOLDS

Dr. Marleta Reynolds is Associate Professor in Clinical Surgery at Northwestern University Medical School, Chicago, Illinois, and Director of the ECMO Program at Children's Memorial Hospital, Chicago. She received her M.D. from Tulane University School of Medicine, New Orleans, Louisiana, in 1976. Specializing in neonatology (the care of premature and critically ill newborn babies), she has written numerous works on this subject and cardio-thoracic and pediatric surgery, as well as lecturing extensively.

LINDA SCHELE

Dr. Schele first visited a Maya site in 1970. The experience changed her life and began a twenty-three-year journey into the world of the ancient Maya. Dr. Schele has co-authored three books on the Maya and published numerous articles. During her research at sites such as Palenque and Copan, she has been a participant in the decipherment of the writing system and recovering the lost history of the Maya. She received her Ph.D. from the University of Texas in 1980 and is now John D. Murchison Professor in Art there.

PAUL C. SERENO

Dr. Sereno is an Assistant Professor at the University of Chicago, where his main projects are mapping dinosaur evolution, dinosaur discovery, and the origin of birds. Dr. Sereno's hunt for dinosaurs has taken him to Europe, Siberia, Argentina, China, North Africa, and Outer Mongolia. In Argentina he discovered the most complete remains of a dinosaur ever found and in 1990, in China, he discovered a fossilized sparrow-sized bird nearly 135 million years old, an important link in the evolution of birds.

LARRY L. SMARR

Dr. Smarr is Professor of Physics and Astronomy at the University of Illinois. An internationally recognized astrophysicist, he has published over fifty scientific papers. He is actively involved in research on the dynamics of black holes in general relativity. He was one of the first to work to increase the number of academic and industrial researchers using supercomputers to attack critical problems in basic and applied research, development, and manufacturing. Since 1985, he has been the Director of the National Center for Supercomputing Applications. Dr. Smarr is a Fellow of the American Physical Society and is the 1990 recipient of the Franklin Institute's Delmer S. Fahrney Medal.

WILLIAM B. STAPP
Dr. Stapp is Arthur Thurnau Professor and Professor of Natural Resources at the School of Natural Resources, the University of Michigan. He was the first Director of the United Nations Environmental Education Program for Unesco. He is the author of numerous audiovisual instructional aids, articles, and books, including the widely used *Field Manual for Water Quality Monitoring*. He is the current Director of the Global Rivers Environmental Education Network, operating in 130 nations, and on all continents.

KAREN B. WACHS
Karen Wachs has a B.A. with a major in Zoology from Miami University, Oxford, Ohio. She has been associated with the Cincinnati Zoo Center for Reproduction of Endangered Wildlife (CREW) since 1983. Her experience includes surgical and nonsurgical embryo collection and transfer procedures, embryo handling, and semen collection and cryopreservation with various exotic and domestic species. She has extensive writing experience, and currently serves as Conservation Officer for CREW.

DAVID E. WILLARD
Dr. Willard gained a Ph.D. in Ecology and Animal Behavior from Princeton University. For the next two years, he studied fish-eating birds at the Cocha Cashu Biological Station in Manu National Park, Peru. From 1978 to the present, he has been the Collection Manager of the bird collection of the Field Museum of Natural History in Chicago. As a part of this position he has taken frequent research trips to many parts of South America, as well as Africa and the Philippines.

ROBERT N. YONOVER
Dr. Yonover first became interested in volcanoes during his field course in geology. His Masters degree centered on the development of a laser system to analyze high-temperature fluids associated with gold deposits. His work with lasers led to the development of the laser mass spectrometer and a three-year fellowship at NASA Johnson Space Center. He also participated in the monitoring of Kilauea volcano on the Island of Hawaii. Following a postdoctoral/faculty position at the University of Hawaii, Dr. Yonover became the director of research and development with a high-technology company.

Acknowledgments

The publishers would like to thank the following people for their assistance in the preparation of this book:

Sharon Barrett; Linnea Berg; Michelle Boustani; John Dittmer; Joseph Donovan; Selena Quintrell Hand; Veronica Hilton; Dr. Deborah C. Hockman; Alan Jenkins; Heather Menzies; Emma Skidmore; Natalie Vellis; Peter Vesk; James Young; George Miksch Sutton Avian Research Center Inc., Bartlesville, OK, USA; and The Children's Hospital, Camperdown, NSW, Australia

ILLUSTRATIONS BY:

DR. LEVENT EFE: p. 47; p 48; p. 50

MIKE GORMAN: p. 16; pp. 22–23; p. 29; p. 30 (based on illustration by David Macaulay, *The Way Things Work*, Reader's Digest Press, 1988, p. 206); p. 58; p. 59; p. 60; p. 61; p. 65; p. 73; p. 74 (based on information provided by the Electron Microscope Unit, University of Sydney, NSW, Australia); p. 82; p. 99; p. 100; p. 125 (top); p. 144; p. 157; p. 181; p. 188 (inset computer-generated map of Hawaii provided by Dynamic Graphics, Raven Press, Medford, OR, USA); pp. 192–93; p. 195; p. 211; p. 215

DAVID KIRSHNER: pp. 112–13; p. 161; p. 173

FRANK KNIGHT: p. 40–41 (based on illustrations by Joyce Turner, *Cincinnati 300 Wildlife Research Society*, Vol. 2, No. 1, Summer 1984, p. 3 and Vol. 2, No. 2, Winter 1984, p. 2); p. 43; p. 80 (based on reference provided by Dr. David Stuart); p. 113; pp. 114–15; pp. 116–17 (based on references provided by George Miksch Sutton Avian Research Center, Inc. Bartlesville, OK, USA); p. 121;

pp. 122-23 (based on R.T. Sauey, "The behavior of Siberian cranes wintering in India", J.C. Lewis, [ed.] *Proceedings of the International Crane Workshop*, 3–6 September 1975, The International Crane Foundation, Baraboo, WI, Oklahoma State University, 1976: 336) p. 125 (bottom); p. 132; p. 135; pp. 138–39; p. 143; p. 153; p. 159; p. 160; pp. 162–63; p. 177; p. 179; p. 182; p. 187

MIKE LAMBLE: pp. 62–63; p. 110 (based on data from US Fish and Wildlife Service); p. 166 (top); pp. 220–21 (based on information supplied by WMX Technologies, Inc.); p. 227 (based on illustrations in G. Lean and D. Hinrichsen, *WWF Atlas of the Environment*, Helicon, 1992, p. 87); p. 228; p. 233 (based on illustrations in G. Lean and D. Hinrichsen, *WWF Atlas of the Environment*, Helicon, 1992, p. 59)

ULRICH LEHMANN: pp. 32–33 (based on reference provided by Chicago Institute of NeuroSurgery and NeuroResearch Medical Group, S.C., Chicago, IL, USA); p. 72; p. 91; p. 102; p. 204 (based on photograph provided by NASA); p. 216 (based on information provided by WMX Technologies, Inc.)

NICOLA ORAM: p. 15; p. 17; p. 18; p. 20; p. 21; p. 23

TONY PYRZAKOWSKI: pp. 134–35; p. 168 (based on *A Field Guide to Dinosaurs*, NY, The Diagram Group, Arrow Books, 1983, pp. 34–36); p. 213; pp. 218–19

PATRICK WATSON: pp. 146–47; p. 149

Other than those specified here, most illustration references were provided by the contributors.

Index